T0375524

THE TRINITY

FROM GENESIS TO REVELATION

DR. GARY L COX

WestBow Press books may be ordered through booksellers or by contacting:

WestBow Press
A Division of Thomas Nelson & Zondervan
1663 Liberty Drive
Bloomington, IN 47403
www.westbowpress.com
844-714-3454

ISBN: 979-8-3850-1950-2 (sc)
ISBN: 979-8-3850-1951-9 (hc)
ISBN: 979-8-3850-2075-1 (e)

Library of Congress Control Number: 2024904575

Print information available on the last page.

WestBow Press rev. date: 03/05/2024

CONTENTS

PREFACE

Among many Christians today there seems to be a never-ending controversy regarding God and the subject of the Trinity. Entire denominations have been established on the topic of the Trinity.

Those who adopt the belief that there are three persons in the Triune Godhead are usually known as "Trinitarian," and those who reject the Trinity are usually known as "non-Trinitarian."

Trinitarians believe there is only one God, yet manifested in three persons, and are still monotheistic. Monotheism believes that there is only one God, one deity that is all supreme. Polytheism is the belief that there are multiple deities, in other words multiple gods.

Trinitarians believe in only one God and are monotheistic.

> Hear, O Israel: The Lord our God, the Lord is one! (Deuteronomy 6:4)

Trinitarians believe that verse and are monotheistic.

Trinitarians do not believe that there are three gods, rather there is only one God manifested in three persons: God the Father, the Son, and the Holy Spirit.

Modalism is another term that needs attention. Those who are "non-Trinitarian" usually adopt modalism. The doctrine teaches that there is only one God and that God can appear in any "mode" even simultaneously such as at the baptism of Jesus. Modalism also teaches that God has multiple "personalities" rather than three distinct "persons" in the Godhead. Modalism believes that God can switch between different ways in which He desires to be manifested and that the Father, Son and Holy Spirit are simply different titles for the same person. Trinitarians believe modalism denies the true nature of the Godhead. Trinitarians do not accept modalism and believe in one God yet three unique persons in the Triune Godhead, God the Father, God the Son and God the Holy Spirit. Trinitarians believe the three persons in the Godhead are co-equal and co-eternal.

It is the purpose of this book to provide sound doctrine for the believer in Christ and also explain the position to many who are under a misunderstanding concerning the belief of Trinitarians. You will see that we have practically taken every verse of scripture related to the Trinity, both from the Old and New Testaments, and included them in this book. (Approximately nine hundred verses from Genesis to Revelation are referenced to validate the doctrine of the Trinity)!

The verses will be categorized by the books of the Bible, which will make it easy for one to find all passages related to the Trinity and their individual writers (Genesis, Psalms, Isaiah, Daniel, etc.).

We will also be taking a look at important definitions and biblical terminology that will make the Trinity much easier to understand. We have striven to write the book in layman's terminology, yet even the avid Bible scholar will see the book is a deep dive on the subject of the Godhead.

We also address the arguments used many times by non-Trinitarians and give the answers to those arguments.

Regardless of which position the reader takes on this subject, I believe this book will help one understand the "why" in the doctrine of the Trinity.

This book should also assist both the minister and teacher in presenting the Trinity to their congregations. An entire series on the Trinity could be taught from this book. It is my prayer that the Lord will bless every reader as we progress through the upcoming chapters.

CHAPTER 1

THE TRINITY

Godhead is a scriptural word that is found multiple times in the Bible, and it thereby establishes the doctrine of the Godhead. Here are a few references:

> For since the creation of the world His invisible attributes are clearly seen, being understood by the things that are made, even His eternal power and Godhead, so that they are without excuse. (Romans 1:20)

> For in Him dwells all the fullness of the Godhead bodily. (Corinthians 2:9)

In the following verse, we see the term divine nature. Most Bible translations use this term, while some others actually use Godhead. Godhead means divine nature:

> Therefore, since we are the offspring of God, we ought not to think that the Divine Nature is like gold or silver or stone, something shaped by art and man's devising. (Acts 17:29)

No one can fully understand everything about God, God is so great that He goes beyond the comprehension of man's finite mind. Still, there are thousands of references about God in the Bible, this means that mankind has no reasonable excuses for the ignorance of God. God wanted us to know about Him so He gave us the scriptures to tell us what the Godhead is like.

Today, here are many ideas about God and many misunderstandings about Him. When the believer reads the Bible as God gave it to us, they will see that God has much to say concerning the Trinity.

Many no non-Trinitarians argue that the English word "Trinity" is not found in the scriptures. This is true however, neither are other words like monotheism, deity, divine, and rapture, omnipresent, omniscient, omnipotent, incarnation; however, the Word of God teaches these irrefutable truths. To deny the Trinity based on the word not being found in the scripture is unfounded—as one would have to deny the above doctrines as well.

Many have been taught that God cannot be understood, and while it is true that God cannot be completely understood, Romans 1:20 clearly states the Godhead can be comprehended by the things He has made. Let's look at that verse once more.

> For since the creation of the world His invisible attributes, that is, His eternal power and divine nature, have been clearly perceived, being understood by what has been made, so that they are without excuse. (Romans 1:20)

As we just mentioned, the term Godhead means "God's divine nature." These two terms are synonymous.

It is worth noting that there are some things about God that God does not intend for us to know, such as how God originated. We know that God always has been; there never has been a time when God was not. He is the Alpha and the Omega and has always existed in eternity past and will always exist in eternity future (Revelation 1:8; Psalm 90:2, 93:2; Micah 5:2; Hebrews 9:14). God being eternal is something that goes beyond our human comprehension (since everything in our realm has a beginning and end). The things we do not know and understand about God are to be left with God alone.

> The secret things belong to the Lord our God, but those things which are revealed belong to us and to our children forever, that we may do all the words of this law. (Deuteronomy 29:29)

From the scriptures we mentioned above, we already know a few things about God:

- He is not a God made with human hands (gold, silver, stone, and art).
- We know that the eternal Godhead is "clearly seen" and "understood."
- The scriptures use the term "the Godhead" (in the singular), so in the beginning, the Godhead is the one and only Deity.
- However, there are many things about God that God does reveal to us about Himself.

CHAPTER 2

A FEW DEFINITIONS

To understand properly what the Bible teaches about God, it's critical to understand a few biblical terms and give their definitions. Let's look at a few.

God (Godhead)

In the scriptures in our text, different Greek words are used; fortunately, they all have the same meaning: "deity," "divine," or "divine nature." The word Godhead is used to refer to the concept of the Triune God, or one God in three persons, that includes God the Father, God the Son, and God the Holy Spirit.

One

The term one means "to unify or to be in agreement." We will see the following terms in the scriptures:

- one Lord,
- one God,
- one flesh (Genesis 2:24)
- the people are one (Genesis 11:6)

Whether one means one in number or one in unity (agreement) must be determined by the complete context of the scriptures and not by the English word itself. Sometimes the word in scripture means one in number; other times, it means one in unity. For example, the word date might mean a day on a calendar, yet it could also mean a meeting, such as a dinner date. The word park might refer to parking one's car, but it could also mean a city park. The word play might mean what a child does in the park, yet play might reference a performance in a theater. The word fast may refer to how fast are we traveling, but it could also mean we are on a fast and not eating. The list just goes on. The point is that sometimes a word may have more than one meaning, as does the biblical word one. One might mean one in number, but it could also mean one in agreement or one in unity or harmony:

> Therefore, a man shall leave his father and mother and be joined to his wife, and they shall become one flesh. (Genesis 2:24)

Now, is this one in number or one in unity? We, of course, know that there is no possible way that two physical people can become one individual person. We must then conclude this means one in unity or in agreement. Here's another verse with the same concept. Here, Jesus is praying to the Father:

> That they all may be one, as You, Father, are in Me, and I in You; that they also may be one in us, that the world may believe that You sent Me. And the glory which You gave Me I have given them, that they may be one just as We are one: I in them, and You in Me; that they may be made perfect in one, and that the world may know that You have sent Me, and have loved them as You have loved Me. (John 17:21–23)

We ask again, Do these verses mean one numerically or one in agreement? Again, it is impossible that the entire body of multiple believers could become one individual person. Jesus clearly says that "they" may be one "even as we" are one.

One must ask the question regarding the word "they," which of course is plural: How can we, the many individual members of the church, be made one (singular) in number? We can't; however, we can be made one in unity, harmony, and agreement.

> But he who is joined to the Lord is one spirit with Him. (1 Corinthians 6:17)

Everyone would agree that there are very many individuals who are joined to the Lord, yet it doesn't make sense that our multiple spirits are joined to the Lord's spirit, becoming one in number.

In

Our next word is in. It's very important to understand the proper definition of this little word, as it is sometimes used to disavow the Trinity. Consider the following biblical examples:

> Therefore, if anyone is in Christ, he is a new creation. (2 Corinthians 5:17)

> Do you not believe that I am in the Father, and the Father in Me? The words that I speak to you I do not speak on My own authority; but the Father who dwells in Me does the works. Believe Me that I am in the Father and the Father in Me, or else believe Me for the sake of the works themselves. … At that day you will know that I am in My Father, and you in Me, and I in you. (John 14:10–11, 20)

> But you are not in the flesh but in the Spirit, if indeed the Spirit of God dwells in you. Now if anyone does not have the Spirit of Christ, he is not His. And if Christ is

> in you, the body is dead because of sin, but the Spirit is life because of righteousness. (Romans 8:10)

Next, we have a verse concerning Judas at the Lord's betrayal:

> Satan entered him. Then Jesus said to him, "What you do, do quickly." (John 13:27)

This doesn't mean (and cannot mean) a physical or bodily entering of Satan (an angel) into the body of Judas; we all know one body cannot get inside another body. (Satan is an angel with a body, unlike demon spirits, which have no bodies.)

Next, Paul writes to the church at Corinth:

> I do not say this to condemn; for I have said before that you are in our hearts. (2 Corinthians 7:3)

> Just as it is right for me to think this of you all, because I have you in my heart. (Philippians 1:7)

Again, having people in your heart is not a physical entrance. However, people can be in unity (agreement and harmony) with one another without bodily being in one another. In fact, in this context, different people can be in one another yet be many miles apart.

When the Bible says that God dwells in Christ and Christ dwells in God, it means they are in agreement, in unity, with each other, not physically inside each other.

The next verse tells us how many persons there are in the Godhead. There are three persons (witnesses) in the Godhead, and they all "agree" in one:

> For there are three that bear witness in heaven: the Father, the Word, and the Holy Spirit; and these three are one. And there are three that bear witness on earth: the Spirit, the water, and the blood; and these three agree as one. (1 John 5:7–8)

Here, the scriptures plainly say the Godhead is one in agreement (unity and harmony). Next, we move on to the term both.

Both

Anyone with even elementary knowledge of the English language understands the word "both." In case one is struggling with it, here is the definition. As a pronoun, it is plural in construction, as in "the one as well as the other" or "he loves both children and the elderly."

Conjunction. It is used as a function word to indicate and stress the inclusion of each of two or more things specified and by coordinated words, phrases, or clauses. As in "he loved well both children, middle aged and elderly."

Adjective. Being the two: affecting or involving the one and the other; used to refer to two people or things regarded and identified together. As in both eyes, both ears, both hands, both feet, both persons, etc.

Now let's take a look at the word "both" and how it relates with the Trinity in scripture.

The upcoming verse is a promise to those who abide in the doctrine of Christ. The verse uses the word "both" to relate to the Father and the Son

> He who abides in the doctrine of Christ has both the Father and the Son. (2 John 1:9)

To further validate how the word "both" is used in relation to the Trinity, here are two more verses:

> But now they have seen and also hated both Me and My Father. (John 15:24)

> That their hearts may be encouraged, being knit together in love, and attaining to all riches of the full

> assurance of understanding, to the knowledge of the mystery of God, both of the Father and of Christ. (Colossians 2:2)

The Holy Spirit guided the hands of Paul as he wrote using the word "both" and refers to the mystery of God including "both" the Father and Christ.

Now we progress to the word "and."

AND

"And" is a conjunction connecting grammatically equal elements.

Conjunctions are words that join together other words or groups of words.

A coordinating conjunction connects words, phrases, and clauses of equal importance. The main coordinating conjunctions are and, or, either, and but.

And is a coordinating conjunction. We use "and" to connect two words, phrases, clauses, or prefixes together:

Here are some examples of "and" as a coordinating conjunction:

- Men like meat and potatoes.
- Smartphones and computers are changing our lives.
- My best friend and my father's father both come from Ireland.

In the upcoming chapters, we will often see the word "and" in reference to the Trinity. This little word and will be used multiple times—even in greetings and the salutations of the epistles. For now, let's look at just one verse.

> Grace to you and peace from God our Father and the Lord Jesus Christ. (Romans 1:7)

ALSO

Our next word is "also," which can apply to more than one. Even though this seems elementary, it's an important word that we will see in relation with the Trinity. Here's the definition.

Adverb

When we use the word "also," we are giving more information about something:

- I like meat and also potatoes.
- I'd like a fishing rod for my birthday and also a tackle box.

Now let's see the word in scripture.

> He that hates me hates my Father also. (John 15:23)

A synonym for also is "likewise" or the phrase "as well." The scripture could also read "He that hates me hates my Father likewise." Most "word-for-word" Bible translations use the word "also," and some of the "thought-for-thought" translations use the word "likewise" or "as well."

As we progress through the upcoming chapters, we will see many references using these terms. But there's more!

Now we move to the definition of the word "by."

BY

Preposition. Identifying the agent performing an action

Let's see a biblical example:

> No one can say that Jesus is Lord except by the Holy Spirit. (1 Corinthians 12:3)

The definition here is so self-evident, we now advance to the word "the."

THE

Determiner. Denoting one or more people or things already mentioned or assumed to be common knowledge. Used as a function word to indicate the following noun or noun equivalent is a unique or a particular member of its class.

Here we see the word "the" in scripture:

> Go therefore and make disciples of all the nations, baptizing them in the name of the Father and of the Son and of the Holy Spirit. (Matthew 28:19)

In the above verse, the Godhead is the class, the unique nouns are the Father, the Son and the Holy Spirit. We still are not finished our next word is "with."

WITH

Preposition. Used as a function word to indicate combination, accompaniment, presence, or addition. To be accompanied by another person or thing.

> How God anointed Jesus of Nazareth with the Holy Spirit and with power, who went about doing good and healing all who were oppressed by the devil, for God was with Him. (Acts 10:38)

Note that all three members of the Godhead are in the first line. It is (1) God who anointed (2) Jesus "with" the (3) Holy Spirit. We also saw in the last four words "God was "with" him."

THROUGH

Adjective. Of a means of transportation continuing to the final destination.

Adverb or Preposition. As to continue in time toward the completion of a process.

This is just one example, yet we will see many verses using the word through:

> Therefore, He is able to save forever those who draw near to God through Him, since He always lives to make intercession for them. (Hebrews 7:25)

In this verse, our final destination is God, and we draw near to God through Christ.

TO

Preposition. Used as a function word to indicate movement or an action or condition suggestive of movement toward a place, person, or thing reached. Used as a function word to indicate combination, accompaniment, presence, or addition. To be accompanied by another person or thing.

The following are a couple of examples of how "to" is used in scripture to reference the Trinity:

> All things have been delivered to Me by my Father, and no one knows the Son except the Father. Nor does anyone know the Father except the Son, and the one to whom the Son wills to reveal Him. (Matthew 11:27)

In the above verse Jesus Himself is speaking and clearly states that all things were given "to" Him by His Father. In the following verse Daniel sees a vision of God (the Ancient of Days) with the Son of Man (Jesus) being brought "to" God on the throne. Here are the words of Daniel:

> I watched till thrones were put in place and the Ancient of Days was seated and behold, one like the Son of Man coming with the clouds of heaven. He came "to" the ancient of days, and they brought Him near before Him then "to" Him was given dominion and glory and a kingdom. (Daniel 7:9, 13)

We are almost done with definitions; there is just one more.

From

As a preposition "from" can indicate the source of someone or something; or a point at which a journey or action begins; (as in, "as I mentioned before, I am from New York"). The word can also indicate a distinction (as in, "John saw the traffic accident from that of Mary").

Now let's take a look at the word "from" in scripture referring to the distinction between the Father and the Son. We will also see the starting point from which Jesus began His journey from the Father to earth, and that the source from which Jesus came was from the Father.

> For I have given to them the words which You have given Me; and they have received them, and have known surely that I came forth from You; and they have believed that You sent Me. (John 17:8)

Again, as we progress in this book from one chapter to another, please pay close attention to all of the following terms and definitions:

- in
- both
- and
- also
- by
- the
- with
- through
- to
- from

CHAPTER 3

PLURAL PRONOUNS

Let us first establish that the scripture says "there are three" in the Godhead.

> For there are three that bear witness in heaven: the Father, the Word, and the Holy Spirit; and these three are one. And there are three that bear witness on earth: the Spirit, the water, and the blood; and these three agree as one. (1 John 5:7–8)

All through the scriptures, we find plural pronouns referencing the Trinity. Even a child can understand the list below.

Beginning in Genesis, our first plural pronoun is the word "us."

Us

Here are some examples of how we use the word "us" in the English language:

- just the two of us
- between us
- both of us
- one of us

- all of us
- like us
- with us
- of us

If you research similar words for "us," you will come across "ourselves." All of these examples show that the word "us" is always plural and never singular.

On the sixth day of creation, God made man, and before God made man, an interesting conversation took place. As far as we have record of, when God created man, only the Godhead and angels existed. Angels have no power to create and played no part whatsoever in the creation of man. In the next verse, who else could the "us" refer to rather than the three persons of the Godhead?

> Then God said, "Let Us make man in Our image, according to Our likeness." (Genesis 1:26)

After the fall of Adam and Eve, God again uses the plural pronoun of "us." This verse could not refer to angels since man was not made in the image and likeness of the angels; only man was made in the "image and likeness of God." There is no possible way the word "us" could refer to anyone other than the Godhead. Again, it is a plural pronoun that shows plurality in the Godhead.

The following verse further substantiates multiple persons in the Godhead using the word "us."

> Then the Lord God said, "Behold, the man has become like one of Us, to know good and evil." (Genesis 3:22)

Regarding earth's first couple, the scriptures use the word "us" twice regarding the Triune God.

Coming to Genesis chapter 11, we arrive at the Tower of Babel in the days of Nimrod. The scripture says, "The Lord said, 'Let us go down.'" This verse does not refer to angels in any way whatsoever;

it was God, not angels, who confounded the languages at the Tower of Babel. Once again, the Godhead is used with a plural pronoun:

> And the Lord said, "Indeed the people are one, and they all have one language, and this is what they begin to do; now nothing that they propose to do will be withheld from them. Come, let us go down and there confuse their language, that they may not understand one another's speech." (Genesis 11:6–7)

Seven hundred years before the birth of Christ, God called a prophet who would end up being the most quoted prophet by New Testament writers. His name was Isaiah, and he records the following:

> Also, I heard the voice of the Lord, saying, "Who shall I send, and who will go for us?" (Isaiah 6:8)

Isaiah, the prophet himself, answered this call and told the Lord (who is referenced with the plural pronoun "us"), "Here am I Lord, send me."

If one wants more confirmation, the pronoun "us" is used in the Old Testament, and in the New Testament Jesus Himself uses it to reference Himself and the Father.

> That they all may be one, as You, Father, are in Me, and I in You; that they also may be one in "us", that the world may believe that You sent Me. (John 17:21)

We have presented scriptures showing the word "us" five times and how it is used in reference to the Godhead both in the Old and New Testaments.

Continuing with plural pronouns, we come to the word "our." Examples of the ways we use the word "our" include "our home," "our Father," "our material goods," etc.

When Jesus taught His disciples to pray, He used the word "our" to refer to the multiple disciples. He used "our" in the plural. It is very obvious that the Lord's prayer was packed with plural pronouns using the words "our," "us" and "we," and "them."

> He said to them, "When you pray, say: our Father in heaven, hallowed be Your name. Your kingdom come, Your will be done on earth as it is in heaven. Give us day by day our daily bread. And forgive us our sins, for we also forgive everyone who is indebted to us. And do not lead us into temptation, but deliver us from the evil one. (Luke 11:2–4)

Please keep the Lord's Prayer in mind as we progress through this book. Each of these pronouns will be used to call attention to the Godhead. If the Holy Spirit here is using plural pronouns to address the disciples, why would He change and go to singular persons in the Godhead using the same terms?

Beginning again in creation where we just saw the word "us," in that same verse, the Holy Spirit inspires Moses to also use the word "our." It will be used twice in this one verse. Again, we repeat, this could not refer to angels as man was not made in the image and likeness of angels but only of God, and we have already established that angels had no part in man's creation. Man was made from the dust of the ground by God alone.

Our

> Then God said, "Let Us make man in our image, according to our likeness. (Genesis 1:26)

In the famous chapter of John 14, Jesus also uses the word "our" to refer to Himself and the Father:

> Jesus answered and said to him, "If anyone loves Me, he will keep My word; and My Father will love him,

> and We will come to him and make our home with him." (John 14:23)

So far, we've seen "us" and "our" both in the Old and New Testaments, and next is the plural pronoun "we." We find Jesus using the word on three different occasions, and they all concern the Godhead.

We

> Jesus answered and said to him, "If anyone loves Me, he will keep My word; and My Father will love him, and we will come to him and make our home with him. (John 14:23)

> Now I am no longer in the world, but these are in the world, and I come to You. Holy Father, keep through Your name those whom You have given Me, that they may be one as we are. And the glory which You gave Me I have given them, that they may be one just as we are one. (John 17:11, 22)

Multiple people cannot be one in number, but they can be one in unity, in agreement, and so it is with the Father and the Son.

Our last plural pronoun will be the word "their." The writer will be David in the book of Psalms, the man after God's own heart. David knew about the Trinity:

> The Lord said to my Lord, "Sit at My right hand, Till I make Your enemies Your footstool." (Psalm 110:1)

> Do not cast me away from Your presence, and do not take Your Holy Spirit from me. (Psalm 51:11)

Yes, David was aware that the Lord said unto his Lord, "Sit at my right hand," and then he mentions the third person in the Godhead asking God not to take His Holy Spirit from him.

Right now we are on the subject of plural pronouns, and we conclude this chapter with the word "their."

THEIR

> The kings of the earth set themselves, and the rulers take counsel together, against the Lord, and against his anointed, saying, "Let us break their bands asunder, and cast away their cords from us." (Psalm 2:2–3)

All one has to do is use common sense when reading the Bible and speak just as we do when we speak to each other.

To recap, our plural pronouns related to the Trinity are us, our, we, and their.

CHAPTER 4

GOD'S ORDER OF COMMUNICATION WITH MAN

In this chapter, we will see that each person of the Godhead did their own speaking, and each had their own time to speak.

The first speaker is God the Father during Old Testament times, and then God the Son speaks on earth during His earthly ministry. Last of all, it is the Holy Spirit speaking for the past two thousand years (since Pentecost). We will see each speaker speaking in their own time. Let's begin.

DURING THE OLD TESTAMENT, GOD THE FATHER WAS THE SPEAKER

God mostly spoke through the prophets, and when He spoke through the prophets, He sometimes spoke audibly, such as when God spoke to Moses from the burning bush. At other times, He spoke through dreams and visions, such as with Daniel, Isaiah, Jeremiah, and Ezekiel. In the Old Testament, God the Father was the speaker.

As one can see by now, everything we are putting in print is validated by scripture:

> God, who at various times and in various ways spoke in time past to the fathers by the prophets. (Hebrews 1:1)

Before Jesus came—before the last days in times past—God the Father did the speaking. Here's another verse to confirm:

> Whom heaven must receive until the times of restoration of all things, which God has spoken by the mouth of all His holy prophets since the world began. (Acts 3:21)

An Old Testament example of multiple persons in the Godhead spoken by the mouth of a holy prophet is Daniel's vision. Daniel, a prophet, saw the Father and the Son simultaneously. He saw the Son standing before God the Father on His throne, God the Father was seated on the throne, and God the Son was "brought near before" the throne. The Father is called the "Ancient of Days," and the Son is called the "Son of Man."

> I watched till thrones were put in place, and the Ancient of Days was seated. And behold, one like the Son of Man coming with the clouds of heaven. He came to the Ancient of Days, and they brought Him near before Him. Then to Him was given dominion and glory and a kingdom. (Daniel 7:9, 13)

As one can see, Daniel saw both God the Father (the Ancient of Days) sitting on the throne and God the Son who was "brought near." Both are obviously different persons within the Godhead. No one can deny it is God who sits on the throne and that it is Christ who stands before Him being "brought near." Also note the line that says the Son of Man was brought "to" the Ancient of Days.

In case anyone is wondering, God the Father did speak in the New Testament. In fact, He spoke on three different occasions during the ministry of Jesus on earth:

- At the Lord's baptism (Matthew 3:17, Mark 1:11, and Luke 3:22). A voice came from heaven, saying, "This is My beloved Son, in whom I am well pleased."
- On the Mount of Transfiguration (Matthew 17:5, Mark 9:7, and Luke 9:35). A voice came out of the cloud, saying, "This is My beloved Son, in whom I am well pleased. Hear Him!"
- After the Lord prayed after His triumphal entry and just before the last Passover. "Father, glorify Your name." Then a voice came from heaven, saying, "I have both glorified it and will glorify it again." (John 12:28–30)

God the Father did speak during the four Gospels; however, we will see next that Jesus was the primary speaker during His three and a half years of ministry on earth.

In the Four Gospels, God the Son (Jesus) Was Doing the Speaking

> For if you believed Moses, you would believe Me; for he wrote about Me. But if you do not believe his writings, how will you believe My words?" (John 5:46–47)

> I have many things to say and to judge concerning you, but He who sent Me is true; and I speak to the world those things which I heard from Him." I do nothing of Myself; but as My Father taught Me, I speak these things. (John 8:26, 28)

> I speak what I have seen with My Father, and you do what you have seen with your father." (John 8:38)

> And if anyone hears My words and does not believe, I do not judge him; for I did not come to judge the world but to save the world. He who rejects Me, and does not receive My words, has that which judges him—the word that I have spoken will judge him in the last day. For I have not spoken on My own authority; but the Father who sent Me gave Me a command, what I should say and what I should speak. And I know that His command is everlasting life. Therefore, whatever I speak, just as the Father has told Me, so I speak." (John 12:47–50)

Note the clear distinction that Jesus makes between Himself and the Father as He says, "I have not spoken of myself but the Father." The main point we are making is that Christ is doing the speaking in the four Gospels:

> For I have given to them the words which You have given Me; and they have received them, and have known surely that I came forth from You; and they have believed that You sent Me. (John 17:8)

How much clearer does it need to be? It was Christ who did the speaking for three and a half years while He was here on earth. The words He spoke were "given" to Him by the Father.

The first words we have recorded of Jesus are at the age of twelve when He was speaking in the temple in Jerusalem. He was sitting with the teachers and listening and asking questions. Those who heard Him listened in astonishment. We can certainly learn much about the Godhead simply by listening to Jesus Himself. This is what He said.

> And He said to them, "Why did you seek Me? Did you not know that I must be about My Father's business?" (Luke 2:49)

The first words recorded by Jesus in scripture give a clear distinction between Himself and the Father. The last words Jesus said on the cross just before He breathed His last breath are recorded in Luke:

> Father, into your hands I commit my spirit. (Luke 23:46)

As with His first words, the last words of Jesus on the cross gave a distinction between Himself and the Father. Now we go to the last words of Christ before He left the disciples on the Mount of Olives. The last words that Jesus spoke before His ascension were recorded by Luke in Acts:

> Until the day in which He was taken up, after He through the Holy Spirit had given commandments to the apostles whom He had chosen, to whom He also presented Himself alive after His suffering by many infallible proofs, being seen by them forty days and speaking of the things pertaining to the kingdom of God.
>
> And being assembled together with them, He commanded them not to depart from Jerusalem, but to wait for the Promise of the Father, "which," He said, "you have heard from Me; for John truly baptized with water, but you shall be baptized with the Holy Spirit not many days from now."
>
> Therefore, when they had come together, they asked Him, saying, "Lord, will You at this time restore the kingdom to Israel?"
>
> And He said to them, "It is not for you to know times or seasons which the Father has put in His own

> authority. But you shall receive power when the Holy Spirit has come upon you; and you shall be witnesses to Me in Jerusalem, and in all Judea and Samaria, and to the end of the earth." Now when He had spoken these things, while they watched, He was taken up, and a cloud received Him out of their sight. (Acts 1:2–9)

Did you notice Jesus was speaking all the way until He was taken up?

In the Great Commission, it is very obvious that Jesus addresses the three persons of the Triune God. He uses the phrases "the Father" and "the Holy Spirit." After the Holy Spirit comes on the Day of Pentecost, Jesus tells the disciples, "You will be witness of Me." Jesus is saying, "The Father, the Holy Spirit, and Me." That's three in the Trinity.

Since the Day of Pentecost, the Holy Spirit Has Been Doing the Speaking

Although Jesus did speak after His ascension, the Holy Spirit would become the primary speaker.

An example of Christ speaking after Pentecost would be when Jesus spoke to Saul of Tarsus on the road to Damascus. Saul saw a light from heaven, and then he heard a voice. The voice he heard was the voice of Jesus as He spoke audibly to Saul. When Saul asked who was speaking to him, Jesus said that He was Jesus whom Saul was persecuting. You can read the story in Acts 9:3–5.

Now that God the Father has spoken through the prophets in the Old Testament and Jesus spoke while on earth between His birth and ascension, are we now left without a voice? Certainly not! We have the third person of the Triune Godhead speaking with us today. Here are a series of verses to confirm.

The Holy Spirit is our "Teacher." In some translations, the word "Comforter" is used rather than "Helper." Regardless of the translation, it's clear that Jesus was referring to the Holy Spirit. In fact, the verses state that the "Helper" is the "Holy Spirit."

Jesus told us the Holy Spirit would teach us all things and that He would testify of Jesus (see John 14:26 and 15:26).

From these verses, please note that we even know of whom the Holy Spirit will speak: He (the Holy Spirit) testifies of Christ and only of Christ. For further verification that the Trinity is spoken of here, the following verse tells us that the Holy Spirit doesn't speak of Himself. This is very important; it's a powerful verse!

> Whatever He hears He will speak; and He will tell you things to come. He will glorify Me, for He will take of what is Mine and declare it to you. (John 16:13–14)

The Holy Spirit is vocal! Again, note the distinction between Jesus and the Holy Spirit. The Holy Spirit does not speak of Himself; the Holy Spirit glorifies Christ.

Something needs to be said concerning this verse. There are some churches today that glorify the Holy Spirit. Do not misunderstand me. The Holy Spirit is God, but the work of the Holy Spirit is to glorify Christ. Jesus said, "The Holy Spirit will not speak of Himself!" Don't miss that.

This includes the gifts of the Spirit. None of the nine gifts of the Spirit should glorify the Holy Spirit. The gifts are His gifts, and the Holy Spirit does not glorify Himself. The Holy Spirit speaks only of Christ; if that is true, then this is the way His gifts operate. The gifts of the Spirit should leave one glorifying none other than Jesus Himself—never the Holy Spirit—for He doesn't even speak concerning Himself at all.

A body of believers that glorifies the Holy Spirit rather than Christ is missing the mark! The Holy Spirit does not glorify man; He doesn't even glorify Himself. He only glorifies Jesus, the Son of God. By the way, didn't the heavenly Father do the same when He spoke? When God the Father spoke out of heaven at the Lord's baptism and the Mount of Transfiguration, He spoke only of the

Son! We can all learn a lesson from this. The Father didn't speak of Himself; the Holy Spirit doesn't speak of Himself. When one reads the words of Jesus, it's amazing how much He spoke of the Father and of the Holy Spirit. We should not be wrapped up in speaking of ourselves. We should be speaking of Him who has saved and redeemed us!

John the Baptist said that Jesus must increase—and he (John) must decrease (John 3:30).

We live in an age when many glorify man. Many glorify their TV and radio ministers, their pastors, and their men of talents. Any minister whose followers speak more about the "wonderfulness of the minister" than how wonderful Jesus is has missed the mark! Even Jesus taught us by example not to receive the honor of men and to even beware when men speak well of us (John 5:41).

These are the main points I want to bring to the table:

- God the Father spoke of the Son.
- God the Son spoke of the Father and the Holy Spirit.
- God the Holy Spirit speaks of the Son.

We should follow their examples and seek not the glory and honor of men. Each of our lives should bring glory to Christ. Paul said:

> But God forbid that I should boast except in the cross of our Lord Jesus Christ. (Galatians 6:14)

It is the Holy Spirit speaking today. I have never heard Him audibly, and I don't know of anyone who ever has. However, I've certainly had Him lead and direct me. There have been times when I have had experiences where I didn't have the wisdom and didn't know the answer within myself and had Him do exactly what Jesus said He would do: lead me and guide me into all truth. In fact, the Holy Spirit can even speak to God for us when we pray, as we will see later, especially when we don't know what to pray.

On the day of Pentecost, the Bible says that the Holy Spirit gave them "utterance" (Acts 2:4). Have you ever had someone come to you for advice and you didn't know what to tell them? The Holy Spirit can give us the words, and He can give us the "utterace." Jesus told the disciples that they should not be concerned with what they would say when they were brought before councils because the Holy Spirit would give them the words.

> Now when they bring you to the synagogues and magistrates and authorities, do not worry about how or what you should answer, or what you should say. For the Holy Spirit will teach you in that very hour what you ought to say. (Luke 12:11-12)

My friends, The Holy Spirit can give us the "utterance." Wouldn't it be marvelous if the Holy Spirit used us as His voice!

It is the Holy Spirit speaking in this age of God's grace. As you see from scripture, the Holy Spirit can give us utterance, and that, my friend, is "speaking" and being "vocal." We should be uttering not that which comes from our own hearts but from the Holy Spirit that lives in our hearts. On that note, the Holy Spirit can also help us be quiet! James told us that the tongue no man can tame, but the good news is that the Holy Spirit can tame it! He can tell us when not to speak (James 3:7-8).

What does the Bible say about the Holy Spirit speaking today? When Paul and Barnabas were at the church at Antioch, they departed on their first missionary journey. The Holy Spirit "spoke" with the following instructions to the church. Yes, the Holy Spirit can give direction to our churches. Remember how Jesus gave the book of Revelation to John—and John was to give it to the seven churches of Asia Minor?

Didn't the Lord say if we had an ear we should hear what "the Spirit would say" to the churches (Revelation 2:29)? That statement was said seven times in Revelation 2–3 (Revelation 2:7, 11, 17, 29; 3:6, 13, 22).

In Antioch, the Holy Spirit gave the church direction concerning

Paul and Barnabas, and the Holy Spirit did it by speaking to them. If one is doubtful that the Holy Spirit can speak today, please read the following verse:

> The Holy Spirit said, "Now separate to Me Barnabas and Saul for the work to which I have called them." (Acts 13:2)

Did you get that? "The Holy Spirit said." This is the church of the New Testament book of Acts. This is after the resurrection and ascension; this is in our church age. The church at Antioch is receiving their marching orders from the Holy Spirit Himself!

God's people can really get into trouble when they listen to man instead of waiting on the direction of the Holy Spirit. Let us not forget about those ten spies who came back from Canaan. Israel listened to man rather than God, and it dearly cost them. They lost their lives dying in the wilderness for 40 years because they listened to man.

I've seen that in church business meetings. I've heard people speak, and I knew for certain that what I was hearing wasn't the Holy Spirit.

Like Israel, I've seen God's work really held back because of failing to hear what the Spirit says and follow His leading. We live in an era of church growth mechanics. Although I'm all for church growth, the early church certainly was—and they grew big and fast. I'm all for church growth, but I'm more for following the voice of the Holy Spirit. I promise you that we can hear it! And He can speak expressly!

Concerning how the Holy Spirit speaks, remember what Paul wrote to Timothy? Paul told him how the Holy Spirit speaks. He can "express" what He wants us to know:

> Now the Spirit speaks expressly, that in the latter times some shall depart from the faith, giving

> heed to seducing spirits, and doctrines of devils. (1 Timothy 4:1)

Everything the Holy Spirit says isn't always pleasant. What the Holy Spirit was saying here was to "be aware."

Many Christian believers today listen far too much to the word of man. I know some folks who want to do all of the talking even when they pray. Prayer is two-way communication.

All of us should take the time to be quiet and listen to the Holy Spirit. I sincerely believe that many of our problems could be avoided if we'd only take the time to "hear what the Spirit says." By the way, He will always be 100 percent in agreement with the Word of God. Frankly, that's one of the best ways He speaks to us. Jesus told us when the Holy Spirit would come that He would bring things back to our remembrance of the things Jesus told us (John 14:26).

Have you ever had the Holy Spirit bring a scripture back to your mind that you haven't thought of in a long time? I've had Him do that for me when I was in a situation that I didn't know how to handle. Jesus said the Holy Spirit can remind us!

I forget where I heard it, but someone said, "If you're worried about losing your memory, just forget about it!" It's so wonderful that the Holy Spirit still speaks to us today. Far too many of us sometimes place too much confidence in the word of man. Folks, the Holy Spirit will never lead us wrong. When David found himself in trouble, he said to Gad,

> "Don't let me fall into the hand of man." (2 Samuel 24:14)

It was David again who told us it's better to trust in the Lord than to put confidence in man; in fact, he once wrote that "in man there is no help". David also cautioned us to be careful about placing confidence in man.

> Do not put your trust in princes, nor in a son of man in whom there is no help. (Psalms 146:3)

> It is better to trust in the Lord than to put confidence in man. (Psalms 118:8)

Many times, the person we trust has as many issues as the person seeking help. Man can lead us wrong, but the Holy Spirit never will!

There are people today who flock to preachers who claim to have heard from the Holy Spirit but really haven't. The buzzword among these churches is "personal prophecy," which is 100 percent unscriptural. By personal prophecy, we mean the preachers who "call people out" of the congregations and tell them that God told them things about them and prophesy over them concerning the future. That is unscriptural because no one can prophesy ahead of the Rapture.

If the scripture teaches (which it does) that the Rapture can happen at any moment, then how can one prophesy ahead of that? If God has really spoken to the preacher that—in the near future—God is going to bring them into money, give them a spouse, or use them to reach thousands for Christ, then God is going to have to put the Rapture on hold, He's going to have to pause the possibility that the Rapture can happen today because "God has said" these things are going to take place in the future.

The same is true with what the scriptures say about the possibility of our deaths. The scripture says that we are not to boast about things that will happen tomorrow for "we know not" what tomorrow holds (Proverbs 27:1).

Concerning the possibility that the disciples could die at any moment Jesus told them, "Your time is always ready" (John 7:6). According to scripture, we can die at any time. The Holy Spirit will never speak in disagreement with the Word of God!

Prophecy was sealed up in Revelation 22, and anyone who says, "God has shown me things about your future" is in danger of having the plagues of the tribulation added to them, which means that they will miss the Rapture and go through the tribulation with the plagues being placed upon them (Revelation 22:18).

Personal prophecy is dangerous because it leads Christians to place their faith in man. My friend, the Holy Spirit can lead us and guide us in life, day by day, one day at a time. Jesus commanded, "Take no thought for tomorrow, that tomorrow will take care of itself" (Matthew 6:34). We don't have to cross tomorrow's bridges today! We are to pray, "Give us This day our daily bread" (Matthew 6:11). Preachers who give personal prophecy to individuals are causing the person to "give thought about tomorrow" which is contrary to what Jesus taught.

I personally feel cautious when I hear ministers saying, "God told me" or Christians saying, "Thus saith the Lord," (especially if they say it a lot). I have known people who have made some of the most unwise decisions because they listened to men. There are people who have quit serving the Lord because they ended up being disappointed by what was said to them in personal prophecies that never came to pass.

Take, for instance, the gift of "interpretation of tongues." The interpreter usually begins by saying, "Thus saith the Lord" and then begins a prophecy. This is going to ruffle some feathers, but I hope I can provoke us to stop and ask, "Is what we are doing scriptural?"

Before I upset the reader, let me say that I am not saying that tongues and interpretation of tongues are unscriptural. I am, however, saying that the way these gifts are exercised by many is unscriptural. Allow me to give an example.

The Bible teaches that when one speaks with tongues that it is not God speaking to man; it is man speaking to God. I challenge anyone to find even one instance in the scriptures where it is God speaking to man when they spoke with tongues. It is always a person speaking to God. Speaking with tongues is never man speaking to man, and it is never God speaking to man. Without exception, every Bible instance is man speaking to God. Consider the following verses:

> For he who speaks in a tongue does not speak to men but to God. (1 Corinthians 14:2)

> Likewise, the Spirit also helps in our weaknesses. For we do not know what we should pray for as we ought, but the Spirit Himself makes intercession for us with groanings which cannot be uttered. (Romans 8:26)

In every instance in the scripture, when anyone spoke with tongues, it was never God speaking to them—not one single time. On the day of Pentecost, when they spoke with tongues for the first time, what did they speak? The scripture declares exactly what they said:

> We hear them speaking in our own tongues the wonderful works of God. (Acts 2:11)

This scripture clearly says that they spoke the "wonderful works of God," not from God:

> But you, beloved, building yourselves up on your most holy faith, praying in the Holy Spirit. (Jude 1:20)

When one speaks with tongues scripturally, it is always a person speaking to God and not the other way around. In fact, the scripture says when one speaks with tongues, it is not to a person; it is to God.

A while back, someone brought me a sample of two popular television ministers and asked my opinion about them. The two ministers were on the platform in a worship service and were having a conversation with each other in tongues. One would say something in tongues to the other minister, and the other would answer in tongues and they would just laugh and slap the other one's arm. The congregation was loving it.

Is there a problem here? Paul told the Corinthians (we just read it) that when a person speaks with tongues, he speaks not unto men. This is an example of how Paul said that if any come in who are unlearned and uninformed or unbelievers, they would say you're mad and out of your mind:

> Therefore if the whole church comes together in one place, and all speak with tongues, and there come in those who are uninformed or unbelievers, will they not say that you are out of your mind? (1 Corinthians 14:23)

In verse 40 of that same chapter, Paul also told us that all things were to be done decently and in order. Now that we have established that, according to scripture, if one speaks with tongues, it is always man speaking to God and never man speaking to man or God speaking to man, let's continue with the interpretation of tongues.

If it is true by scripture that when a person speaks with tongues, what is being spoken are words to God and not from God, then when a person gives what many call a "message" in tongues, they are speaking to God rather than it being a message from God. When one gives the interpretation of the tongues, how then can the interpretation of the tongues begin with "Thus saith the Lord?" In scripture, it is not the Lord speaking to man; they have it backwards.

According to scripture, what is being spoken is spoken to God, therefore, the interpretation cannot be from God. Any interpretation of tongues that says, "Thus saith the Lord" is unfounded scripturally.

I very well realize that I have just opened a can of worms for many readers. Please don't take me wrong; I find no place in the scriptures where the Holy Spirit has taken His gifts away from the church. The Holy Spirit is still here with us today—and so are His gifts. My point is that what we have seen for years in many circles has become "tradition," and it is nothing less than a repeat of the Corinthians who Paul had to correct because of their abuse in the operation of the gifts.

This is not a contradiction in what I said earlier; the Holy Spirit is still speaking today. He has been speaking since Pentecost, and we in the church need to hear what the Spirit says and turn our ears away from the words of men.

My friends, we can hear from the Holy Spirit ourselves, learn to trust Him, and wait for His direction. I have known many people who can't make decisions on their own. I have had church members who wanted to come to me with every little problem they encountered. The strong Christian is the one who has learned that they don't have to run to man with all of their needs; Jesus said the Holy Spirit was our Helper, and He will show us all things and give us guidance.

Many Christians have been saved with the Holy Spirit living within them for fifty years who have never said one time "thank you" to the Holy Spirit much less lean on Him for daily direction.

For many believers, the Holy Spirit has been completely ignored. How would you feel if you were living (dwelling permanently) in someone's home for years, and the person never even acknowledged that you were there and never spoke a single word to you? We would be grieved. That's one of the reasons the Bible tells us not to grieve the Holy Spirit. (Ephesians 4:30)

How grieved the Holy Spirit must feel to know that He is a permanent resident within our hearts—and we never even acknowledge His presence! We should tell Him that we "love Him and are thankful that He dwells within us." Jesus told us the Holy Spirit would abide with us forever. (John 14:16)

The Holy Spirit does not lead us to worship Him; He speaks only of Christ. I am not saying that we should pray to Him. (This is a topic we'll take up in a future chapter). For now, Jesus told the disciples that we pray to the Father in His name, and we will see in our discussion on the Trinity that we are not to pray to Jesus or the Holy Spirit.

Our Lord's clear instructions for our prayer life is that we pray to the Father in the name of Jesus and to no one else. (John 16:23)

I've had people tell me that the Bible doesn't have answers for everything we face today. According to 2 Peter, it does: "God has given us all things that pertain to life." (2 Peter 1:2–4)

If you look at that verse, it teaches us that "all things" that pertain to life have already been given to us through the knowledge of God and Jesus our Lord. Everything we need in life can be found in Christ. Again, we don't need to be habitually running to ministers and counselors for things that pertain to our lives, God has already given us everything we need to know that pertains to our own lives.

The mature Christian will learn how to pray and trust on their own instead of running to man with every problem we come across. It's also crucial to listen. It's very important that we learn to wait until the Holy Spirit guides us. One of the main reasons God has given every Christian the Holy Spirit to dwell in our hearts is for guidance. Jesus said so Himself:

> However, when He, the Spirit of truth, has come, He will guide you into all truth; for He will not speak on His own authority, but whatever He hears He will speak; and He will tell you things to come. (John 16:13)

There comes a time for each of us when we don't know what to do; during those times, we find the Holy Spirit (our Helper) there to guide us. Are you ready for this? He'll even intercede for us when we don't know what to pray. Do you mean the Holy Spirit will even pray for us?

Paul wrote in the great chapter of Romans 8 that sometimes we don't know what we should pray for as we should, and during those times, the Holy Spirit will make intercessions for us according to the will of God. When we do this, Paul gives us that wonderful promise that everything will work out for our good for those who love God.

> Likewise, the Spirit also helps in our weaknesses. For we do not know what we should pray for as we ought, but the Spirit Himself makes intercession for us with groanings which cannot be uttered.

> Now He who searches the hearts knows what the mind of the Spirit is, because He makes intercession for the saints according to the will of God.
>
> And we know that all things work together for good to those who love God, to those who are the called according to His purpose. (Romans 8:26–28)

Did you see that? There are things we can know when we don't know the will of God for our lives. We can know that everything is going to work out for our good when we love God, and we can also know that the Holy Spirit does know the will of God for us. He will intercede for us according to God's will.

I've been there more than once in my life, and I can testify that the Holy Spirit can intercede to God for us. That's the Trinity right there. The Holy Spirit (the third person in the Godhead) intercedes for us according to the will of God (the first person in the Godhead).

I know this from many experiences in my life. There have been times when I did not know the answer, which will happen with all of us sooner or later, and there have been times I didn't know which way to turn. In those times, I would simply worship, praise God, and love the Lord. I've had the Holy Spirit intercede on my behalf many times.

When you don't know the way, worship. When you don't know the path, praise. When you don't know which way He's leading, love Him! I can promise you, by His Word, that the Holy Spirit will be there on your behalf.

As we recap the above, we conclude that we have three distinct and primary speakers at three different periods in biblical history:

- God the Father spoke in the Old Testament.
- Jesus spoke during His earthly ministry.
- The Holy Spirit has spoken since the Lord's ascension and Pentecost.

CHAPTER 5

SINGULAR TERMINOLOGY

The Godhead and the church, which are made up of multiple persons, are spoken of with plural pronouns—and they also are both used in the singular. This is very important because it addresses an argument used by non-Trinitarians.

It is similar to how one sports team can include many players or how one church with multiple members can be referenced in the singular. The Godhead can be spoken of in the singular, yet it includes three distinct persons.

We can see this in our government and military branches with terms like Congress, Senate, Army, Navy, and Air Force. Even though we are using singular terms, multiple members are included in each of them.

With terms like the "First Christian Church of New York," we have one church (singular) that contains multiple members (plural).

Think of your family name. With the Smith family or the Jones family, aren't they made up of multiple family members but referenced as a single family?

Some have used the example of an egg. One egg has three parts. The egg is still called a single egg although it has three parts: the outer shell, the white, and the yoke.

Let's relate this principle to the Godhead in scripture.

THE GODHEAD (SINGULAR)

God is spoken of in scripture in singular terminology. Isaiah and Hosea speak of God in the singular. They will let us know there is no God beside Him, that God is the Lord, and that there is no other. (Isaiah 44:6, 8; 45:5; 46:9; Hosea 13:4)

Trinitarians believe in one God—not three. We believe in one God, including three persons in the Triune Godhead. Trinitarians believe these verses wholeheartedly. There is only one God!

The Godhead in scripture is addressed in singular terminology. Can there actually be multiples within one singular? This is where many get tripped up. Can more than one be in a single entity?

Our first example will be the church. The church is spoken of many times in the Bible in singular format, yet we know that the church is made up of more than one person. This is completely scriptural as we will see.

THE CHURCH (SINGULAR)

> Husbands, love your wives, just as Christ also loved the church and gave Himself for her, that He might sanctify and cleanse her with the washing of water by the word, that He might present her to Himself a glorious church, not having spot or wrinkle or any such thing, but that she should be holy and without blemish. (Ephesians 5:25–27)

The NKJV, ESV, NASB, NIV and TLV all use the word "her" in the above verses. Some translations such as the ASV and KJV actually use the word "it" rather than "her". Either way, regardless of whether we use "her" or "it" we are speaking in the singular. We know that "a" church or "the" church (singular) is comprised of multiple members (plural).

The above quoted verse is the NJKV, instead of using "it," uses the words "her" and "she." Both are still singular in form, but there's more.

The Greek word *autos* can refer to he, she, it, himself, herself, itself, or themselves. Whether the translation uses "it" or "her," either word is still appropriate. Most word-for-word translations use the word "her." Our emphasis is that all these terms are singular.

Although the church is spoken of in singular, the church still is comprised of multiple members. The same is true of God; there is one God including three persons.

OK, buckle your seat belts. The verses we just read use the word "her." Would you believe it if I told you that the Bible also calls the church a "man?" The following verse references the church as "a man," which is singular.

> And He Himself gave some to be apostles, some prophets, some evangelists, and some pastors and teachers, for the equipping of the saints for the work of ministry, for the edifying of the body of Christ, till we all come to the unity of the faith and of the knowledge of the Son of God, to a perfect man, to the measure of the stature of the fullness of Christ. (Ephesians 4:11–13)

Did you notice the singular terms of "the body" of Christ, unto a "perfect man, and "to the measure of the statue of the fullness of Christ?" Therefore, the church can be known as a "her" or a "man" that is growing into the stature of Christ. The "body" of Christ can be described as a man or a woman.

I'm sure you can see that all of these terms are singular, yet in each case, they are comprised of multiple persons. One can contain multiples.

If one applies this same scriptural principle to God, we can understand (just as the scripture says) there are "three that bear witness in heaven" and these three "agree in one" (1 John 5:8).

Still not convinced? Paul continues on in Corinthians with the exact same logic, and he is going to spell it out for us.

> For as the body is one and has many members, but all the members of that one body, being many, are one body, so also is Christ.
>
> For by one Spirit we were all baptized into one body—whether Jews or Greeks, whether slaves or free—and have all been made to drink into one Spirit.
>
> For in fact the body is not one member but many. But now God has set the members, each one of them, in the body just as He pleased.
>
> And if they were all one member, where would the body be? But now indeed there are many members, yet one body. (1 Corinthians 12:12–14, 18–20)

As we can see from the above verses, "one" spoken of in the singular can include "many members" spoken of in the plural. I'm sure you saw the following phrases:

- one body (singular) being many (plural)
- all members (plural) are of one body (singular)
- one body (singular) being Jews, Greeks (plural)
- the body (singular) is not one but many (plural)
- God has set the members, each one (plural) in the body (singular)
- indeed there are many members (plural) yet one body (singular)

Concerning the Godhead, this addresses the argument of "how can one be three?"

The divine nature of God is that there is one God, which includes three persons: God the Father, God the Son, and God the Holy Spirit.

CHAPTER 6

THE TRINITY IN GENESIS

Although some of the scriptures related to the Trinity in the Old Testament were covered in the first five chapters, we felt it would be good to dedicate a chapter placing all of the scriptures in one single chapter. You will see there will be many other verses confirming the Trinity in this chapter that were not referenced in the previous chapters as well.

When we open the Bible to the book of Genesis, the Trinity is immediately before us in chapter 1 and the first two verses.

In the following verses, we see that God was in the beginning—and it was the Holy Spirit that was moving (hovering) over the face of the waters. The Holy Spirit had a part in creation (or we could say "re-creation" if one holds to the doctrine of a world that existed before Adam. Moses, Jeremiah, Jesus, and Peter have much to say on that topic, but it goes beyond the scope of this subject. Regardless of which belief one has concerning this, we all can agree that God was in the beginning (whenever that was, sometime in eternity past), and the Holy Spirit moved on the face of the world's first flood that is mentioned in Genesis 1:2.

> In the beginning God created the heavens and the earth. The earth was without form, and void; and darkness was on the face of the deep. And the Spirit of God was hovering over the face of the waters. (Genesis 1:1–2)

Next, we see God uses the plural pronouns of "us" and "our" at the creation of Adam. God uses the terminology of "our" image and "our" likeness.

> Then God said, "Let *Us* make man in *Our* image, according to *Our* likeness." (Genesis 1:26)

Once we get into chapter 2, we see that the word "one" can be one in unity and agreement rather than one in number. Adam and Eve were made "one" flesh, which would be impossible if we interpreted this verse as one in number.

In the New Testament, when the scripture says that there are three that bear witness both in heaven and in earth, the scriptures will tell us that these three "agree in one." In this case, we interpret "one" here to be one in agreement.

> Therefore, a man shall leave his father and mother and be joined to his wife, and *they shall become one flesh.* (Genesis 2:24)

Remaining in Genesis, we now go to chapter 3. We will see the plural pronoun "us" used in relation with the Godhead. After Adam and Eve fell in the Garden of Eden, God said that both of them had become as one of "us." This shows plurality in the Triune God.

> Then the Lord God said, "Behold, the man has become like one of *Us*, to know good and evil." (Genesis 3:22)

We conclude in the eleventh chapter of Genesis, at the Tower of Babel, concerning Nimrod. During this time, all people of the earth were of one language. This happened after Noah's flood and is where the languages of the earth were established by God. Again, we will see the word "us" where our Holy God is spoken of in plurality, giving proof of more than one person in the Godhead:

> And the Lord said, "Indeed the people are one, and they all have one language, and this is what they begin to do; now nothing that they propose to do will be withheld from them.
>
> Come, *let us go down* and there confuse their language, that they may not understand one another's speech. (Genesis 11:6–7)

In Genesis, we have seen the Trinity in chapters 1, 2, 3, and 11.

CHAPTER 7

THE TRINITY IN EXODUS

The Hebrew name for God is Elohim. In another chapter, we will go much more in detail with Elohim. For now, Elohim is plural for "El," which is singular.

Elohim was used many times in the scriptures, and it was even used in relation to false gods. In Exodus 12, Elohim is spoken of in plurality with these false gods:

> And against all the gods (Elohim—plural) of Egypt I will execute judgment: I am the Lord. (Exodus 12:12)

Elohim is plural and is the same name for God in the Old Testament (Hebrew Bible). This again gives validity to plurality in the Godhead. Even though this is a brief chapter, there much more information concerning "El" and "Elohim" later.

The purpose of placing this one verse in a chapter of its own is to show that Elohim is found in plural reference in Exodus. This is good to remember for later.

CHAPTER 8

THE TRINITY IN PSALMS

David will give us information about plurality in the Godhead. We will show three separate instances of how the psalmist, the sweet singer of Israel, speaks of the Trinity. We will see in these three passages that all three persons of the Godhead will be acknowledged.

FIRST EXAMPLE

This passage is one of my favorites, and it is quoted by Jesus (Matthew 22:4), Paul (Hebrews 1:13), and Peter (Acts 2:34). This is the verse Jesus used to "hush up" the Pharisees; after Jesus quoted this verse, the Pharisees asked Him no more questions:

> The Lord said to my Lord, "Sit at My right hand, Till I make Your enemies Your footstool." (Psalm 110:1)

Who are these two Lords? One Lord is speaking to David's Lord. The conversation is happening in heaven. One Lord tells the other Lord to sit at His right hand and tells Him that He will make "your" enemies "your" footstool.

The terminology is straightforward. There is a conversation taking place in heaven between these two separate Lords. Don't forget that Jesus, Paul, and Peter all confirm that this conversation took place. David is certainly not the only reference we have.

SECOND EXAMPLE

Did the psalmist have another verse to confirm that the Lord speaks to His Son? In the next verse, notice the words "I," "My," "You," and "Me." Like the previous scripture, this verse uses the phrase "The Lord said." The one He is speaking to is called His Son whom He has begotten. John also used the word "begotten" when he told us that God gave "His only begotten Son" (John 3:16).

> Yet I have set My King on My holy hill of Zion. I will declare the decree: The Lord has said to Me, "You are My Son. Today I have begotten You." (Psalm 2:6–7)

The "I have set" is God the Father, the "My" is God the Father, "King" is God the Son, "The Lord" is God the Father, "Me" is God the Son, "You" is God the Son, "My" is God the Father, "Son" is God the Son, "I have begotten" is God the Father and "You" is God the Son.

By the way, this verse was quoted by Paul three times in the New Testament (Acts 13:33 and Hebrews 1:5; 5:5). Both the Old and New Testaments confirm the Trinity with this verse. When we compare Psalms 2:7 with Acts 13:33 Paul actually verifies the identities of both God the Father and Jesus whom He raised from the dead. Paul also states in Hebrews 5:5 that it was not Jesus who glorified Himself to be High Priest but God the Father who had spoke the words "You are My Son, Today I have begotten You." God gave Jesus the High Priest position, not Jesus Himself.

Third Example

In the first two examples, only two persons of the Godhead are mentioned. Does the book of Psalms have any references to the Holy Spirit in relation with the Trinity? David had committed the terrible sins of murder and adultery. We have his prayer of repentance in Psalm 51. No one disputes that David's prayer is "to God."

As Jesus used the word "God" while He was separated from His Father on the cross, crying, "My God, My God, why have you forsaken me?" The psalmist usually called God his Lord (as in Psalm 23), but he is now calling his Lord "God."

David goes now to God. After we go to "God" for forgiveness, He becomes our "Father" and "Lord."

Jesus said that in the Day of Judgment, many will say, "Lord, Lord, have we not cast out devils and done many wonderful works and prophesied?" Jesus then said, "I say unto them, 'Depart from me you that work iniquity, I never knew you.'" Jesus is not "Lord" to all who call Him Lord. Jesus also said, "Why do you call me Lord and do not do the things that I say?"

From that, we see that Jesus is not our Lord until we have made Him the Lord of our lives. Confessing that Jesus is Lord along with faith in His sacrifice on the cross is what brings salvation (Romans 10:9–10, 13). Not all are God's children; we are all His creation, but not all are His children.

In Psalms 51, David uses the word "God" six times, but he never calls Him "Lord."

- Have mercy upon me, O God.
- Create in me a clean heart, O God.
- Deliver me from the guilt of bloodshed, O God.
- The God of my salvation.
- The sacrifices of God are a broken spirit.
- These, O God, You will not despise.

I will let you read David's complete prayer yourself in Psalm 51.

Something very interesting is about to happen in verse 11. David has been praying to God, and after using the word "God" five times, he asks God not to take the Holy Spirit away from him.

We have already established that the Holy Spirit is God. He was there in the beginning (Genesis 1:1–2) when He moved (hovered) over the face of the waters. David now prays to God and asks that God does not take away the Holy Spirit from him.

> Do not cast me away from Your presence, and do not take Your Holy Spirit from me. (Psalm 51:11)

David is praying to God and ask that God's Holy Spirit not be taken from him. Notice the word "Your." He makes two things crystal clear:

- God is the one who does the "taking."
- The Holy Spirit is who David does not want God to take away.

This is one of the worst things that happened to King Saul (the first king of Israel). The Spirit of the Lord left Saul and never returned to him:

> But the Spirit of the Lord departed from Saul, and an evil spirit from the Lord troubled him. 1 (Samuel 16:14)

We call attention to three words: "of the Lord." It was the Holy Spirit of the Lord who departed from Saul. David knew this. After the Spirit of the Lord left Saul, David would come in and play music to drive away the evil spirits. He had seen this firsthand as an eyewitness.

> David would take a harp and play it with his hand. Then Saul would become refreshed and well, and the distressing spirit would depart from him. (1 Samuel 16:22–23)

David had seen the Spirit of God depart from Saul, and he didn't want the same thing to happen to him. Remember what the scripture says about Samson? Samson had taken a "nap in the lap" of Delilah, and she cut his seven locks and cried that the Philistines were upon him. This reminds us of Samson when the Lord had departed from him:

> So he awoke from his sleep, and said, "I will go out as before, at other times, and shake myself free!" But he did not know that the Lord had departed from him. (Judges 16:20)

Before we close this chapter, I want to remind the believer that Jesus said to the those who believe in Him that the Holy Spirit would come and abide with us "forever" (John 14:16). In the Old Testament, before the Holy Spirit came at the Day of Pentecost, He would sometimes come upon men and empower them to do certain things—and then He would leave. In other words, He didn't stay permanently.

After Jesus ascended to the Father, He prayed that the Holy Spirit would come, and Jesus told us that when He came, He would stay with us forever!

> In Him you also trusted, after you heard the word of truth, the Gospel of your salvation; in whom also, having believed, you were sealed with the Holy Spirit of promise, who is the guarantee of our inheritance until the redemption of the purchased possession, to the praise of His glory. (Ephesians 1:13–14)

This is a wonderful verse. We are sealed with the Holy Spirit, and He is our guarantee. The Greek word for *seal* is *sphragizo*, which means that when something has been purchased, a mark is placed to show it's already been bought. In other words, it's a seal of ownership. It's like if you bought something and hadn't yet picked it up, they might put a "sold" sign on it.

When we were saved, the Holy Spirit placed a seal on us that says "sold!" Jesus bought us, and at the Rapture, Jesus is going to come and pick us up! And we have been sealed until that day of redemption. Jesus bought us at Calvary's cross!

Peter told us this as well:

> Knowing that you were not redeemed with corruptible things, like silver or gold, from your aimless conduct received by tradition from your fathers, but with the precious blood of Christ, as of a lamb without blemish and without spot. (1 Peter 1:18–19)

Paul jumps in on this too:

> For you were bought at a price; therefore glorify God in your body and in your spirit, which are God's. (1 Corinthians 6:20)

Jesus bought us, we are His, His Spirit is within us, we are the temple of the Holy Spirit, and He is our guarantee!

My friend, we are God's property. He bought us at Golgotha's hill, and we belong to Him lock, stock, and barrel. By that, I mean spirit, soul, and body! Head to toe, we belong to God completely.

The word guarantee means down payment or a pledge. This scripture is saying that when Jesus saved us, He placed the Holy Spirit within our hearts. The Holy Spirit is the "deposit." Today, we don't have all of the benefits of being saved, but right now, in our hearts, we have the Holy Spirit. This is our guarantee that, at the Rapture, Jesus is going to come and pick us up!

How wonderful it is to be a part of that Bible-taught, heaven-sought, devil-fought, God-wrought, blood-bought band of believers! Redeemed! That will be our theme song when we get to glory!

I guess I got a little carried away here. We're supposed to be talking about the Trinity in the book of Psalms:

- The Lord said (first person in the Godhead) to my Lord (second person in the Godhead).
- Sit at My (first person in the Godhead) right hand.
- Until I (first person in the Godhead) make Your (second person in the Godhead) enemies Your (second person in the Godhead) footstool.
- The Lord said (first person in the Godhead) to Me (second person in the Godhead).
- You (second person in the Godhead) are My (first person in the Godhead) Son (second person in the Godhead).
- Today, I (first person in the Godhead) have begotten You (second person in the Godhead).
- Do not take Your (first person in the Godhead) Holy Spirit (third person in the Godhead) from me.

Yes, the Psalmist David, the Darling of Israel spoke in the Old Testament of the Trinity.

CHAPTER 9

THE TRINITY IN ISAIAH

Isaiah will tell us much about the Trinity. We begin in Isaiah 6:8. Isaiah had been a man of unclean lips and dwelled among people of unclean lips. (Peter wasn't the only one who had a little difficulty with cursing.) In the year that King Uzziah died, Isaiah actually saw the Lord. He saw God sitting on a throne, and he even saw the Lord's clothing. He said that God's robe filled the temple.

Seraphim angels were crying three Holies before the Lord. Isaiah felt his unworthiness and cried, "Woe is me. I am undone. I'm a man of unclean lips." The next thing Isaiah said is that he had seen the King.

In another book, we'll discuss whether or not God can be seen. Actually, there were quite a few people in scripture who saw God. Moses saw God face-to-face and his hinder parts (although he did not see God in "all His glory," no human man could see God in all His glory and live").

Abraham saw God and ate with Him. Daniel saw God and the Son simultaneously and called God the "Ancient of Days" and Jesus the "Son of Man." Job said, concerning the resurrection, that in his flesh, he would see God. John saw Him on Patmos. Adam and Eve saw him in the Garden of Eden. Jacob saw God face to face at Peniel and even wrestled physically with Him. Aaron and his sons Nadab and Abihu and seventy elders saw God at Mount Sinai. Jesus told us in the Sermon on the Mount that the pure in heart would see God.

Isaiah will be among this list as well. Isaiah says that he saw The Lord high and lifted up.

My friends, God is not some phantom or ghost floating around on clouds. He is a real God with a real body, sitting on a real throne, and at this moment, Jesus in His glorified body is sitting right next to Him as our High Priest, Advocate, and Mediator.

We are on the topic of the Trinity, so the question arises, "Did Isaiah mention the Trinity?"

Isaiah 6

> Also, I heard the voice of the Lord, saying, "Who shall I send, and who will go for us?" (Isaiah 6:8)

Did you notice the plural pronoun "us?" This is a glorious record of the Trinity. Isaiah goes on to answer the call by saying, "Here am I Lord, send me."

Isaiah prophesied some seven hundred years before the birth of Christ. He will tell us that Jesus will be born of a virgin and would be a son (male). If one reads Isaiah's prophecies concerning Jesus, they will find words such as Son, His, He, and Him. The Messiah was prophesied to be a male child.

After the child was born, He was to be crucified. Isaiah predicted this in chapter 53. When we read these verses, please note the things that "God will do with Christ" on the cross. This will help with understanding the Trinity. Pay close attention to what "God does" rather than what "man does."

ISAIAH 7

Here are Isaiah's prophecies:

> Therefore the Lord Himself will give you a sign: Behold, the virgin shall conceive and bear a Son, and shall call His name Immanuel. (Isaiah 7:14)

Isaiah goes on to say that the Messiah would be "given" to us. That's an important word. If the Messiah is "given," then who is the giver? We all know from John that God "gave" His only begotten Son (John 3:16). God the Father is the Giver, and the Messiah (Christ) is the gift. This proves more than one in the Godhead:.

> For unto us a Child is born, Unto us a Son is *given*; and the government will be upon His shoulder. And His name will be called Wonderful, Counselor, Mighty God, Everlasting Father, Prince of Peace. (Isaiah 9:6)

In Isaiah 53, we see the Trinity again.

Of course, this is without a doubt the most popular chapter in Isaiah. It declares the distinction between God the Father and the Son. Verse 4 will tell us that Jesus will be "smitten by God."

ISAIAH 53

> Smitten by God, and afflicted. (Isaiah 53:4)

Verse 6 tells us that "the Lord" lays all our iniquities on Jesus.

> The Lord has laid on Him the iniquity of us all. (Isaiah 53:6)

Verse 10 says that "the Lord bruised Him, places grief upon Him, makes His soul an offering for sin and the pleasure of the Lord's hand would prosper in His hand."

You will hear me say this many times in the book: the Crucifixion was not an assassination, it was an offering to God and a sacrifice "to" God. It was not the Romans who bruised Jesus:

> Yet it pleased the Lord to bruise Him; He has put Him to grief. When You make His soul an offering for sin, He shall see His seed, He shall prolong His days, And the pleasure of the Lord shall prosper in His hand. (Isaiah 53:10)

From these verses, we have to ask certain questions:

- By whom was Jesus smitten?
- Who was it that "afflicted" Him?
- Who laid our iniquities on Him?
- Who bruised Him?
- Who placed grief on Him?
- Who made His soul and offering for sin?
- To whom was Jesus offered?
- Whose pleasure was placed in the hands of Jesus?

Now let's go to Isaiah 61. When Jesus went to the synagogue in His home town Nazareth, He stood to read and then sat down and taught. We will deal with this in detail when we see the Trinity in the New Testament.

These passages Jesus read from Isaiah almost cost Him His life. After Jesus quoted this verse, He sat down and told the people that "today this scripture was fulfilled in their ears." Jesus grew up in Nazareth, and at that time, it was a small town where everyone knew everyone.

Nazareth did not accept Jesus, and after Jesus quoted Isaiah, they took Him to thc top of a mountain to cast Him off the cliff to kill Him. This mountain is believed to be Mount Precipice, which is just outside Nazareth on the southern side. When I visited there, I saw the steep drop. Anyone falling from this mountain would have no chance of survival.

Jesus had a time to die, and He would say, "My hour has not yet come." (John 7:6, 30) The Holy Spirit would see to it that Jesus would not die until He reached Golgotha.

When Jesus went into the synagogue, what did He read? When we look at what He read, is there any information regarding the Trinity? If you want to jump ahead, this story starts in Luke 4:16. For now, the minister of the synagogue handed Jesus the scroll that contained the following from Isaiah.

Isaiah 61

> The Spirit of the Lord God is upon Me, Because the Lord has anointed Me to preach good tidings to the poor; He has sent Me to heal the brokenhearted, to proclaim liberty to the captives, and the opening of the prison to those who are bound; to proclaim the acceptable year of the Lord. (Isaiah 61:1–2)

In the first line alone, we see the Trinity, and it continues through the rest of the verse.

First, we see the Holy Spirit in the first line.

Second, the Holy Spirit is called the Spirit "of the Lord."

Third, we see that the Holy Spirit would rest on "Me." We know who "the Spirit" is, and we know who "the Lord" is. We have to ask, "Who is the Me? Jesus said in Luke 4 that "He" was the "Me." When Jesus read this passage in Nazareth, He sat down, looked at the people, and said, "Today is this scripture fulfilled in your ears." He was the Me!

Fourth, the verse says, "He has anointed Me." Certainly Jesus did not anoint Himself. The scripture says it was the "Lord" who anointed Jesus.

Fifth, Isaiah next prophesies that the Messiah would be "sent." The line says, "He has sent me." If He was sent, who sent Him? The scripture says it was "the Lord." The scripture is filled with verses saying that God sent Jesus. (John 3:17)

We see the Trinity in this verse in the following phrases:

- The Spirit (third person of the Godhead).
- Of the Lord (first person of the Godhead).
- Is upon Me (second person of the Godhead).
- The Lord has anointed Me (first and second persons of the Godhead).
- He has sent Me (first and second persons of the Godhead).

Was the Holy Spirit mentioned in the Old Testament? Yes, the Holy Spirit is called in the Old Testament (Hebrew Bible):

- my Spirit
- the Spirit of God
- the Spirit of the Lord
- His Spirit
- the Spirit
- your Spirit

Here are the scriptures for verification:

- The Spirit of God (Genesis 1:2; 41:38; Exodus 31:3; 35:31; Numbers 24:2; 1 Samuel 11:6; 19:20, 23; 2 Chronicles 15:1; 24:20; Job 33:4; Daniel 5:14)
- The Spirit of the Lord (Judges 3:10; 6:34; 11:29; 13:25; 14:6, 19; 15:14; 1 Samuel 10:6; 10:10; 16:13, 14; 2 Samuel 23:2; 1 Kings 18:12; 2 Kings 2:16; 2 Chronicles 20:14; Isaiah 11:2; 40:13; 59:19; 61:1; 63:14; Ezekiel 11:5; 37:1; Micah 2:7; 3:8)
- The Spirit (Numbers 11:26; 27:18; 1 Chronicles 12:18; Ezekiel 3:12, 14; 8:3; 11:1, 24; 43:5; Malachi 2:15)
- Holy Spirit (Isaiah 63:11)

- Spirit of the Holy God (Daniel 4:8, 9, 18; 5:11)
- Spirit of Wisdom (Isaiah 11:2)
- Spirit of Counsel (Isaiah 11:2)
- Spirit of Knowledge (Isaiah 11:2)
- Spirit of Grace (Zechariah 12:10)
- My Spirit (Isaiah 30:1; 59:21; Ezekiel 39:29; Haggai 2:5; Zechariah 4:6)
- His Spirit (Isaiah 34:16; 42:1; 44:3; Zechariah 7:12)
- Your Spirit (Nehemiah 9:30; Psalm 51:12; Psalm 104:30; 143:10)

Isaiah, the most quoted of all Old Testament prophets gave us the truth about the Trinity. Isaiah saw God high and lifted up in the temple (chapter 6), he told us that God would give us a virgin born Son (chapter 7), he told us of all the God would do to Jesus on the cross, (chapter 53) and he told us of how the Holy Spirit would anoint Jesus to do many wonderful things (chapter 61). Isaiah references all three persons of the Triune Godhead.

CHAPTER 10

THE TRINITY IN DANIEL

Daniel (a prophet) saw both the God the Father and the Son simultaneously. He saw the Son standing before God the Father on His throne. God the Father was seated on the throne, and God the Son was "brought near before" the throne. The Father is called the "Ancient of Days," and the Son is called the "Son of Man."

> I watched till thrones were put in place, and the Ancient of Days was seated; and behold, one like the Son of Man, coming with the clouds of heaven! He came to the Ancient of Days, and they brought Him near before Him. Then to Him was given dominion and glory and a kingdom. (Daniel 7:9, 13)

Daniel saw God the Father (the Ancient of Days) sitting on the throne and God the Son as He was "brought near." Both are obviously different persons within the Godhead. No one can deny it is God who sits on the throne and that it is Christ who stands before Him being "brought near." Also note the line that says the Son of Man was brought "to" the Ancient of Days.

Let's go through this slowly. First, Daniel sees God sitting on His throne. Daniel gives a full description of his garments (clothing), hair, and throne. He says a fiery stream was issued from before Him. He saw the thousands of thousands standing before Him. He then speaks of the books that were opened.

What happens next is remarkable. He sees the Son of Man, and the Son of Man came "to" the Ancient of Days as He was sitting on the throne. The Son of Man came to Him, and the Son of Man was brought "near before" Him.

We know the Son of Man is Jesus (the second person in the Godhead) because the Ancient of Days "gives" to him dominion, glory, and a kingdom.

Daniel says that His dominion is an everlasting dominion that will never pass away or be destroyed. This proves the Son of Man can be none other than Jesus Himself.

When God promised David that the Messiah would come from his family, he told him that His throne would be established forever (2 Samuel 7:16; 2 Chronicles 13:5; Psalm 89:29, 36, 37). Isaiah said that the Messiah's government and kingdom would be established forever. Gabriel told Mary that Jesus would be given the throne of David and His kingdom would have no end (Luke 1:32, 33).

The Son of Man seen by Daniel is "given" from the Ancient of Days the everlasting kingdom that would never pass away or see destruction. Notice how the Ancient of Days on the throne gives to the Son of Man this kingdom. This shows plurality in the Godhead.

Daniel also calls attention to the Holy Spirit. He calls the Holy Spirit the "Spirit of the Holy God" and the "Spirit of God." (Daniel 4:8, 9, 18; 5:11, 14)

Each of these names are in capital letters, and these are names of each person in the Trinity as written by Daniel:

- Ancient of Days (first person in the Godhead)
- Son of Man (second person in the Godhead)
- Spirit of the Holy God (third person in the Godhead)

CHAPTER 11

THE TRINITY IN OLD TESTAMENT TYPES

We could write an entire book on the types and shadows of Jesus and the Holy Spirit in the Old Testament. We will only give just a few of the most popular.

Abraham Sending Forth Eleazar to Bring Back a Bride for Isaac

In Genesis 24 we have the story of Abraham sending his servant Eleazar to bring back a bride for his son Isaac. Although Eleazar is not mentioned by name and is only called the oldest servant in this chapter, almost all scholars agree this servant is Eleazar.

- Abraham is a type of God the Father who desires a bride for his son Isaac.
- Isaac is a type of Jesus.
- Eleazar is a type of the Holy Spirit who has been sent to get the bride.
- Rebekah is a type of the church who is brought back and presented as a bride for Isaac.

This is one of the most romantic chapters in the Bible, and I encourage everyone to read it. Notice that we have listed "in type" all persons of the Trinity in the above bullet points.

Abraham Offers Isaac on Mount Moriah

The event happens in Genesis 22. Abraham (a type of God the Father) is told to take his "only" son to Mount Moriah for a sacrifice. He is actually told to sacrifice his only son, Isaac. Abraham did have another son (Ishmael), yet God tells Abraham to take his "only" son (verse 2). God had promised that the Messiah would come from Isaac, and Abraham only has one son in the eyes of God.

When Abraham and Isaac reach Mount Moriah, Abraham took wood and placed it on Isaac's back (verse 6).

Most are familiar with the rest of the story of how Abraham and Isaac go up the mountain. Isaac (I believe voluntarily) submitted to his father and laid himself on the altar (no mention is recorded of Isaac putting up any type of a struggle). We do not know exactly how old Isaac was at this time, but we do know he was strong enough to carry wood up the mountain on his back (Genesis 22:6). We also know that Abraham had journeyed "many days in the land of the Philistines" (Genesis 21:34). Abraham did tell the servants to wait while he and "the boy" went to worship (Genesis 22:5). Since the trip to Moriah was a three-day journey, Isaac had to be old enough to make the journey. When Abraham lifted the knife to take Isaac's life, God intervened and spared the son.

Abraham is a type of God the Father providing His only son as a sacrifice, and the wood on Isaac's back and taking the wood to the top of the mountain is a type of the cross that Jesus bore and carried to Calvary. Isaac rising from the altar is a type of the resurrection of Jesus who arose from the dead after being placed on the cross. Isaac being Abraham's "only" son is a type of what John wrote in John 3:16 that God so loved the world that He gave His "only" begotten Son.

Joseph and Jacob

The story of Jacob and Joseph begins in Genesis 30 and continues all the way to Genesis 50.

There is probably no better type of the Father-and-Son relationship between God the Father and Jesus the Son than that of Jacob and Joseph.

- Joseph was the beloved son of his father, and Jesus told us that the Father loves the Son.
- Joseph was a miracle baby at birth because his mother, Rachel, was barren. Jesus was a miracle baby born of a virgin.
- Jacob's heart was torn when the saw the blood of his son on the coat of many colors. God the Father darkened the heavens between noon and 3:00 p.m. when Jesus was crucified. How God the Father's heart must have hurt as he beheld the blood of His Son.
- Joseph was the firstborn from Rachel, and Jesus was God's only begotten Son.
- Joseph and Jesus were both shepherds. Jesus, of course, is our Good Shepherd.
- Joseph was rejected by his brothers. Jesus came to "His own," and His own did not receive Him. They were both hated by their brethren.
- Jacob sent Joseph to the brothers who hated him, and God the Father sent Jesus to the lost house of Israel.
- Both Joseph and Jesus were predicted to be exalted.
- Both were exalted.
- Joseph was exalted and was only second to Pharaoh. Jesus was exalted and sits at the Father's right hand.
- Joseph was thrown in a pit, and Jesus was placed in a tomb.
- Joseph was raised from the pit and exalted, and Jesus was raised from the tomb and exalted.
- Joseph was stripped of his coat of many colors, and Jesus was stripped of His robe.

- Joseph was sold for twenty pieces of silver, and Jesus was betrayed for thirty pieces of silver.
- Joseph was carried to Egypt, and Jesus was carried to Egypt after His birth.
- Joseph was falsely accused, and Jesus's accusers made false accusations.
- The Bible says that "God was with Joseph," and the scriptures say, "God was with Jesus."
- Joseph revealed his identity to his brothers, and they bowed before him. Israel will bow before Jesus at the Second Coming, and Jesus will reveal Himself and show His identity with the piercings in His hands.
- It is believed that Joseph was around thirty years of age when he began serving Pharaoh, and Luke said Jesus was about thirty when He started His ministry of working for His Father.
- Joseph forgave those who wronged him. On the cross, Jesus forgave those who crucified Him.
- Joseph saved the people of Egypt, and Jesus is the Savior of the world.
- Joseph's bride was given to him by Pharaoh, and she was a Gentile. The bride of Christ (the church) is Gentile.
- It is worth noting that not one sin is spoken of concerning Joseph. The Bible said that Jesus knew no sin, lived a sinless life, and was our Lamb without blemish. The thief on the cross said Jesus had done nothing amiss, and Pilate even had to say, "I find no fault in Him."

The relationship of Jacob and Joseph is a type of the relationship between God and His Son. Jacob is a type of God the Father, and Joseph is a type of God the Son.

MOSES

Moses prophesied that a prophet would rise up from among the Jews, and he said that the prophet would be like himself (Deuteronomy 18:15). This was part of Peter's inaugural message on the day of Pentecost (Acts 3:22). Even Stephen, the church's first martyr, spoke of it in his discourse before the Sanhedrin council (Acts 7:37).

- Moses and Jesus were miracle babies, and they both came into the world with a death sentence. Moses was to be cast into the Nile, and Herod sought to kill Jesus. Their lives were spared at birth.
- Moses and Jesus both lived in Egypt.
- Moses and Jesus both were sent to the house of Israel to deliver them.
- Moses is known to the Jews as a lawgiver, and when Jesus arrived, He preached His longest message during the Sermon on the Mount. In that sermon, Jesus went even stronger than Mosaic law. Moses gave "commandment" to Israel, and Jesus told us that we will "keep His commandments" if we love Him.
- Moses fasted in mount Sinai for forty days, and Jesus fasted on the Mount of Temptation (close to Jericho) for forty days.
- Moses was an adopted son who placed him in line for the throne of all Egypt, and Jesus was adopted by Joseph and will return as the "King of kings."
- Moses served as a shepherd, and Jesus said that He was the "Good Shepherd." He spoke of His followers as His flock, sheep, and fold, and He told us that His sheep hear His voice.
- The Bible says that Moses was the "meekest man in all of the earth." Jesus told us that He was "meek and lowly in heart."
- Moses was a man who performed outstanding miracles as none had ever seen, and Jesus did the same. The miracles of Jesus surpassed Moses, Jesus even raised the dead.

- Moses is known as the deliverer who led people from bondage. Jesus said the Spirit of the Lord had anointed Him to preach deliverance to the captive and set at liberty those who are bruised.
- Moses fed multitudes with bread and meat that came from heaven. Jesus fed thousands with five loaves and two fishes.
- When Moses was on the mountain with God, his face shone as an angel and couldn't be looked at without a veil. Jesus was transfigured on a mountain, and his face shone like the sun.
- There were times that Moses had to intercede for Israel to withhold God's destruction. The Bible says that Jesus today intercedes for us at the right hand of God.
- Moses had to contend with evil Israelites. Jesus had to contend with Pharisees and scribes who were Jews.
- Moses did miracles with water. He turned the Nile to blood, opened the Red Sea, and cured the waters of Marah. Jesus turned water into wine, sent a blind man to water at the pool of Siloam, and even walked on the water. He said, "If any man thirst let him come unto me and drink."
- Moses was discredited by his family when Miriam and Aaron rebelled against him. The brothers and sisters of Jesus did not believe in Him. James and Jude became believers after the resurrection, but before that, they were unbelievers. Jesus, in his hometown of Nazareth, said, "A prophet is not without honor except in his own country and in his own house."
- Moses had seventy elders who assisted him, and Jesus had seventy disciples who followed Him.
- Moses showed himself alive after his death at the Mount of Transfiguration. Jesus showed Himself alive for forty days after His death.
- Moses would have died for His people. Jesus was willing, and He did die for you and me.

God sent Moses with all these attributes, and God sent Jesus into the world with the same characteristics.

CHAPTER 12

THE TRINITY IN THE NEW TESTAMENT

In this chapter, we will take a look at New Testament "concepts" related to the Trinity and will introduce a few more terms. Some of the new terms will refer to God the Father, and others will be related to Jesus.

The Most High God Compared with the Son of the Most High

The definition of the Most High God means supreme and highest.

The title of the "Most High God" only refers to God the Father. The title "Son of the Most High" only refers to Jesus.

In scripture, Jesus is never called the Most High God. He is, however, called the "Son of the Most High God."

Both Mark and Luke record the story of Jesus casting out the legion of demons from the man in the tombs in the country of the Gadarenes. Both record that the demons called Christ the "Son of the Most High God." (Mark 5:7; Luke 8:28). In Mark's record, the demon actually says to Jesus, "I implore you by God" and asked not to be tormented. That's extremely interesting. The demons are talking to

Jesus and imploring Him by God! They called Him the "Son of the Most High God" and implored Him by God. Therefore, how can the Most High God and the Son of the Most High God be one and the same person?

Here's more. In Luke's Gospel, the angel Gabriel was "sent by God" to Mary in Nazareth. After his salutation, Gabriel gives the good news to Mary, a virgin, that she will have a son. The angel tells Mary that Jesus will be great, will be called the "Son of the Highest," and "God will give Him" his throne.

Because she was a virgin, Mary asked, "How?"

Gabriel told her that the "Holy Spirit" would come upon her, and then he said the "power of the Highest" would overshadow her. To nail it down, he tells her that the Holy One who will be born will be called the "Son of God."

> He will be great, and will be called the Son of the Highest; and the Lord God will give Him the throne of His father David.
>
> And He will reign over the house of Jacob forever, and of His kingdom there will be no end."
>
> Then Mary said to the angel, "How can this be, since I do not know a man?"
>
> And the angel answered and said to her, "The Holy Spirit will come upon you, and the power of the Highest will overshadow you; therefore, also, that Holy One who is to be born will be called the Son of God. (Luke 1:32–35)

But the story doesn't end there. We have to talk about some shepherds. Can what happened with them contribute to our topic? What we have read so far happened nine months earlier, and now we pick up with His birth.

The Bible says that we have angels appearing to shepherds in the fields of Bethlehem. I've been to that shepherd's field, and you can still visit the place to this day.

Luke does not record that the angels sang—we've been traditionally taught that—but he says they were praising God and speaking. One might ask, "Do angels sing?" Of course they do. God asked Job where he was when He laid the foundations of the earth when the "morning stars sang together" (Job 38:7). I like that it says that they sang "together." They made up an angelic choir when God created this world.

Angels sing and play musical instruments. Lucifer was a musician, and we have record in the book of Revelation that angels play trumpets. The Bible says that we are going to play harps in heaven (Ezekiel 28:13; Revelation 8:12, 14, 15).

Back to the shepherd's field! These angels had something to say in their praise to God. The Bible says that the angels were praising God. Where was the God they were praising? Jesus was on earth, in a manger, and the angels were saying, "Glory to God in the highest!"

> And suddenly there was with the angel a multitude of the heavenly host praising God and saying: "Glory to God in the highest, and on earth peace, goodwill toward men!" (Luke 2:13–14)

The God in the Highest they were praising was in heaven, Jesus was on earth in a manger to bring peace and goodwill to men.

Now we have established with four different verses of scripture that Jesus is called the "Son of the Most High God," and God is called "God in the Highest" and the "Most High God."

Even though the scripture teaches that Jesus thought it not robbery to be equal with God, Christ voluntarily set aside the expression of His deity and was made lower than the Godhead. (I bet you're thinking I misquoted that). Some translations use "lower than the angels."

The word that was translated angels in the book of Psalms is Elohim. Elohim is the Hebrew name for God. Jesus was made a little lower than God, or even better, since Elohim is in plural form, Jesus was made a little lower than the Godhead:

> For You have made him a little lower than the angels,
> And You have crowned him with glory and honor.
> (Psalm 8:5)

Don't miss the word "made." Jesus was made at the incarnation and conceived of the Holy Spirit a little lower than Elohim. God crowned him with glory and honor.

- Who made Jesus lower than Elohim?
- Who crowned Him with glory and honor?

It was the Holy Spirit by whom He was conceived and made flesh. The way John wrote it in his Gospel is that the Word "became" flesh, and then he goes on to say that they beheld his glory, the glory as of the only begotten of the Father (John 1:14).

Just as David said that Jesus would be crowned with glory, John wrote that he saw His glory. When did they did see it? He saw it on the Mount of Transfiguration!

My friends, Jesus was made lower than Elohim. This is how Paul could later write that the "head of Christ is God" (1 Corinthians 11:3).

Again, this was written by Paul after the resurrection and ascension and is still valid to this day. We conclude that God the Father is the Most High God, and Jesus is the Son of the Most High.

The Trinity in the Great Commission

When Trinitarians begin to teach the Trinity in their churches, this is usually one of the first places they begin because it's so easy to understand without having to go into a deep dive. It's people who make the Trinity hard and confusing.

Before the Lord ascended, He took His disciples to what the Bible calls a high mountain at the Sea of Galilee. Most scholars believe this to the highest mountain known as Mount Arbel. I've been there, and one can overlook the entire Sea of Galilee and the surrounding locations where Jesus spent more than 70 percent of His ministry. Jesus wanted the disciples to have a great vision in taking the Gospel to the ends of the earth. What better mountain than Arbel?

Jesus will now give the disciples the Great Commission. He will tell them to go and make disciples and then give them the formula for baptism. He tells them to baptize in the name of the Father and of the Son and of the Holy Spirit. Jesus includes the entirety of the Godhead in these instructions (Matthew 28:19).

Those who are non-Trinitarians say that these are not names but titles. To address this argument, let's go to the dictionary.

Definition of Title

The "name" given to something to identify or describe it. A title is defined as a name. One will also notice that all these names begin with capital letters since they are names. By the way, did you notice the word the? It shows the distinction between the Father, Son, and Holy Spirit?

The Father, the Son, and the Holy Spirit

- The word "Father" in the New Testament is never used to reference Jesus.
- The word "Son" is never used to reference the Father.
- The words "Father and Son" are never used to reference the Holy Spirit.

Let's look for a moment at God's Hebrew name.

Elohim

In Hebrew (Tanakh), God's name is Elohim. It is plural in its form, yet it's singular in its meaning. In other words, one Godhead (singular) includes God the Father, God the Son, and God the Holy Spirit (plural).

So that we are very clear, there are not three gods; there is only one God, including the Father, Son, and Holy Spirit. There are three distinct persons in the Godhead.

Elohim means majestic and mighty. It is the common Hebrew name for God. El is the singular form of God. Have you ever noticed how many names in the Bible include the two letters "El?"

- Daniel (God is my judge)
- Ezekiel (the strength of God)
- Ishmael (God will hear)
- Gamaliel (the Lord is my reward)
- Samuel (God has heard)
- Joel (Jehovah is the Lord)
- Nathanael (God has given)
- Gabriel (God is my strength)
- Michael (gift from God or who is like God)
- Israel (although Israel is a nation, God changed Jacob's name to Israel, which means "one who prevails with God."
- Immanuel (a name given to Christ, which means God with us)

The last two are the most important. There are many more, but these are some of the most recognizable ones. They are all in the singular. El is singular. To prove this, let's see Elohim in the plural. Elohim (plural) is used for the three persons of the Trinity. Let's take a look at the first book in the Bible.

Genesis 1:1

In the beginning, God (Elohim) is the plural of El. In verse 2, we have mention of the third person in the Godhead: "And the Spirit of God" moved upon the face of the waters.

The word Elohim is found more than 2,750 times in the Bible, and it is even used to reference false gods (plural). This is proven in the next verse:

> And against all the gods (Elohim—plural) of Egypt I will execute judgment: I am the Lord. (Exodus 12:12)

Some people have told me that Matthew 28:19 should read "names" rather than "name." If an ambassador goes to a foreign country and does business in the "name" (singular) of the United States, which is made up of multiple states, it would not be proper to say that the ambassador is wrong for not going "in the names of."

We have fifty (individual) states (plural) that make up one (singular) union. Are we now also going to say Florida isn't a name or California isn't a name?

Some claim that the scripture would read like this: "In the name of the Father, in the name of the Son, and in the name of the Holy Spirit." Would we expect the ambassador to say, "In the name of Texas and in the name of Washington" and state the names of all the states?

Look at the first part of the scripture: "All power is given unto me in heaven and in earth."

Should we rewrite this verse? "All power is given unto me in heaven and all power is given to me in earth." I guess we should go back to Genesis 1:1 and rewrite it: "In the beginning, God created the heaven, and in the beginning, God created the earth." Instead of saying, "The God of Abraham, Isaac, and Jacob," we should say "The God of Abraham, the God of Isaac, and the God of Jacob."

Someone once said, "Humans have five senses, but along with those five senses, we need two more: common and horse!" Understanding what Jesus meant in the Great Commission only requires common sense.

What does "in the name of" mean? It means "by the authority of." The phase "in the name of" is used both in the Old and New Testaments, and it always means by the authority of.

> And these signs will follow those who believe: In My name they will cast out demons; they will speak with new tongues. (Mark 16:17)

Jesus was telling the disciples that using the Lord's name to do these works was by the Lord's authority. Here's another verse spoken by Jesus.

> I have come in My Father's name, and you do not receive Me; if another comes in his own name, him you will receive. (John 5:43)

What did Jesus mean? He was saying that He did not come in His own authority but by the authority of the Father—and what authority He did have!

There are quite a few verses pertaining to the Lord's authority. I'll reference a couple in case you want to look them up. Authority was a big thing to the scribes and Pharisees. They asked Jesus about whose authority He did His works, and they asked Him who gave Him His authority. Those who believed in Him said He spoke with authority and not as the scribes (Matthew 7:29; John 14:10; Matthew 21:23).

Jesus clearly said He had come in His Father's name; therefore, He spoke by His Father's authority. "In the name of" means by the authority of. When we baptize in the name of the Father, the Son, and the Holy Spirit, we have the full backing and authority of the Triune Holy God to do so. If we baptize in the name of Jesus only, we would be robbing the Father and the Holy Spirit of their authority in baptism.

Imagine if you were to do a job for "Company A and B Inc." If you did the job in the name of "A" only, wouldn't you be robbing Company B of their proper authority? Baptizing according to Matthew 28:19 automatically includes the "Son."

What if you went to the doctor, and the doctor gave you a prescription to take three times per day with food? A family member tells you, "I don't think you have to take it three times a day. Don't use all three pills—just take one." Whose instructions would you follow—the physician or your family member?

Our Great Physician gave us the prescription for how we should baptize—and He gave us three names. He said, "In the name of the Father, and the Son, and the Holy Spirit." Imagine if a fellow church member said, "Well, I don't think we should baptize that way. We don't have to use all three names. Let's only use one." Who should we follow: the Great Physician or the church member? It should be obvious which prescription is best to follow.

What is most tragic is that the churches that claim that one must be baptized in the name of Jesus only make baptism a prerequisite for salvation, which makes salvation by means of works rather than a free gift of God.

Baptism is something we do; therefore, it is works. Baptism in scripture always follows salvation. Being baptized by any formula never produces salvation! Never forget that salvation is not a product of our own works; by grace, it is given as we place our faith in the sacrifice that Jesus made on Calvary when He died in our place.

We are not baptized to be saved; we are baptized because we have been saved. Baptism is only an outward testimony before others that we have been crucified with Christ, buried with Him, and raised to new life! It is the same with taking the Lord's Supper (communion).

The Lord only gave two ordinances for us to observe—water baptism and communion—and neither of these saves anyone! We are justified by faith in the price Jesus paid on Calvary. That alone brings salvation. The scripture is crystal clear that by the works of the law, no flesh can be justified (Galatians 2:16).

Eternal Life Is a Free Gift from God

Baptism is scriptural, and every Christian should be baptized. Jesus was baptized and walked approximately seventy miles to be baptized when he went to Bethabara at the Jordan, but He was not baptized to be saved. He was sinless when He was baptized. If the purpose of baptism is to produce salvation, why was Jesus baptized?

Baptism is an outward display to others that one has been saved. It's like a wedding ring, which is an outward display of being married. If a married person takes off their wedding ring, do they become unmarried? If one took off their wedding ring and placed it on an infant, would the infant become married? My friend, that's the way it is with infant baptism. Infant baptism does not confirm that any child is ready for heaven.

Can a person become married without a ring? You're following this, right? A person is not married because they wear a wedding ring, and a person is not saved because they have been baptized and given an outward display that they have been saved. I've met many people who have been baptized but have never been born again. As a person wears a ring to show that they are married, a born-again believer becomes baptized to show others that they are saved. Let's take a look at a verse many take out of context.

> He who believes and is baptized will be saved; but he who does not believe will be condemned. (Mark 16:16)

Many people have taken this scripture completely out of its intended meaning. The main point is at the end of the verse: "He who does not believe will be condemned."

Imagine if you were at the airport gate, and the attendant said, "He who boards the plane and is seated will arrive in New York, and he who does not board will not arrive." Would you agree that the main thing is to get on board.?

Suppose you got on board, and all of the seats were taken. The plane takes off—and you still haven't gotten a seat. Will you get to New York? You boarded the plane, but you never sat down.

My friend, when it comes to salvation, the main thing is to get on board! If you've boarded by faith in Christ and what He did on Calvary's cross, you are going to arrive at heaven's gate!

CHAPTER 13

THE TRINITY IN THE LIFE OF CHRIST

In the life of Christ—from His conception to His ascension—the Triune Godhead is seen many times. One cannot read the four Gospels without seeing the Trinity.

LUKE'S RECORD OF THE INCARNATION

> And the angel said to her, "Do not be afraid, Mary, for you have found favor with God. And behold, you will conceive in your womb and give birth to a son, and you shall name Him Jesus. He will be great and will be called the Son of the Most High; and the Lord God will give Him the throne of His father David; and He will reign over the house of Jacob forever, and His kingdom will have no end."
>
> But Mary said to the angel, "How will this be, since I am a virgin?"
>
> The angel answered and said to her, "The Holy Spirit will come upon you, and the power of the Most High will overshadow you; for that reason also

> the holy Child will be called the Son of God. (Luke 1:30–35)

In this passage, we saw several things:

- Christ will be the Son of the "Highest."
- The Lord God will be the one to "give" to Him His throne.
- It will be the "Holy Spirit" who comes upon Mary.
- Mary will be overshadowed by the "power of the Highest."
- The Holy One born of Mary will be called "the Son of God."

Matthew's Record of the Incarnation

Matthew tells us quite a bit about the Trinity and the birth of Jesus:

> Now the birth of Jesus the Messiah was as follows: when His mother Mary had been betrothed to Joseph, before they came together she was found to be pregnant by the Holy Spirit.
>
> And her husband Joseph, since he was a righteous man and did not want to disgrace her, planned to send her away secretly.
>
> But when he had thought this over, behold, an angel of the Lord appeared to him in a dream, saying, "Joseph, son of David, do not be afraid to take Mary as your wife; for the Child who has been conceived in her is of the Holy Spirit." (Matthew 1:18–20)

From Matthew, we see the following things:

- Mary was found with child of the Holy Spirit.
- Gabriel tells Joseph that which is conceived in Mary is of the Holy Spirit.

Just like in the beginning, when the world was "spoken" into existence, the Holy Spirit says, "Let there be conception." Christ was conceived of the Holy Spirit. Jesus had no earthly father; he was the earthly son of a heavenly Father and the heavenly Son of an earthly mother. No one was born like Him before or after His incarnation.

Have you ever noticed that those who don't believe in the virgin birth also don't believe in the new birth? Being born again and being given new life requires that they believe that Jesus is the Son of God.

A person once came to my office, he was having some struggles because he was adopted. I told him that two of the greatest people in scripture were adopted. Moses was adopted by Pharaoh's daughter and grew up to be the greatest leader in the Old Testament. I also told him about Jesus. Joseph was His foster father, and the Father of Jesus was "in heaven." I told him you have to be adopted to get to heaven, which really got his attention.

> For you did not receive the spirit of bondage again to fear, but you received the Spirit of adoption by whom we cry out, "Abba, Father." (Romans 8:15)

That man went away with a different point of view! Isn't it wonderful to be accepted by the Father? That scripture is a wonderful pillow to rest your head on at night.

At the Age of Twelve, Christ Confirms the Trinity in the Temple

> And He said to them, "Why did you seek Me? Did you not know that I must be about My Father's business?" (Luke 2:49)

Those are the first words recorded of Jesus in the Bible, and they deal with the subject of the Trinity. Jesus did not come to do His own will or tend to His own business. He came to do the work of the Father who sent Him. He tended to His Father's work.

> Jesus said to them, "My food is to do the will of Him who sent Me, and to finish His work." (John 4:34)

The Baptism of Christ Confirms the Trinity

The baptism of Jesus was so vital that all four writers of the four Gospels record this event. One of the easiest ways to teach the Trinity is to point to the Lord's baptism. The Trinity was in full display for the world to see when Jesus was baptized by John.

Matthew's Record

According to Matthew, when Jesus was "in the water," He "saw" the Holy Spirit coming down from God, which is where the anointing of the Holy Spirit took place:

> When He had been baptized, Jesus came up immediately from the water; and behold, the heavens were opened to Him, and He saw the Spirit of God descending like a dove and alighting upon Him. (Matthew 3:16)

Let's see how Mark would write the event. As we blend these records together, we keep accumulating more information.

Mark's Record

Mark's record is probably the most descriptive. John the Baptist states that it will be Jesus who baptizes with the Holy Spirit, and as Jesus is coming up out of the water, John sees the Holy Spirit descending from heaven. A voice out of heaven says, "This is My beloved Son in who I am well pleased." The Holy Spirit drives Jesus into the wilderness to be tempted by the devil for forty days.

> "I indeed baptized you with water, but He will baptize you with the Holy Spirit." It came to pass in those days that Jesus came from Nazareth of Galilee, and was baptized by John in the Jordan. And immediately, coming up from the water, He saw the heavens parting and the Spirit descending upon Him like a dove. Then a voice came from heaven, "You are My beloved Son, in whom I am well pleased." Immediately the Spirit drove Him into the wilderness. (Mark 1:8–12)

There is a lot in those verses:

- Jesus will baptize with the Holy Spirit.
- Jesus is in the water.
- The Holy Spirit descends from heaven.
- A voice from God in heaven declares Jesus to be His Son.
- The Father is pleased with Jesus.
- The Holy Spirit drives Jesus into the wilderness.

Luke's Record

Luke echoes Matthew and Mark and gives us the third written account of the Trinity in the Gospels.

> When all the people were baptized, it came to pass that Jesus also was baptized; and while He prayed, the heaven was opened. And the Holy Spirit descended in bodily form like a dove upon Him, and a voice came

> from heaven which said, "You are My beloved Son; in You I am well pleased." (Luke 3:21–22)

Luke says that Jesus was praying when He came out of the water. Who was He praying to? It could be none other than the Father who is speaking out of heaven.

JOHN'S RECORD

John confirms the words of Matthew, Mark, and Luke. He also gives some interesting information concerning the Holy Spirit. He says that the Holy Spirit lit upon Jesus and "remained" upon Him. The Holy Spirit "remaining" on Jesus is what God told John the Baptist would happen when Jesus was seen by John. This is how John knew Jesus was the one sent from the Father and would baptize with the Holy Spirit.

> And John bore witness, saying, "I saw the Spirit descending from heaven like a dove, and He remained upon him. I did not know Him, but He who sent me to baptize with water said to me, 'Upon whom you see the Spirit descending, and remaining on Him, this is He who baptizes with the Holy Spirit.' And I have seen and testified that this is the Son of God." (John 1:32–33)

This is easy enough for a child to understand! This is the record of the Trinity in full display. Everything that happens is simultaneous. Everything happens at the same time, and it was so important that all the writers of the four Gospels record it!

- Christ is (in His body) on earth and in the water.
- He was praying to the Father.
- The Holy Spirit descended in a different body than that of Jesus.

- The Holy Spirit is descending from heaven.
- The voice of the Father speaks from heaven.
- The Holy Spirit in the bodily form of a dove remains on Jesus, and John sees this.
- The Holy Spirit drives Jesus into the wilderness to be tempted by the devil.

It's so wonderful that we have the four Gospels complementing each other and giving us their own detailed accounts of the Lord's baptism and how all four show us the Trinity.

The Mount of Transfiguration Confirms the Trinity

The transfiguration of Christ is similar to the Lord's baptism. This is a double whammy. We discussed this earlier concerning Peter's confession that Jesus was the Son of the Living God. Jesus told Peter that flesh and blood had not revealed this to Him, but the revelation came from the Father.

Who told Peter this revelation? It could not have been Jesus because Jesus had flesh and blood while He was here on earth. At the crucifixion, the soldiers pierced His flesh, and blood flowed forth from His side. If flesh and blood had not revealed it to Peter—and Jesus had flesh and blood—it could not have been Jesus who told Peter that He was the Son of God. After Jesus arose, He appeared to the disciples and told Thomas to handle Him and see that a spirit had not flesh and bones. Notice that Jesus did not say "blood."

This is not our topic, but there is some debate about whether we will have blood in our glorified bodies once we are in heaven. John said that we would be like Jesus when we see Him as He is. There are some who state we will have no blood in our glorified bodies. We'll talk about it in our book on the spirit, soul, and body.

We discussed the Mount of Transfiguration earlier. I believe this happened on Mount Tabor. Some believe it was Mount Hermon because of the distance from Caesarea Philippi and Mount Hermon is less, but Jesus had plenty of time to reach Mount Tabor by foot. They didn't arrive at the Mount of Transfiguration until six days after leaving Caesarea Philippi. They had plenty of time to arrive. Traditionally, Mount Tabor is the location.

Peter's declaration that Jesus was the Son of the Living God happened before Peter arrived at the Mount of Transfiguration. Jesus said, "My Father which is in heaven." He was the one who revealed this to Peter. The Father who gave Peter the revelation earlier is about to speak audibly to Peter on the Mount of Transfiguration.

God interrupted Peter while he was still speaking, and He corrected Peter when he wanted to build three tabernacles for Moses, Elijah, and Jesus. God's voice spoke out of heaven and told Peter, James, and John that He was pleased in Jesus and to "hear Him." This validates the Trinity at Mount Tabor (Matthew 17:5–8).

Much like the Lord's baptism, Christ is on earth. It is the Father's voice (for the voice called Christ "his Son") and spoke from heaven. In this passage, we also see the difference between Jesus speaking and the voice from the cloud. These are two different voices; one is of Christ, and the other is of the Father.

Who corrected Peter on the Mount of Transfiguration, it wasn't the voice of Jesus but the voice from the Father? Who did the voice from heaven tell Peter to listen to, the voice wasn't telling Peter to listen to "me" but rather to "Him?"

Jesus Quoting Isaiah in the Synagogue of Nazareth Confirms the Trinity

Isaiah is quoted more in the New Testament than any other Old Testament prophet. Isaiah was an imperfect man with unclean lips, but God raised Him up to write the Book of Isaiah which is known as a little Bible in itself.

The Bible has sixty-six books, and Isaiah has sixty-six chapters. The first thirty-nine books of the Bible are about judgment, and the last twenty-seven books are about redemption. The first thirty-nine chapters of Isaiah are on judgment, and the last twenty-seven chapters are on redemption.

Isaiah was married to an unnamed female prophetess. Isaiah actually said that he saw the Lord high and lifted up and saw the God's clothing (his robe) that filled the temple. Isaiah prophesied seven hundred years before the birth of Christ and said the Messiah would be a male and born of a virgin (Isaiah 7:14).

Could Isaiah have anything to add to our discussion of the Trinity? Isaiah did not let us down and wrote one of the most well-known verses that almost all have heard. Jesus would quote this passage in the synagogue of Nazareth (Isaiah 61). In the very first line of chapter 61, all three persons of the Trinity are acknowledged.

> The Spirit of the Lord God is upon Me, Because the Lord has anointed Me To preach good tidings to the poor; He has sent Me to heal the brokenhearted, To proclaim liberty to the captives, And the opening of the prison to those who are bound; To proclaim the acceptable year of the Lord, and the day of vengeance of our God; to comfort all who mourn. (Isaiah 61:1–2)

We can see the Trinity in one verse:

- The Spirit (the third person of the Godhead)
- Of the Lord (the first person of the Godhead)
- Upon Me (Christ, the second person of the Godhead)

The first line alone gives us all the confirmation we need that there is a Trinity.

Jesus Quoting David in Psalm 110:1 Confirms the Trinity

This is one of my favorite things Jesus ever said. He always had an answer for the religious crowd of His day. Jesus puts a final hush on the Pharisees with a quote from David. The Messiah was promised to come from the lineage of David.

> While the Pharisees were gathered together, Jesus asked them, saying, "What do you think about the Christ? Whose Son is He?"
>
> They said to Him, "The Son of David."
>
> He said to them, "How then does David in the Spirit call Him 'Lord,' saying: 'The Lord said to my Lord, "Sit at My right hand, Till I make Your enemies Your footstool.' If David then calls Him 'Lord,' how is He his Son?"
>
> And no one was able to answer Him a word, nor from that day on did anyone dare question Him anymore. (Matthew 22:41–46)

I can never read this verse without laughing. Christ uses the doctrine of the Trinity to silence the Pharisees. Verse 44 is golden!

Jesus existed before David, and David records that the Lord said unto David's Lord (that's right, the Father and Son are having a conversation). Jesus is told by the Father to sit at His right hand. That verse is so wonderful that it was used multiple times in scripture.

The Prayers of Jesus Confirm the Trinity

Everyone knows about Lazarus being dead for four days. Jesus intentionally delayed His arrival at Bethany to raise Lazarus. Someone said, "God's delays are not always His denials." Jesus is never too late!

Jesus told them to roll away the stone. Have you ever noticed that Jesus doesn't always do everything for us? He told them to do what they could do, and then He did what they couldn't do. Isn't it the same with us? God wants us to do what we can. He will do what we can't, and nothing is ever too hard for Him.

Does the story of Lazarus have any reference to the Trinity? Let's find out.

> Then they took away the stone from the place where the dead man was lying. And Jesus lifted up His eyes and said, "Father, I thank You that You have heard Me."
>
> And I know that You always hear Me, but because of the people who are standing by I said this, that they may believe that You sent Me.
>
> Now when He had said these things, He cried with a loud voice, "Lazarus, come forth!" (John 11:41–43)

Reading this passage we have to ask the following:

- To whom is Jesus praying?
- Who always hears Christ?
- To whom was Jesus lifting His eyes?
- To whom was Jesus giving thanks?

Jesus was not praying to Himself and saying that He always heard Himself. He was in Bethany, on the eastern side of the Mount of Olives, and He looked up to the Father on the throne in heaven. It was the Father to whom He gave thanks.

The Lord's Prayer

This really should be called the Disciple's Prayer, Jesus was giving the disciples the model of how to pray. The disciples really wanted to know how Jesus prayed. They never asked Him how to preach, how to heal, or how to perform miracles, but they did ask Him to teach them how to pray.

If we had walked with Jesus, would we have done the same thing? Would we have said, "Lord, teach us to pray?" So many people today are so taken with signs and wonders. Many people flock like bees to honey to television ministries where manifestations (if we want to call them that) are happening.

Jesus, as busy as He was, always had time for prayer. He who had left heaven's glory and had never been outside the presence of His Father for all of eternity past had come to earth to live among us. He was always in prayer in fellowship with His Father. Let's look at the model of prayer He gave to the disciples.

> In this manner, therefore, pray: Our Father in heaven, Hallowed be Your name. Your kingdom come. Your will be done on earth as it is in heaven. (Matthew 6:9–10)

While Jesus was on earth, He taught the disciples to pray to the Father in heaven.

In John's Gospel, Jesus said that after His ascension we would no longer pray directly to Him. Jesus taught us the proper way to pray: to "the Father using the name of Jesus" (John 16:23). The Father was in heaven before Jesus ascended to heaven, which verifies the Trinity. While Jesus was on earth, He prayed to the Father in heaven.

The Lord's Three Prayers in the Garden of Gethsemane

This is one of the most touching passages in the Word of God. On my last trip to the Holy Land, I visited more than eighty sites, and Gethsemane is one was one of the most touching. They have a church built over the stone where it is believed that Jesus prayed and sweated great drops of blood.

Most of us know the story of how that the disciples slept while Jesus prayed. Judas betrayed Him with a kiss. He would be led to the house of Caiaphas to spend the night in a basement after being falsely accused, mocked, and beaten. Early the next morning, He would be taken to Pilate.

These two places touched my heart more than any other sites I visited. I stood in the room where Jesus most likely was kept. You can see where the ropes were looped through the corners of the walls where Jesus would have been tied and beaten.

Back in Gethsemane, is where the Lord's victory was won. It was there in Gethsemene among the grove of olive trees where He submitted His will to the will of the Father. Our Lord would pray to the Father the same prayer three times:

> Then Jesus came with them to a place called Gethsemane, and said to the disciples, "Sit here while I go and pray over there."
>
> And He took with Him Peter and the two sons of Zebedee, and He began to be sorrowful and deeply distressed.
>
> Then He said to them, "My soul is exceedingly sorrowful, even to death. Stay here and watch with Me."
>
> He went a little farther and fell on His face, and prayed, saying, "O My Father, if it is possible, let this cup pass from Me; nevertheless, not as I will, but as You will."
>
> Then He came to the disciples and found them sleeping, and said to Peter, "What! Could you not watch with Me one hour?
>
> Watch and pray, lest you enter into temptation. The spirit indeed is willing, but the flesh is weak."
>
> Again, a second time, He went away and prayed, saying, "O My Father, if this cup cannot pass away from Me unless I drink it, Your will be done."

> And He came and found them asleep again, for their eyes were heavy.
>
> So He left them, went away again, and prayed the third time, saying the same words. (Matthew 26:36–44)

Anyone who understands the words "I," "My," "Me, "Thy," "Thou," and "Your" (in some translations) can see the Trinity in this prayer.

Evidence of the Trinity is found in the following examples:

- One is being prayed to.
- The other is doing the praying.
- The Father and Jesus have their own separate wills.
- The will of Jesus was submitted to the will of the Father.

It takes two in the equation for all of that to occur.

The Lord's Instructions for How to Pray after His Ascension

Since we covered this in detail in the Gospel of John, we will only review it. here. The scriptures are in John 16:23–30 if you wish to go back to read them again.

- After His ascension, we will ask Him nothing.
- We are to ask the Father in His name.
- Jesus says "He" (not "Me") will give to you.
- Jesus will not pray for us any longer—we are to pray to the Father on our own.
- The Father loves us because we love Jesus.
- Jesus came from God the Father.
- Jesus was leaving to return to the Father.
- The disciples believed that Jesus came from God.

Jesus gave us the proper way to pray after He ascended. We will no longer pray to Jesus. Jesus said, "I won't be praying for you once I get to the Father because the Father loves you, and you know I came from the Father." We can now go directly to the throne of the Father ourselves.

The above verses are self-evident; if we only had this one passage, it would be enough to show that the Father and the Son are two of the three who bear witness in heaven.

The Crucifixion of Christ Confirms the Trinity

The following passages show how Jesus was offered to the Father and by whom He was offered.

The crucifixion was not an assassination or a murder; it was a sacrifice, and Jesus was the "offering." I know that Peter used the word "murdered" in Acts 5 when he told the Jews at the council that they had murdered Jesus and hung Him on a tree, but Jesus was not murdered. He was "offered," which we will see in Hebrews.

When it comes to murder, Jesus taught us that murder proceeds from the heart (Mark 7:21). Jesus condemned the religious Jews and said they were the sons of those who murdered the prophets (Matthew 23:31). It was in the Ten Commandments that murder was forbidden (Mark 10:19). In these scriptures, we see that murder is a sin that comes from within the heart of a man—and to murder would mean one had broken the Mosaic law.

In the following verse, we will see that Jesus was "offered" to God on the cross through the Holy Spirit. If Jesus went to the cross through the Holy Spirit, and this had been a murder, the Holy Spirit would have been the One who murdered Jesus, murder would have been in the heart of the Holy Spirit, and the Holy Spirit would have broken the law of Moses.

Even though the religious establishment, Pilate, and the Roman soldiers performed the actions of the crucifixion, it was actually the

Holy Spirit that superintended the death of Christ. This is something that may be new to many of us, but the next verse clearly says that it was the Holy Spirit who did this "offering." We can't say it enough. Jesus was not assassinated. He was "offered to God" as a sacrifice for our sins.

> How much more shall the blood of Christ, who through the eternal spirit offered himself without spot to God, cleanse your conscience from dead works to serve the living god? (Hebrews 9:14)

We see the words "to" and "through," and we see all three persons in the Trinity in one sentence. Jesus was offered to God through the eternal spirit! That is the Trinity.

The Holy Spirit was upon Christ and anointed Him at His baptism, and He was still with Jesus at the crucifixion!

Everything Jesus did on earth, he did as a man (though He was God). Every miracle He performed, every person He healed, and every dead body He raised, He did by the Holy Spirit! Jesus performed no miracles or healings before the Holy Spirit descended on Him at His baptism. He never performed one great feat as God; every miracle was performed as a man anointed with the Holy Spirit.

Beginning at His birth, His conception was by the Holy Spirit. On the cross, at His death, Christ offered Himself to God though the Eternal Spirit! Even after the crucifixion, the Holy Spirit was still present and raised Jesus from the dead! The next verse is so wonderful, and it even gives us hope concerning our mortal bodies.

> But if the Spirit of Him who raised Jesus from the dead dwells in you, He who raised Christ from the dead will also give life to your mortal bodies through His Spirit who dwells in you. (Romans 8:11)

The Holy Spirit that raised Jesus from the dead, dwells within us, and can give us victorious lives in our mortal bodies. What a comforting and powerful verse.

On the Cross, the Trinity Was on Full Display

We have seen that Christ was offered though the Eternal Spirit. On the cross, He was praying to the Father in heaven. The crucifixion was a sacrifice to satisfy the demands of a Thrice Holy God. Jesus was the offering to God, and Jesus was offered "through the Eternal Spirit."

The scripture also tells us the "Lord" bruised "Him." Many of us are prone to think that it was Pilate, the religious Pharisees, or even the Roman soldiers who bruised our Lord. The next verse tells us who did the "bruising:

> Yet it pleased the Lord to bruise Him; He has put Him to grief. When You make His soul an offering for sin. (Isaiah 53:10)

It was God who bruised the Lord, it was God who put Him to grief, and it was God who made Jesus's soul and offering for sin. The crucifixion was a sacrifice to God. It was not a defeat; it was a victory that was promised all the way back in Genesis 3:15. God told the serpent the "seed of the woman" would bruise Satan's head. That happened at Calvary. That is where Jesus crushed the head of the serpent.

I wish we had time to go back and look at the sacrificial system of the Jews and talk about the whole burnt offering. I'll give the reader this much as it pertains to Jesus being a sacrifice to satisfy the demands of our Holy God. There were different offerings under the old Mosaic sacrificial system: the whole burnt offering, the sin offering, the meal offering, the peace offering, and the trespass offering. The purpose of the whole burnt offering was to satisfy the demands of God. This offering was not for the one bringing the offering; that was done under the sin offering. The other offerings were for the benefits of man, but the whole burnt offering was solely to satisfy the demands of God Himself. The details of the whole burnt offering are found in Leviticus 1. The animal was sacrificed in its entirety because it shows that God gave us His all. That's what the crucifixion accomplished. Jesus was completely given and completely offered as the whole burnt offering that satisfied the demands of God. Sin had separated man from God, and God's holiness had to be satisfied to reconcile man to God. The whole burnt offering was for this purpose.

What is wonderful is that the sacrifices offered by the Israelites were not a permanent satisfaction. These offerings had to be repeated by the priests. Paul tells us why in Hebrews; the offerings in the Mosaic sacrificial system could only cover sins. The sacrifices could not permanently take away our sins; they only covered the sins.

> For it is not possible that the blood of bulls and goats could take away sins. (Hebrews 10:4)

When Jesus appeared on the banks of the Jordan, John the Baptist beheld Him and cried out!

> Behold! The Lamb of God who takes away the sin of the world! (John 1:29)

The sacrifice on Calvary is the permanent solution for sin! There is no other solution. He was the one and only sacrifice that took care of man's sin problem forever. Sin cannot be remedied by any other means. He was completely offered, and we should completely receive Him!

I wish we had the time to discuss the differences between all of the sacrifices, but that discussion will have to be for another day. We should all be thankful that Jesus was the whole burnt offering who was offered to God through the Holy Spirit. None of us could have done it. None of us are qualified to be an offering that would satisfy perfect holiness without spot or blemish to God. Jesus knew no sin and became sin so that we might be made the righteousness of God through Him (2 Corinthians 5:21).

While we are still here at the foot of the cross, let's continue.

Every time Jesus referenced the Father, He always called him "Father." Other than when Jesus spoke to Mary at the tomb, when He was giving a message to the disciples, this is the only time Jesus ever called His Father "God."

> Jesus said to her, "Do not cling to Me, for I have not yet ascended to My Father; but go to My brethren and say to them, 'I am ascending to My Father and your Father, and to My God and your God.'" (John 20:17)

Other than on the cross, this is the only time Jesus called the Father "My God." In this verse, we see the distinctions between the Father and Jesus. Jesus is saying, "I have not ascended to my Father; I am ascending to my Father and your Father; my God and your God."

Jesus could always call God His "Father" because God was always with Him. We have seen that one of our key words is the word "with". From His conception, Jesus was always "with" the Father.

Why did Jesus here on the cross call the Father God? Sin "separates" us from God. On the cross, Jesus was made sin for us—and Jesus, for the first time, called His Father "God." Sin means separation from God. We have seen that since Adam was expelled from the Garden of Eden. It took a blood sacrifice to bring man back into fellowship with God. God is a holy God, and sin "separates" us from God.

> For He made Him who knew no sin to be sin for us, that we might become the righteousness of God in Him. (2 Corinthians 5:21)

When Jesus called His Father "God," for the first time, Jesus was separated from the presence of the Father. Jesus made this cry of anguish when God covered the earth with darkness between noon and three o'clock. Man, because of sin, was now separated from God, and Jesus endured that separation for us. He alone endured that separation.

This was the first time in all eternity past that Jesus was alone without His Father. One should really pause a moment and take that in. Jesus suffered alone. My dear friends, when we go through loneliness, when we go through betrayals, when those we love the most have forsaken us and disappeared, Jesus knows that feeling. Jesus was forsaken when He called the Father "God" He asked, "Why have you forsaken me?"

In Psalm 22, David prophesied the crucifixion:

> My God, My God, why have You forsaken Me? Why are You so far from helping Me, And from the words of My groaning? O My God, I cry in the daytime, but You do not hear; And in the night season, and am not silent. (Psalm 22:1–2)

Jesus was forsaken by both God and man. Mark tells us that every disciple forsook Christ and departed.

> Then they all forsook Him and fled. (Mark 14:50)

How comforting it is when we have gone through times when our friends—and maybe even our families have turned and forsaken us, leaving us alone. Jesus knows that feeling. He suffered alone, forsaken by all, even by His heavenly Father. How wonderful it is that we can take our loneliness to Jesus. When no one can be found to stand by our side, Jesus will be there. He went through what we are going through. Hebrews tells us that He sympathizes with our weaknesses in all points.

Maybe loneliness touched your heart when you stood next to the cold casket of a departed loved one. It may have been when divorce came and left you alone. It might have been when your closest friends left. Jesus knows and understands.

I have heard many people say that we should not question God, but even Jesus questioned God. When our Lord cried, "My God, My God," He also asked, "Why?" It's OK to bring our questions to the Lord. He invites us to. When we go through times of suffering it's only normal that we wonder why. If there was something wrong with asking God why, Jesus would have sinned on the cross. He asked, "Why have you forsaken me?" During these times, we have somewhere to go! We can take that hurt and that broken heart to the Lord. He understands when no one else can. This is why the cross of Christ is so important. None of us will ever understand everything Jesus did for us on the cross. Everything He endured on the cross was for you and me.

Many of us know that Jesus died for us on the cross, but do we stop to think of the price it took to accomplish that? Jesus was never once without the Father in all of eternity past, but He was separated from His Father on the cross.

Can the Father be "separated" from the Son? When Jesus was made sin for us, He called His Father "God." At that moment, Jesus was "forsaken" by the Father. Blackness and darkness covered the scene, and Jesus called His Father God and asked why the Father had forsaken Him.

In these verses, there are three thoughts I hope we will take away:

- Jesus is now separated from the Father on the cross, which is proven by the fact that Jesus calls the Father "God."
- For someone to be forsaken, they have to be forsaken by another.
- Someone has to do the forsaking.

Who forsook Jesus while He was on the cross? Jesus did not forsake Himself. For Jesus to be forsaken, it implies that another had to forsake Him. When Jesus and the disciples were in the Garden of Gethsemane, just before His arrest, the disciples—every last one of them—forsook the Lord and left Him:

> Then they all forsook Him and fled. (Mark 14:50)

Jesus was forsaken, and the disciples did the forsaking.

For one to be forsaken implies that there has to be at least two in the equation. In the above verse, Mark uses the words "they all." For anyone to be forsaken, they must be forsaken by another. The following verses recorded by Matthew and Mark will verify that Jesus was forsaken by and separated from the Father.

> And about the ninth hour Jesus cried with a loud voice, saying, "Eli, Eli, lama sabachthani? That is to say, My God, My God, why hast thou forsaken me?" (Matthew 27:46; see also Mark 15:34)

The phrase "Eli, Eli, lama sabachthani" is Aramaic, which was the primary language that Jesus spoke. The verse itself gives us the interpretation. Jesus is using the word "My." This shows He was calling to God. He is not calling to Himself; He is calling to the other who has forsaken Him.

Next, we look at two more prayers of Jesus on the cross. In the upcoming verse, we will see that Jesus prays to the Father for the forgiveness of those present at the cross.

Jesus tells the dying thief that today he will be with Him in paradise, which was in the heart of the earth at that time (Matthew 12:40). Of the three being crucified, Jesus died first. We know this because the soldiers broke the legs of both thieves to speed up their deaths. The legs of Jesus were not broken, showing that He had already died (John 19:33). When Jesus died, He went straight to paradise in the heart of the earth and not to heaven. The Father—to whom Jesus had been praying while on the cross—was still in heaven. There are no verses to support that the Father in heaven ever went to paradise in the heart of the earth.

When the repentant thief died, he joined Jesus in paradise. Jesus said, "Today you will be with Me." The thief did not go to the Father; he went to Christ in paradise. This shows that the Father and the Son are in two different locations, supporting the Trinity.

Paradise was moved to heaven after the resurrection of Jesus. Paul recorded that he was caught "up" into paradise (2 Corinthians

12:4). When Jesus arose, He emptied paradise in the heart of the earth. Ephesians tells us He "led captivity captive." Like Moses led the children out of bondage, Jesus led those captive in paradise out of captivity and transported them to heaven.

Paradise is no longer "down" in the heart of the earth; it is now "up." When a believer dies, they go to be with Jesus at the Father's right hand in heaven. Paradise is now up! Unlike the Old Testament saints who went down when they died, now that Jesus has risen and paradise has been moved to heaven, we go up when we die. When we leave our bodies at death, our souls are in the presence of the Lord immediately (2 Corinthians 5:8).

For a moment let's go back to the Mount of Transfiguration. Here Moses came "up" and Elijah came "down" to meet Jesus on the mountain. Moses was still in paradise in the heart of the earth, and Jesus had not yet emptied paradise. Moses had died at Mount Nebo. His body was buried, and his spirit went to paradise. God did not allow him to enter Canaan before his death, but God did let him get to the Promised Land at the transfiguration of Christ!

Elijah had never died and been taken "to heaven" (not paradise). Enoch and Elijah are the only two in the Old Testament who went to heaven. All the others—from Abel on—went to the heart of the earth.

What I'm going to say next will make you shout. When Moses and Elijah met Jesus on the mountain, they still had their same names. The death of Moses and the rapture of Elijah had not removed their identities. After we go to heaven, we will still be known as we are known right now (1 Corinthians 13:12)!

Remember when the Sadducees (who did not believe in the resurrection) asked Jesus the ridiculous question about the wife who had seven husbands on earth? They wanted to know, in heaven, which man would be her husband. Jesus told them "Have you not read what God has spoken, saying "I am the God of Abraham, Isaac, and Jacob?" He then told the Sadducees that God was not the God of the dead but the living. Jesus was telling them that Abraham, Isaac and Jacob were still alive and had their same names (Matthew 22:31-32).

We also have Jesus telling of the true event (not a parable) of the rich man and Lazarus who went to paradise (Abraham's Bosom). The rich man asked Abraham to send Moses back from the dead to speak to his five brothers. Abraham, Moses, and Lazarus still had their same names (identities) after death (Luke 16:19–31). Folks, we're still going to have our identities after we die!

What does all of this have to do with the Trinity? We have already given the proof that it was the Holy Spirit who offered Jesus on the cross.

Jesus on the cross prays to His Father who is in heaven. When Jesus breathed His last breath, He went to paradise in the heart of the earth. The thief died and went to be with Jesus—not the Father. The thief went to paradise and not heaven. Jesus said that's where he would go, and Jesus told him it would be "today." This places Jesus in paradise while the Father is still in heaven. God the Father never left the throne. Three days later, the Holy Spirit will raise Jesus from the dead. The Trinity is seen during the crucifixion and all the way through to the resurrection.

We are still not done here. Afterward, Jesus prayed to the Father and committed His Spirit into the Father's hands.

> Then Jesus said, "Father, forgive them, for they do not know what they do." And they divided His garments and cast lots.
>
> And Jesus said to him, "Assuredly, I say to you, today you will be with Me in paradise."
>
> And when Jesus had cried out with a loud voice, He said, "Father, into Your hands I commit My spirit." Having said this, He breathed His last. (Luke 23:34, 43, 46)

Did you see the last line? Jesus uses the words "Your" hands and "I" commit "My" spirit. The hands of Jesus were nailed to the cross. While His hands are nailed, He places His spirit into the Father's hands. Both had a different pair of hands. Jesus says that it is "My" spirit that He is committing into "the Father's" hands.

Jesus still lives in the same body today in which He was crucified and resurrected (although it's now a glorified body). Jesus showed His body to His disciples and told them to handle His body. He displayed to them His body with flesh and bones. He later showed to Thomas that He was in the same body with proof of the scars. Israel will see those wounds in His body when they are restored to God at the Second Coming (John 20:27; Luke 24:39, 42, 43; Zechariah 12:10; 13:6). Jesus will have that same body with those scars forever—through all eternity. Jesus even ate in that glorified body. I really like that because I like to eat. I'm really looking forward to the Marriage Supper of the Lamb. What a feast we will have in our glorified bodies!

God the Father has a body, a real body, that sits on a real throne in a real place called heaven. Jesus, today, in His body, is seated in His throne at the right hand of the Father. One day, every overcomer will get to sit with Jesus in His throne as He overcame and sat down with His Father in His throne! Allow me to ask the following:

- To whom was Jesus praying while on the cross?
- Into whose hands was His spirit committed at the time of His death?
- Why did Jesus say "Your" hands "I" commit "My" spirit?
- When Jesus cried "My God," who was He calling to?
- Why did Jesus tell the dying thief "You will be with Me in paradise?"
- Why did Jesus call the Father "My" God?
- Who was Jesus forsaken by?
- Why did Jesus call the Father "God" instead of Father?

All three persons in the Godhead were present at the crucifixion!

In Hebrews, we saw that it was "through the eternal Spirit" that Jesus was offered. Jesus is offered through the Holy Spirit, and Jesus committed His spirit to the Father when He died. There is no way that all three who bear witness in heaven would not be at this event. All three persons of the Godhead witnessed the crucifixion.

The Resurrection of Christ Confirms the Trinity

> But if the Spirit of Him who raised Jesus from the dead dwells in you, He who raised Christ from the dead will also give life to your mortal bodies through His Spirit who dwells in you. (Romans 8:11)

The Trinity is found in the first words alone, and we don't even have to read the entire verse:

- The Spirit
- of Him (God the Father) who raised
- Jesus from the dead.

Paul goes on to say that the same Spirit that raised Jesus is the Spirit that dwells within us. There is no possible way that the Spirit that raised Jesus could be one and the same person. It was "the Spirit" that raised "Jesus."

Since we are observing the Trinity in the resurrection, let's consider what Jesus said to Mary after the resurrection.

> Jesus said to her, "Do not cling to Me, for I have not yet ascended to My Father; but go to My brethren and say to them, 'I am ascending to My Father and your Father, and to My God and your God.'" (John 20:17)

We simply read the verse as it is written. Jesus had not yet ascended to his Father. Jesus is returning to his Father, and the Father is the same Father as the Father of His brethren.

Now we move to Jesus speaking with Thomas after the resurrection.

> Behold my hands and my feet, that it is I myself: handle me, and see; for a spirit hath not flesh and bones, as ye see me have. (Luke 24:39)

After the resurrection, Jesus tells Thomas to handle Him. Earlier, Jesus had told Mary not to cling to Him. What happened between the Lord's appearance to Mary and the time he appeared to Thomas? Jesus told Mary not to touch him because He had not yet ascended to His Father. Jesus had to have ascended to the Father between His appearance to Mary and His appearance to Thomas. The Father was on His throne in heaven while Jesus was speaking with Mary on earth. After Jesus ascended to the Father, He returned to Thomas. This event occurs after the resurrection and confirms the Trinity.

The Results of the Ascension

In the next passage, Jesus tells the disciples that He is about the leave them. This is why Jesus said that sorrow had filled their hearts. They had been with Jesus for three and a half years, and they were about to be without Him.

Jesus then tells them the comforting words that He will send to them another Helper. The disciples would not be left alone to carry out the Great Commission on their own. They would be sent another "Helper" (some translations use the word "Comforter").

Jesus tells them who the Helper is. He says it is the "Spirit of truth." We are about to notice some things the Spirit will do for the disciples:

> But now I go away to Him who sent Me, and none of you asks Me, "Where are You going?"
>
> But because I have said these things to you, sorrow has filled your heart.
>
> Nevertheless, I tell you the truth. It is to your advantage that I go away; for if I do not go away, the Helper will not come to you; but if I depart, I will send Him to you.
>
> However, when He, the Spirit of truth, has come, He will guide you into all truth; for He will not speak

> on His own authority, but whatever He hears He will speak; and He will tell you things to come.
>
> He will glorify Me, for He will take of what is Mine and declare it to you. (John 16:5–7, 13, 14)

He (the Holy Spirit is a person of the Godhead and is called a "He"). The Holy Spirit is not an "It." I've heard Christians use the phrase "I've got it." No, they have "Him," and more importantly, when He regenerates us and washes us in the blood of Christ, "He has us." Do you mean the Holy Spirit has a part in our redemption? Notice the past tense in the following verse.

> And such were some of you. But you were washed, but you were sanctified, but you were justified in the name of the Lord Jesus and by the Spirit of our God. (1 Corinthians 6:11)

Yes, it is the Holy Spirit who washes us, sanctifies us, and justifies us in the sight of God. Again, it's all in the past tense! We don't have to wait to get to heaven to be washed, sanctified, and justified; it's already been done by the Holy Spirit.

Did you see the Trinity in that verse as well?

- Name of the Lord Jesus
- By the Spirit
- of our God.

Let's go back to what Jesus told the disciples about Him leaving them and sending them a Helper. Jesus said that He will send the Helper (the Holy Spirit) after He returns to the Father.

The Helper will do many things:

- He will guide them.
- He will not speak of his own authority.
- He will hear.

- He will tell of things to come.
- He will glorify Jesus (rather than Himself).
- He will take what is Christ's and declare it.

To do all of the above, the Holy Spirit could not be a mere "force," as some claim. One would have to have power and intellect with the ability to guide, speak, hear, tell, glorify, and declare.

Let's not forget that the Holy Spirit will be sent to the disciples from Jesus. He said, "I" will send you the Helper. The Holy Spirit is the third person in the Triune Godhead.

As we progress, Jesus has more to say about the Holy Spirit. Jesus gives us another verse where the Trinity is found in one scripture.

> And I will pray the Father, and He will give you another Helper, that He may abide with you forever. (John 14:16)

Notice the words "I," "the Father," and "the Helper." Some translations use the word "Comforter" rather than Helper. The Greek word *parakletos* means "counselor, intercessor, helper, one who encourages and comforts."

That my friend is who the Holy Spirit is and what He does.

I hope you didn't miss the word "another" in that verse. Jesus said I'm sending you "another" Helper. Jesus was not going to return to the disciples. He was going to send "another." Jesus remains even to this day at the right hand of God, and He will return to this earth and establish His kingdom in Jerusalem. He will not come back and touch this earth until then. Even at the Rapture, which I personally believe will happen before the tribulation, Jesus does not return and touch the earth. He stops in the air, and we who are "in Christ" will rise to meet Him. Although Jesus is now bodily in heaven, He has not left us alone. He sent us "another" (the Holy Spirit).

Jesus had so many times been of such help to the disciples. When Peter was sinking on the Sea of Galilee, Jesus reached forth His hand and helped him. We could go on forever with this thought. Jesus would help the disciples catch a haul of fish, and He helped Peter pay his taxes. Jesus helped many others.

Jesus had been their helper for three and a half years, and now He was telling them He was going to leave them. One can only imagine the sorrow in their hearts and the loneliness they immediately felt; they probably were feeling helpless. Were they going to be left on their own? Would they have to carry on the Lord's work without any help?

Jesus calms their fears and tells them that He is going to the Father and will pray to the Father that "another" Helper will be sent. There is the Trinity in one verse!

- "I" will pray (Jesus)
- to the "Father" who will send you (the Father)
- "another Helper" (the Holy Spirit)

Praise the Lord! We are not left to go through this life alone. Jesus said that once the Helper came, He would abide with us forever. The Holy Spirit never leaves us! He is with us right now! Whatever one may be facing or going through—illness, the loss of a loved one, a broken home, financial burdens—we never go through anything alone. The Holy Spirit is with us forever!

Let's now move on to what Jesus is doing for us right now at this moment.

The Intercessory Work of Christ Confirms the Trinity

> It is Christ who died, and furthermore is also risen, who is even at the right hand of God, who also makes intercession for us. (Romans 8:34)

Isn't it wonderful that we know where Jesus is and exactly what He is doing at this very moment? Physically, in His body, He is seated at the right hand of God.

When a Christian sins, Jesus makes an intercession for us to God the Father.

In the days of Job, Satan had access to the throne room of God (Job 1:6–12). Satan is the "accuser of the brethren," and he will continue to do so until the middle of the seven-year tribulation. After three and a half years of tribulation, Satan will be cast out of heaven for good (Revelation 12:7–10).

Satan can still accuse you and I before the Father, but when he does, we have someone at the Father's right hand. We will see in just a moment that Jesus is our intercessor, our "Mediator, our High Priest, and our Advocate."

This should make the heart of every child of God rejoice. Jesus, with His mere presence at the right hand of God, says that all our sins—yes, all of them, past, present, and future—have been taken care of at Calvary's cross. Jesus paid the penalty of our sins, and the wages of sin is death. That's exactly the price that Jesus paid when He died in our place.

If Satan ever bothers us about any of our sins or any of our failures—or even if he accuses us before God—the price has already been paid. Christians can rest in the truth that Jesus is at the Father's right hand, living to make intercession for us.

Jesus told Peter, "Satan has desired to have you that he may sift you as wheat, but I have prayed for you that your faith fails not." The scripture today says that Jesus makes intercession for us!

We know that Jesus is currently at the Father's right hand, and now we'll see further evidence of the Trinity continuing with the same thought. The following verse makes it obvious that Jesus is our Mediator.

A mediator is a go-between who attempts to make people involved in a conflict come to an agreement. For there to be a mediator, there must be at least three parties: the two that are in conflict and the mediator as the go-between. You and I are one of the parties, God is the other, and the mediator who is our go-between is Jesus Christ. We will see that there is only one mediator, just one, who is our go-between.

> For there is one God and one Mediator between God and men, the Man Christ Jesus. (1 Timothy 2:5)

Between man and God is our one and only mediator—Jesus Christ—who died for us and is seated at the Father's right hand.

Let's travel to the book of Acts and find the first martyr in the early church, Stephen. Stephen was one of the first seven deacons selected to take care of providing charity to the widows after the church began on the day of Pentecost.

Stephen was strong in the scriptures and full of the Holy Spirit. His faith in Christ brought about his death. He was stoned near the Lion's Gate (also known as Stephen's Gate) at Jerusalem. I've been to this gate, which is marked with emblems of lions on both sides of the gate entrance.

Stephen, at his death, saw God the Father on His throne and Jesus standing right where we expect Him to be—at the Father's right hand.

> But he, being full of the Holy Spirit, gazed into heaven and saw the glory of God, and Jesus standing at the right hand of God. (Acts 7:55)

Again we see the Trinity in one verse:

- The Holy Spirit is in Stephen's heart on earth
- Jesus is standing in heaven at the Father's right hand.
- Stephen see's both Jesus and the Father in heaven

To further verify the Trinity is seen here, we ask, "What is Jesus doing at the right hand of God?" The book of Hebrews will give us the answer.

Jesus is now our High Priest. A priest was one who went to God on behalf of the people of Israel. On the Day of Atonement, in the month of Tishrei the tenth (Yom Kippur), the high priest would go into the holy of holies—where the presence of God dwelt in the temple—to offer sacrifice for the sins of the people of Israel. The high priest did this once every year on this day. The purpose of the high priest was to go into the presence of God on the people's behalf.

Today, there is only one High Priest. Since the cross, the veil in the Temple was rent from top to bottom, giving everyone access to God's throne of grace. This eliminates the need for an earthly high priest as Jesus is now our High Priest. When He ascended back to the Father, He entered into the presence of God in heaven, and is there today on our behalf. Let's take a look at the following verse:

> Seeing then that we have a great High Priest who has passed through the heavens, Jesus the Son of God, let us hold fast our confession.
>
> For we do not have a High Priest who cannot sympathize with our weaknesses, but was in all points tempted as we are, yet without sin.
>
> Let us therefore come boldly to the throne of grace, that we may obtain mercy and find grace to help in time of need. (Hebrews 4:14–16)

Remember how we said the high priest would have to repeatedly go every year to offer sacrifices for the sins of the people. On the Day of Atonement, he would have to return because the blood of bulls and goats could not remove sin permanently. The high priest had to repeat the sacrifice every year.

When Jesus died, He said, "It is finished." The atonement work was now complete, the veil to the Holy of Holies was finally rent, which happened at the cross, and Jesus only had to provide one sacrifice.

Another point to make is that the earthly priest never sat down because his work was ongoing. Once Jesus ascended to the Father—I love this—He sat down. His work in the atonement of our sins was forever complete.

> But this Man, after He had offered one sacrifice for sins forever, sat down at the right hand of God. (Hebrews 10:12)

The next verse lets us know that His intercessory work continues, and we see the Trinity in that Jesus saves to the uttermost. He is the means by which we are able to be reconciled to God. Jesus says that He is the Way and that no one can come to the Father except through Him (John 14:6). The only way for any person to come to God is through Jesus Christ. Jesus, in John 14, used the word through, and we are about to see that word again:

> Therefore, He is also able to save to the uttermost those who come to God through Him, since He always lives to make intercession for them. (Hebrews 7:25)

Jesus has gone to God on our behalf. Everything He did—coming into the world, living His spotless life, enduring the cross, raising from the dead, and sitting at the right hand of God—was all for us! He did all of this for you and for me. He is the only one who is worthy of sitting at the Father's right hand. This is why we only have one High Priest. There is no earthly man alive who is worthy of priesthood. Because of His blood, Jesus alone is worthy.

> Seeing then that we have a great High Priest who has passed through the heavens, Jesus the Son of God, let us hold fast our confession. (Hebrews 4:14)

Hebrews describes "a High Priest." That's singular. There is no longer any need for earthly priests today; in fact, they don't even exist. There is only one High Priest: Jesus the Son of God. There is not a man on earth who can bring us to the Father. Jesus is "the" Way, and the only way to God is through Him. There is also only one mediator:

> For there is one God and one Mediator between God and men, the Man Christ Jesus. (1 Timothy 2:5)

Hebrews continues with the same theme; this time, the word "the" is singular. Here are three back-to-back verses. It's like the book of

Hebrews can't say it enough times. There's no excuse for us to not grasp this.

> He is the mediator of a better covenant (Hebrews 8:6)

> And for this reason, He is the Mediator of the new covenant, by means of death, for the redemption of the transgressions. (Hebrews 9:15)

> And to Jesus the mediator of the new covenant. (Hebrews 12:24)

One who understands the Trinity certainly has a proper understanding of Christ in His role as High Priest and Mediator. It is impossible for a person who does not understand the Trinity to comprehend Jesus as our High Priest and Mediator because it's the role of the High Priest to go to God on our behalf and the role of a Mediator to be our go-between.

When we sin and fail God—as we all do—and Satan accuses us to God as he did Job, Christ is at the Father's right hand to claim that the payment for our sins was paid in full at Calvary with His blood! He is the Mediator between God and humanity.

CHAPTER 14

THE TRINITY IN MATTHEW'S GOSPEL

Since Matthew was a tax collector, he knew how to count and was good with numbers.

Let's take a look at Matthew confirming the Trinity.

Christ Sends the Disciples

> For it is not you who are speaking, but it is the Spirit of your Father who is speaking in you. (Matthew 10:20)

Jesus is speaking to His disciples and sending them forth as sheep among wolves. We have the Trinity in one verse:

- Jesus is speaking and sending the disciples.
- Jesus tells them of the Spirit.
- Jesus says the Spirit is of the Father.

All Things Are Delivered to Jesus from the Father

> All things have been delivered to Me by my Father, and no one knows the Son except the Father. Nor does anyone know the Father except the Son, and the one to whom the Son wills to reveal Him. (Matthew 11:27)

Our key words here are "to" "by," and "my." Jesus clearly states that all things have been delivered "to" Christ "by" the Father. Jesus did not deliver all things to Himself. Jesus references the Father as "My" Father. These key words show a contrast between Christ and the Father.

The Unpardonable Sin Proves the Trinity

> Therefore, I say to you, every sin and blasphemy will be forgiven men, but the blasphemy against the Spirit will not be forgiven men. Anyone who speaks a word against the Son of Man, it will be forgiven him; but whoever speaks against the Holy Spirit, it will not be forgiven him, either in this age or in the age to come. (Matthew 12:31–32)

Jesus makes a difference between sins committed against Him and sins against the Holy Spirit. This verse would not even make sense if Jesus and the Holy Spirit were the same in person and in number.

What is the unpardonable sin? The Pharisees accused Jesus of doing His miracles by the power of Satan (Beelzebub). They were contributing the works of the Holy Spirit to the power of Satan. That is the definition of the unpardonable sin. It is when a person claims the works of the Holy Spirit are of the devil.

If one has a fear that they have committed the unpardonable sin, it's a sure sign that they haven't. If one has committed this sin, God would no longer deal with that person and show them their need for salvation. Jesus said that no one could come to the Father except the Father "draw him" (John 6:44). Since the unpardonable sin cannot be pardoned, God would cease to deal with that person regarding their need to be saved. In other words, God does not "draw" a person to salvation if they cannot be saved.

One can take comfort in knowing that if they see their need for God, it is a sure sign that God is still dealing with that individual. Why would God deal with a person about their need to be saved if they couldn't be saved?

I'm inserting this into the discussion because there are some who have lived in fear, thinking they have gone too far and are beyond redemption. Jesus told us that if any man would come to Him, He would "in no wise" cast him away. Jesus turns no one down; it is still "whosoever will" who can come to Christ. My dear friend, if you want to be saved, you can be—and there's nothing that can keep you from knowing the Lord. Anyone who comes to Christ is accepted by Him.

Getting back to the Trinity, we see two things:

- Sins committed against Christ are forgivable.
- Sins committed against the Holy Spirit are not forgivable.

This is undeniable evidence of the Trinity.

The Feeding of the Five Thousand Proves the Trinity

In the desolate region of the Sea of Galilee, Jesus performed one of His most popular miracles. With five small loaves of bread and two fishes, Jesus fed five thousand men—plus women and children.

Having visited the Sea of Galilee, there is a traditional location believed to be the place where this miracle happened; however, the traditional location is located in a place that was heavily populated during the ministry of Jesus. The secluded place is on the eastern side of the sea. I personally believe this is the true location of this miracle. If they were in the populated area, they could have just returned home and eaten. Matthew tells us that this place was secluded and desolate.

In this miracle, we see proof of the Trinity:

> Then He commanded the multitudes to sit down on the grass. And He took the five loaves and the two fish, and looking up to heaven, He blessed and broke and gave the loaves to the disciples; and the disciples gave to the multitudes. (Matthew 14:19)

Who was Jesus looking up to? In the Lord's Prayer, He said, "Our Father which are in heaven."

At the tomb of Lazarus, "Jesus lifted up His eyes and said, 'Father, I thank You that You have heard Me'" (John 11:41). When Jesus looked up, He was looking to His Father in heaven. Jesus certainly was not looking up to Himself; this is evidence of the difference between Himself and His Father.

The Feeding of the Four Thousand Displays the Trinity

The feeding of the five thousand was not the only time Jesus did this miracle. He repeated the miracle for four thousand men in Matthew 15, and we have a little more information this time. Matthew 14 only said that "Jesus looked up" and then blessed and gave to the disciples who then gave to the multitude.

This time, Matthew records that Jesus gave "thanks."

> And He took the seven loaves and the fish and gave thanks, broke them and gave them to His disciples; and the disciples gave to the multitude. (Matthew 15:36)

To whom did Jesus give thanks? If not to the Father in heaven, then who? He most assuredly would not be giving thanks to Himself!

In both of these miracles of feeding the multitudes, Jesus is looking up and giving thanks.

The Trinity in Peter's Proclamation

In the setting of the upcoming scriptures, Jesus has led his disciples to the northern part of Galilee. The place is called Caesarea Philippi. This is a place where Israel worshipped the false god Pan and other gods. I've been there, and there is a cave entrance where Israel sacrificed their own children to this false god.

In that setting, Jesus asked one of His most popular questions: "Who do people say the Son of Man is?"

Peter is known for speaking and being rebuked, but this time he hit the nail on the head! He got the answer right.

> Simon Peter answered and said, "You are the Christ, the Son of the living God." Jesus answered and said to him, "Blessed are you, Simon Bar-Jonah, for flesh and blood has not revealed this to you, but My Father who is in heaven." (Matthew 16:16–17)

After Peter's declaration, Jesus told Peter that flesh and blood had not given him this revelation. It was the Lord's Father in heaven.

- Where did Jesus (on earth) say the Father was when He revealed to Peter that Jesus was the Son of God? (The Father is in heaven).
- Who did Jesus say revealed to Peter that Jesus was the Messiah? The verse answers itself. Peter received this revelation from the Father in heaven (not from Jesus).
- How could Jesus be the one who revealed this to Peter? Jesus said, "Flesh and blood had not revealed it." Jesus had flesh

and blood, His flesh was scourged and pierced, and His blood was spilled at the cross. This revelation could not have come from Christ Himself.

- Who is the "Living God" who Jesus is the Son of?

In Peter's declaration, it is easy to understand the difference between Jesus and the Father.

THE TRINITY IN PETER'S CORRECTION ON THE MOUNT OF TRANSFIGURATION

In chapter 16, Jesus commended Peter for claiming that Jesus was the Son of the Living God. One chapter later, Peter will speak again. This time, he will be corrected and not commended.

The setting is the Mount of Transfiguration. There are two mountains in Israel that are believed to be candidates for this event, and I personally believe it is Mount Tabor. I've driven to the top of Tabor; it's a little bit of a winding drive to get to the summit. When you reach the top, the view is spectacular. I thought, "That was quite a little drive", yet Jesus took His inner circle of three disciples here—and they climbed this mountain.

There were three times that Jesus took only Peter, James, and John with Him, leaving the other nine behind. Once was the raising of Jairus's daughter, another time was in the Garden of Gethsemane, and the third was at the top of this mountain. Jesus showed these three men His glory, and they would never forget it.

The glory of Jesus was revealed to these three men, and Moses and Elijah also appeared on the scene. They were both alive and had their same names. Moses had died 1,500 years before. He was still alive after he was buried and still had his same name. Elijah (and Enoch) never died and haven't to this day. Elijah had been caught up to heaven in a chariot and whirlwind. Elijah now comes down from heaven, and Moses comes up from paradise, which was in the heart of the earth.

Light illuminated from Christ as He was transfigured in His glory. Peter became excited and said, "Lord, let's build three tabernacles here: one for you, one for Moses, and another for Elijah." That's when God the Father interrupted Peter and corrected him.

We've all heard about someone "talking over" someone else. Peter wasn't even finished speaking when God jumped into this conversation:

> While he was still speaking, behold, a bright cloud overshadowed them; and suddenly a voice came out of the cloud, saying, "This is My beloved Son, in whom I am well pleased. Hear Him!" (Matthew 17:5)

- Whose voice spoke out of the cloud and stated that Jesus was His Son?
- In whom was the voice pleased?
- Who was pleased?
- Who corrected Peter when he wanted to build three tabernacles for Moses, Elijah, and Jesus?
- Who did the voice tell Peter to listen to?
- If Jesus was speaking from the cloud, why didn't He say "hear Me" instead of "hear Him?"

Let's answer these questions. It was the Father's voice speaking from the cloud. It was Jesus in whom the voice was pleased. It was the Father who was pleased. It was God who corrected Peter and not Jesus. The one speaking said to hear Jesus. We can easily see the difference between God the Father and Jesus who is transfigured.

The Angels of Children Show the Trinity

I believe that God has assigned to every child their own angel of protection. It says so in an upcoming verse. Yes, angels are real. I've never seen one, but I've had experiences where I feel they were there when I needed them.

The only angels we know from scripture that have wings are Seraphim and Cherubim; all of the other angels in scripture usually looked like regular men. The Bible tells us that we should be careful how we treat strangers because some have entertained angels without knowing it (Hebrews 13:2). The angels that came to Lot's home in Sodom certainly looked just like men (Genesis 19:5).

Angels go beyond our subject today, but I'm glad the scripture says that the angels of the Lord pitch their tents in our backyards. It's not worded exactly like that, but the Bible says they "encamp" around those who fear the Lord (Psalm 34:7).

Children have angels assigned to them, and we see the Trinity in this verse:

> Take heed that you do not despise one of these little ones, for I say to you that in heaven their angels always see the face of My Father who is in heaven. (Matthew 18:10)

The angels were not facing Jesus on earth; they were facing the Father in heaven. At the same time, Jesus did reference the Father as "my Father."

The Trinity in the Request of the Mother of James and John

Let's set the stage concerning this next passage. The mother of James and John (the sons of Zebedee) had come to Jesus making a request.

Jesus asked her, "What do you wish?"

She said she wanted her two sons to sit next to Jesus in the kingdom; she wanted one seated on the left and the other on the right.

Jesus told her that she didn't know what she was asking because it would require some real suffering. James and John said they were able to drink of the Lord's suffering.

> So, He said to them, "You will indeed drink My cup, and be baptized with the baptism that I am baptized with; but to sit on My right hand and on My left is not Mine to give, but it is for those for whom it is prepared by My Father." (Matthew 20:20–23)

Jesus told the mother of James and John that the one who decided who would be allowed to be seated next to Him was the Father. This means there are some things that the Father decides that are not the decisions of Jesus. We are seeing this, right? There are decisions the Father makes that the Son does not make.

God Is the Father—and Jesus Is the Teacher

Jesus is about to give some guidelines for how to address individuals religiously. Jesus tells the disciples not to call anyone Father or Rabbi (Teacher) from a religious standpoint.

Of course, it's OK to call someone father or teacher from a secular (earthly) setting. The scriptures often use the word "father" in addressing earthly fathers (in the Old and New Testaments).

Jesus is coming from a religious setting in Matthew 23. Jesus is coming down hard on the scribes and Pharisees who love to sit in the "seat of Moses" in the synagogues. Jesus is warning and giving "woes" to the scribes and Pharisees. He is calling them hypocrites who lay heavy burdens on those who follow them. He condemns how they love to stand in the marketplaces and be called "Rabbi" while they outwardly wear their phylacteries (small square boxes with Torah inscriptions inside) and enlarge the borders of their religious garments.

As one can easily see, Jesus is speaking from a religious standpoint. It's not a secular standpoint. It's perfectly fine to call your earthly father "father." Jesus is speaking from a religious setting, and we will see the Trinity in what He is about to tell us:

> Do not call anyone on earth your father; for One is your Father, He who is in heaven. And do not be called teachers; for One is your Teacher, the Christ. (Matthew 23:9–10)

According to this verse, there is only "one" Father and "one" Teacher. Their identities and locations are distinguishable. While Christ was on earth, He stated the Father is in heaven, and the Teacher, the Christ, obviously was on earth.

One Father in heaven and One Teacher, and both Father and Teacher are capitalized in the verse. These are two different names. Jesus tells us who both of the identities are. He says the Father is the one in heaven and the Teacher is "the Christ" (Messiah, Anointed One). The Father is not the Messiah, and He is not the Anointed One. The Father is the one who is anointing the Anointed One.

Some translations use "Rabbi" rather than "Teacher." "Rabbi" in Hebrew is "*rhabbi*," meaning "teacher or master." I'm not all that fond of titles anyway. The one I certainly won't use is "Reverend." Psalm 111:9 says, "Holy and Awesome is his name." It comes from the Hebrew word "yare," which means "revere, revering, reverent, awesome, dreadful, feared." The ASV, KJV translate this verse as "Reverend is His name".

Don't take me wrong. I have no problem with others using titles. Jesus gave us apostles, prophets, evangelist, pastors, and teachers. We also see deacons, elders, and bishops..

From a religious standpoint, calling anyone on earth "father" is forbidden by Christ. I have studied both sides of this argument and still can't see from a religious setting where the practice is allowed. Jesus said, "There is One Father," which is in heaven and "One Teacher," which is the Christ (Messiah).

Remaining on the subject of the Trinity, Jesus is making a clear distinction between the Father in heaven and Himself the Teacher.

The Day and Hour of the Second Advent Confirms the Trinity

There are certain decisions the Father makes that are not made by the Son. The example we gave was that of the mother of the sons of Zebedee when she asked that her two sons sit at the Lord's right and left hands in the kingdom. Jesus said this decision was not His to give; it was to be decided by the Father alone.

The same is true with knowledge. There are some things known only by the Father that the Son does not know.

I guess no one enjoys having to say, "I don't know." We all want to know the answers to questions we are asked. If you were to ask Jesus, "When are you coming back?" He would say, "I don't know." Let's take of look at this in the scripture:

> But of that day and hour no one knows, not even the angels of heaven, but My Father only. (Matthew 24:36)

Jesus uses the word "only." We live in a day when there are some who try to set a date for the Lord's return. The truth is that no one knows. This is something that is known only by the Father.

I recently read a book that said Jesus was going to return on Tishrei the first, which is the feast of trumpets on the Jewish calendar. His position was that the other feast days had a biblical event that happened on them. As an example, Jesus died on Passover on Nisan the fourteenth, which is true. Jesus arose on firstfruits. The Holy Spirit came when Pentecost had fully come. Most likely, Jesus was born during the feast of tabernacles, which I believe as well. This can be proven in two ways (we'll discuss that in another book). However, if you asked any minister, "How old was Jesus when He died?" almost all would say thirty-three and a half years of age. Everyone also agrees Jesus died on Passover. All we have to do is back off that half a year from Nisan, and it places the birthday of Jesus in Tishrei (usually in September or October).

That's the fast way to find out that Jesus was born in the fall. Jesus was not born in December. The second way is proven by calculating the birth of John the Baptist and Jesus. This would take a little time to explain, but we know from scripture that Jesus was born six months after John the Baptist. Using the cycle of the priestly divisions of 1 Chronicles 24, we find that John the Baptist's father Zacharias was on the eighth rotation from the sons of Abijah. Elizabeth became expecting after Zachariah's return, which places the birth of John the Baptist right at Passover. We can prove from scripture that both Elizabeth and Mary went full term (nine months). All we have to do is add another six months, and it takes us to the birth of Jesus, which would be in September at the feast of tabernacles.

- April: first month
- May: second month
- June: third month
- July: fourth month
- August: fifth month
- September: sixth month

Jesus was born six months after John the Baptist. I didn't go into detail with a lot of proof because that's not the topic of this book. I do have a complete series on this, which covers the topic in six lessons. Doing the topic justice would require at least six hours.

What brought up this subject was the book I was reading about setting a date for the Lord's return. It is true that certain biblical events happened on Jewish feast days. However, Jesus clearly taught us that even He didn't know when the Second Coming would happen. If Jesus doesn't know, I don't think any of us know either. In the past, some have tried to set times—only to be embarrassed. Even Jesus doesn't know the time of the Second Coming. For someone to claim they know would be saying they know something that Jesus doesn't know! I don't think any of us want to go there.

Matthew said that no one knows—not even the angels—besides

the Father. He did not say that Jesus didn't know; he only recorded that the angels didn't know. Let's take a look at how Mark wrote it.

> But of that day and hour no one knows, not even the angels in heaven, nor the Son, but only the Father. (Mark 13:32)

Jesus is saying, "I don't know."

How could the Father and the Son be one in the same person? One knows the date, and the other does not know.

We conclude that the day and hour of the Second Advent—the Second Coming of Christ, when His feet touch the Mount of Olives—is known only to the Father. We also conclude that Jesus said that neither the angels nor the Son knows. This gives confirmation concerning the Trinity.

CHAPTER 15

THE TRINITY IN MARK'S GOSPEL

It is believed by some that the book of Mark was the first of the four Gospels to be written.

Although listed as a cross-reference in a previous chapter with Matthew, this verse is certainly appropriate here as we view the Trinity in the Gospel of Mark:

> But about that day or hour no one knows, not even the angels in heaven, nor the Son, but the Father alone. (Mark 13:32)

According to this scripture, the Father knows the day and hour of the Second Advent (Second Coming), but this time is not known by the Son. This clearly states a distinction between the Father and the Son. We discussed this in more detail in the previous chapter of the Gospel of Matthew. With that being said, we progress to the next verse in Mark.

> And He said, "Abba, Father, all things are possible for You. Take this cup away from Me; nevertheless, not what I will, but what You will." (Mark 14:36)

We see many things in this one verse. First, Jesus is praying to the Father. He certainly would not be praying to Himself.

What does the word Abba mean? First of all it, does not mean "Daddy" as many have claimed. "Abba" is actually the Aramaic word for "Father." This is one example of an Aramaic word in the New Testament, which was normally written in Greek. "Abba" was used both by Jesus and Paul (Mark 14:36; Romans 8:15; Galatians 4:6).

Much of the ministry of Jesus was in Galilee, which primarily spoke in Aramaic. Jesus certainly spoke Aramaic, which was the language of Nazareth (where Jesus grew up) and Capernaum (where Jesus moved his headquarters) on the northern shore of the Sea of Galilee.

Jesus spoke in Aramaic on the cross: "Eli, Eli, lama sabachthani," which is "My God, My God, why have you forsaken me." Jesus most likely was familiar with Hebrew and Greek as well. Hebrew was used mainly by the scribes and teachers (rabbis) of Mosaic law. Jesus conversed well with the Pharisees and Sadducees since the religious leaders knew Hebrew well.

According to the scriptures, Jesus was both a Rabbi and a Prophet, which made Him qualified to speak in the synagogues.

Many, including the disciples, called Jesus Rabbi:

- When Judas betrayed Jesus in the Garden of Gethsemane, he called Jesus "Rabbi" (Mark 14:45).
- When Peter addressed Jesus on the Mount of Transfiguration, he called Jesus "Rabbi" (Mark 9:5).
- When Jesus told John's disciples to come and see His home, they called Jesus "Rabbi" (John 1:38).
- When Jesus called Mary by name after His resurrection, she called Jesus "Rabboni" (John 20:16).

As a Rabbi, Jesus most likely knew Hebrew.

Also, Jesus read in the synagogues. Yes, there were copies of scripture translations during the days of Christ, the Septuagint, which translated the Old Testament from Hebrew to Greek, existed then and was sometimes read in synagogues. Jesus may have been familiar with Greek. Greek was the political language of the Romans while they ruled over Israel during the ministry of Jesus. Jesus was a rabbi and a prophet.

- Moses said Jesus would be a prophet that would be like unto himself (Deuteronomy 18:15).
- Jesus was known as a prophet (John 6:14).

Jesus would have had the right to speak in the synagogues as He did in Nazareth when He read from Isaiah 61.

> Then Jesus returned in the power of the Spirit to Galilee, and news of Him went out through all the surrounding region. And He taught in their synagogues, being glorified by all.
>
> He came to Nazareth, where He had been brought up. And as His custom was, He went into the synagogue on the Sabbath day, and stood up to read.
>
> And He was handed the book of the prophet Isaiah. And when He had opened the book, He found the place where it was written: "The Spirit of the Lord is upon Me." (Luke 4:14–18)

Jesus prayed, "Abba, Father, all things are possible for You. Take this cup away from Me; nevertheless, not what I will, but what You will." He was not praying to Himself; He was calling God His Father.

> And He said, "Abba, Father, all things are possible for You. Take this cup away from Me; nevertheless, not what I will, but what You will." (Mark 14:36)

First, Jesus is praying to the Father. He certainly would not be praying to Himself.

Second, He states that all things are possible for the Father, and He asked the Father to take the cup away from Him. If the Father and Son are one and the same, this verse makes no sense.

Third, and this is huge, we see that the will of the Father and the will of the Son are two different wills. Christ submits His will to the will of His Father.

The above scriptures validate the Trinity in the Gospel of Mark.

CHAPTER 16

THE TRINITY IN LUKE'S GOSPEL

We covered much from Luke's Gospel previously and saw the Trinity in the Life of Christ from His conception of the Holy Spirit, through His life and ministry beginning at His baptism, and being driven into the wilderness by the Holy Spirit to be tempted.

We saw Jesus claiming Isaiah 61 was in reference to Himself when he said, "The Spirit of the Lord is upon Me."

In His prayers and thanksgivings, he gave thanks to the Father. Then we progressed to the Gethsemane prayer. We saw Christ offering Himself a sacrifice through the Holy Spirit, and we saw His resurrection performed by the Holy Spirit. After His ascension, Jesus prays to the Father that another Helper (Comforter) would be sent back to His followers.

The following verses will further validate the doctrine of the Trinity in the Gospel of Luke:

> And the Child grew and became strong in spirit, filled with wisdom; and the grace of God was upon Him. And Jesus increased in wisdom and stature, and in favor with God and men. (Luke 2:40, 52)

- Whose grace was upon Jesus when He was a child?
- In whose favor did Jesus increase?

The answers are obvious since the two verses are self-explanatory. It was the grace of God the Father in heaven that was upon Jesus, and it was the Father's favor in which He grew. If God the Father and Jesus the Son are one and the same, how could these verses be true?

The next few verses are extremely interesting:

> Then Jesus, being filled with the Holy Spirit, returned from the Jordan and was led by the Spirit into the wilderness.
>
> Then Jesus returned in the power of the Spirit to Galilee, and news of Him went out through all the surrounding region.
>
> The Spirit of the Lord is upon Me, Because He has anointed Me To preach the Gospel to the poor; He has sent Me to heal the brokenhearted, To proclaim liberty to the captives And recovery of sight to the blind, To set at liberty those who are oppressed. (Luke 4:1, 14, 18)

- With whom was Jesus filled?
- Who led Jesus into the wilderness?
- In whose power did Jesus return to Galilee?
- Whose Spirit was upon Jesus?
- Who anointed Jesus?
- Who sent Jesus to heal the brokenhearted?

We also note that "Spirit" is spelled with a capital "S," proving this to be the Holy Spirit, and He is called the Spirit "of the Lord."

These verses are packed with the doctrine of the Trinity.

Now we come to a verse related to the Second Coming of Christ to the earth:

> For whoever is ashamed of Me and My words, of him the Son of Man will be ashamed when He comes in His own glory, "and" in His Father's, and of the holy angels. (Luke 9:26)

In whose glory will Jesus return?

- First, He comes in His own glory
- Second, (we have our conjunction word "and") in the glory of His Father and lastly of the holy angels.

We note that the glory of Christ and of the Father are listed separately.

I love this next verse because it shows our Lord displayed times of rejoicing. I like to see a preacher smile. I've known quite a few ministers who never smile. I've sometimes wondered how could a minister be a good representative of Christianity without a disposition of joy? The kingdom of God is righteousness and peace and joy in the Holy Spirit (Romans 14:17). Paul wrote that, and I'm sure he had seen some long-faced, unhappy Pharisees in his day. Once Paul was saved, he writes that the kingdom of God is joy in the Holy Spirit. Being from Texas, I've seen some long-faced mules that I thought would make good members in some churches I've visited. My friend, it's OK to be a happy Christian! I really like this verse because it tells me that my Lord could rejoice. Now pay close attention in whom He rejoiced. We're going to bounce right off of what Paul just told us.

> He who hears you hears Me, he who rejects you rejects Me, and he who rejects Me rejects Him who sent Me.
>
> In that hour Jesus rejoiced in the Spirit and said, "I thank You, Father, Lord of heaven and earth, that You have hidden these things from the wise and prudent and revealed them to babes. Even so, Father, for so it seemed good in Your sight.
>
> All things have been delivered to Me by My Father, and no one knows who the Son is except the Father,

> and who the Father is except the Son, and the one to whom the Son wills to reveal Him. (Luke 10:16, 21–22)

There is a lot in these verses that corresponds with the Trinity.

- If one rejects Jesus, does He also reject the Father who sent Him?
- In whom did Jesus rejoice?
- To whom did Jesus give thanks?
- Who delivered all things to Christ?

The answers are straightforward. If one rejects Jesus, they also reject the Father. It was "the Spirit" in which Jesus rejoiced (capital "S"). It was to the Father who Jesus gave thanks to, and it was the Father who has delivered all things to Christ.

Luke records who gives the Holy Spirit to the believers.

> If you then, being evil, know how to give good gifts to your children, how much more will your heavenly Father give the Holy Spirit to those who ask Him! (Luke 11:13)

Jesus is speaking here, and He is speaking about the Father and the Spirit both. Also, it is the Father who gives the Spirit to those who ask. Here we see the Trinity again in one single verse:

- Jesus is speaking.
- The Father is the one who gives.
- The Holy Spirit is the gift.

Luke's Record of the Unpardonable Sin

> And anyone who speaks a word against the Son of Man, it will be forgiven him; but to him who blasphemes against the Holy Spirit, it will not be forgiven. (Luke 12:10)

Again, we see a clear distinction spoken by Christ Himself that He and the Holy Spirit are separate persons in the Godhead.

- To sin against the Son is forgivable.
- To speak against the Holy Spirit is never forgivable.

We covered this in detail earlier. Luke records that Jesus tells us how He will deliver the kingdom. Pay close attention to the words "just as."

> But you are those who have continued with Me in My trials. And I bestow upon you a kingdom, "just as" My Father bestowed one upon Me. (Luke 22:28–29)

We have seen so many scriptures that would make no sense if the Father and the Son were one and the same. This is another one of those verses.

Now we will see how Luke records the Lord's last words on the cross:

> Then Jesus said, "Father, forgive them, for they do not know what they do." And when Jesus had cried out with a loud voice, He said, "Father, 'into Your hands I commit My spirit.'" Having said this, He breathed His last. (Luke 23:34, 46)

- Who did Jesus ask to forgive those who crucified Him?
- To whom did Jesus commit His spirit?

He certainly did not commit His spirit into His own hands, which again would not make sense. Did you see the words "Your" hand "I" commit "My" spirit?" These words were prayed from Jesus on the cross to the Father in heaven.

The Holy Spirit is a promise of the Father, and Jesus will send this promise to the disciples:

> Behold, I send the Promise of My Father upon you; but tarry in the city of Jerusalem until you are endued with power from on high. (Luke 24:49)

Here again we see the complete Trinity:

- First, Christ is the one delivering the promise.
- Second, the promise is a promise of the Father.
- Third, the power from on high is given by the Holy Spirit.

We know the power of which Jesus spoke was the Holy Spirit:

> And He said to them, "It is not for you to know times or seasons which the Father has put in His own authority. But you shall receive power when the Holy Spirit has come upon you." (Acts 1:7–8)

As a reminder from Luke's record, which we covered earlier, here are four more accounts of Luke confirming the Trinity.

The following verse was also covered under the Trinity in the life of Christ, and it deals with the birth of Christ, which we have covered in detail previously. We place the scripture here again because it is appropriate for the topic of the Trinity in the Gospel of Luke.

> Then the angel said to her, "Do not be afraid, Mary, for you have found favor with God. And behold, you will conceive in your womb and bring forth a Son, and shall call His name Jesus. He will be great, and will be called the Son of the Highest; and the Lord God will give Him the throne of His father David. And He will reign over the house of Jacob forever, and of His kingdom there will be no end."
>
> Then Mary said to the angel, "How can this be, since I do not know a man?"

And the angel answered and said to her, "The Holy Spirit will come upon you, and the power of the Highest will overshadow you; therefore, also, that Holy One who is to be born will be called the Son of God." (Luke 1:30–35)

CHAPTER 17

THE TRINITY IN JOHN'S GOSPEL

John was the closest to Jesus during His earthly ministry, and John is called "that disciple whom Jesus loved."

If any of the disciples would have known Jesus the best, it would have been John. Jesus had twelve disciples, and from those twelve was the inner circle of three (Peter, James, and John). Of those three, John was the closest. He was so close to Jesus that he leaned his head on the chest (bosom) of Christ. He was so close to Jesus that he could hear the heartbeat of the Son of God.

We certainly want to hear from John regarding God. John is going to speak much about the Trinity, and this will be one of our largest chapters, but it's John who we want to hear from the most.

These are the references concerning the Trinity from the Gospel of John alone (not counting 1, 2, and 3 John or the book of Revelation, which were also written by John).

We will begin with John's opening words in John 1.

> In the beginning was the Word, and the Word was with God, and the Word was God. He was in the beginning with God. (John 1:1–2)

Genesis starts with "In the beginning," and John begins His Gospel with the same words: "In the beginning was the Word and the Word was with God."

> You have known Him who is from the beginning. (1 John 2:14)

In Genesis 1:1–2, Moses speaks of the Trinity by telling us that God was in the beginning, and the Holy Spirit moved on the face of the waters. He then mentions that God said, "Let us make man in our image and after our likeness." John begins his Gospel in the same way.

In the opening verses, the Triune Godhead is revealed to us. John, like Moses, says that God was in the beginning, but he adds that the Word (Jesus) was with God in the beginning.

Going back to our key words, "with" implies that there is more than one person. How can one be "with" another if there is not another to be with? (You followed that, right)? This verse shows that Jesus was with the Father from the very beginning.

JOHN 3

> For He whom God has sent speaks the words of God, for God does not give the Spirit by measure. The Father loves the Son, and has given all things into His hand. (John 3:34–35)

These verses display all three persons of the Godhead. Let's break it down. John says that God (the first person in the Godhead) gives the Spirit (third person in the Godhead) and goes on to say that it is the Father (first person in the Godhead) who loves the Son (second person in the Godhead) and has given Him (second person in the Godhead) all things.

John tells us whose will Jesus was sent to finish.

JOHN 4

> Jesus said to them, "My food is to do the will of Him who sent Me, and to finish His work." (John 4:34)

Jesus did not come to do his own will; in fact, in Gethsemane, the will of Jesus was different than that of the Father. Jesus prayed, "Not my will but your will be done." Jesus submitted to the will of the Father and on the cross cried, "It is finished."

What was Jesus's food? He did not feed on doing His own will; it was the will of the Father who sent Him. Whose work did He come to finish? Jesus calls the works that He is to finish the works of the Father and not His own. When Jesus cried, "It is finished," it means He had finished the work that the Father had sent Him to do.

We could have a discussion of how old one had to be to be considered an adult among Jewish traditions and how old the disciples were when Jesus called them. That is a discussion for another day; for now, we'll just say that at the age of twelve, we consider someone a child by our modern-day standards.

At the age of twelve, Jesus was already about His Father's business. We saw that in Luke chapter 2:49. Jesus is still at work after His ministry is underway.

I like this next verse a lot because I believe those of us in the ministry should be at "work" when it comes to taking care of the Lord's business. Jesus's work before His ministry was that of a carpenter, and now that He is officially in His ministry, there's not an ounce of laziness within Him. Jesus is still shoulder to the wheel and hard at work. Folks, the ministry is work! Anyone who enters the ministry thinking it's an easy task is under an illusion. It's downright hard work.

I've seen some who thought differently about that, and I've known some preachers who are so lazy they would whittle with an electric knife! I know some preachers who are not afraid of work, and they can lay down right beside it and go to sleep! If one is going to be successful in the ministry, they're going to have to show up for "work." (I think we could write an entire book on that subject alone).

Jesus is going to tell us a little about who has been at work, and it won't just be Him.

John 5

> But Jesus answered them, "My Father has been working until now, and I have been working." Therefore, the Jews sought all the more to kill Him, because He not only broke the Sabbath, but also said that God was His Father, making Himself equal with God. (John 5:17–18)

The Lord's Father has been working, and Jesus uses our conjunction "and" and says, "And I have been working."

My friend, this simple English is easy to understand. There are two who have been at work; the Father of the Lord (Jesus did say "my" Father) has been working, and then He says "and" and "I" have been working.

It's as obvious as a pimple on a pretty girl's nose! In this verse, there are two who have been working.

Jesus is accused of claiming Himself equal "with" God. The accusation was not that Jesus claimed that He was the Father but that He claimed equality with God.

As we travel through John's Gospel, we turn to chapter 5. There are quite a few verses we're about to present, but I'm assuming that one has purchased this book to learn the details. Jesus begins with the words "most assuredly." Those words are used twenty-five times in the NJKV, and all will be from the book of John. What we are about to read is "most assuredly."

- First, the Son can do nothing of Himself but what He sees the Father do.
- Second, it is the Father who loves the Son and shows Him all things that He Himself does.

- Third, the Son gives life as the Father raises the dead and gives life.
- Fourth, the Father judges no man and has committed all judgment to the Son.
- Fifth, all should honor the Son just as they honor the Father.
- Sixth, the Son has been sent from the Father.
- Seventh, Jesus does not seek His own will—but the will of the Father.
- Eighth, Jesus does not witness of Himself; the witness comes from another.
- Ninth, the works done by Jesus are given to Him from the Father.

Everything listed above is confirmed in the following verses:

> Most assuredly, I say to you, the Son can do nothing of Himself, but what He sees the Father do; for whatever He does, the Son also does in like manner.
>
> For the Father loves the Son, and shows Him all things that He Himself does; and He will show Him greater works than these, that you may marvel.
>
> For as the Father raises the dead and gives life to them, even so the Son gives life to whom He will.
>
> For the Father judges no one, but has committed all judgment to the Son, that all should honor the Son just as they honor the Father. He who does not honor the Son does not honor the Father who sent Him.
>
> Most assuredly, I say to you, he who hears My word and believes in Him who sent Me has everlasting life, and shall not come into judgment, but has passed from death into life.
>
> Most assuredly, I say to you, the hour is coming, and now is, when the dead will hear the voice of the Son of God; and those who hear will live.
>
> For as the Father has life in Himself, so He has granted the Son to have life in Himself, and has given

Him authority to execute judgment also, because He is the Son of Man.

Do not marvel at this; for the hour is coming in which all who are in the graves will hear His voice and come forth—those who have done good, to the resurrection of life, and those who have done evil, to the resurrection of condemnation.

I can of Myself do nothing. As I hear, I judge; and My judgment is righteous, because I do not seek My own will but the will of the Father who sent Me.

If I bear witness of Myself, My witness is not true. There is another who bears witness of Me, and I know that the witness which He witnesses of Me is true.

You have sent to John, and he has borne witness to the truth. Yet I do not receive testimony from man, but I say these things that you may be saved. He was the burning and shining lamp, and you were willing for a time to rejoice in his light. But I have a greater witness than John's; for the works which the Father has given Me to finish—the very works that I do—bear witness of Me, that the Father has sent Me.

And the Father Himself, who sent Me, has testified of Me. You have neither heard His voice at any time, nor seen His form.

But you do not have His word abiding in you, because whom He sent, Him you do not believe. You search the Scriptures, for in them you think you have eternal life; and these are they which testify of Me. But you are not willing to come to Me that you may have life.

I do not receive honor from men. But I know you, that you do not have the love of God in you. I have come in My Father's name, and you do not receive Me; if another comes in his own name, him you will receive. How can you believe, who receive honor from

> one another, and do not seek the honor that comes from the only God? Do not think that I shall accuse you to the Father; there is one who accuses you—Moses, in whom you trust. (John 5:19–45)

In the next verse, the Son has been sent from the Father. The believer is told to believe in the Father from whom Jesus is sent.

JOHN 6

> Jesus answered and said to them, "This is the work of God, that you believe in Him whom He sent." (John 6:29)

Now the next verse, we have another "most assuredly." Jesus compares Himself to the manna (bread) that was given to the children of Israel. He begins by saying that it was not Moses who gave the true bread from heaven; that would be done by the Father.

The bread that came down by Moses was not given to the whole world; it was only given to the Israelites who were in exodus from Egypt. Jesus defines the true bread as the bread that comes down from heaven and is given to the entirety of the world. Jesus is the Bread of Life, which comes from the Father:

> Then Jesus said to them, "Most assuredly, I say to you, Moses did not give you the bread from heaven, but My Father gives you the true bread from heaven. For the bread of God is He who comes down from heaven and gives life to the world." (John 6:32–33)

In the next verses, Jesus will say three times that He has been sent from the Father, and twice He will speak to what the Father has given to Christ. Jesus also clearly states that He has not come to do His own will but the will of the Father.

As we read the passage, please note the words "given" and "sent."

> All that the Father gives Me will come to Me, and the one who comes to Me I will by no means cast out. For I have come down from heaven, not to do My own will, but the will of Him who sent Me. This is the will of the Father who sent Me, that of all He has given Me I should lose nothing, but should raise it up at the last day. And this is the will of Him who sent Me, that everyone who sees the Son and believes in Him may have everlasting life; and I will raise him up at the last day. (John 6:37–40)

Remaining still in John 6, Jesus explains the only way in which one can come to God. Jesus distinguishes Himself from the Father with the words "Me" and the "Father who sent me." Note again that it is Jesus who is speaking here. Jesus will claim that all who hear and learn from the Father come to Christ, and he says that only He Himself has seen the Father.

> No one can come to Me unless the Father who sent Me draws him; and I will raise him up at the last day. It is written in the prophets, "And they shall all be taught by God." Therefore everyone who has heard and learned from the Father comes to Me. Not that anyone has seen the Father, except He who is from God. (John 6:44–46)

One more verse before we leave John 6. Jesus once more says He has been sent from the Father and that He lives because of the Father. That is quite a statement! I hope we don't miss it.

> As the living Father sent Me, and I live because of the Father, so he who feeds on Me will live because of Me. (John 6:57)

You probably have noticed how we have been emphasizing that Jesus was sent from the Father. The Greek word for *sent* is *apostello*, which means to "send, send out, send away or send for." The definition is clear; Jesus was "sent out, sent away, and sent for" the Father. The word "sent" is found approximately sixty times in the book of John alone.

"Sent" is found seven times in John 5 and six times in chapter 6. Jesus is making sure we don't miss this. He continues saying that it is the Father who has sent Him. The word sent is found 7,705 times in the New Testament alone. We should be very acquainted with its meaning. When Jesus says the Father has sent Him, it implies someone has to do the sending and another has to be sent. It reminds us of Isaiah saying, "Here am I, Lord, send me." All of us know the meaning of "sent," and there's no way to make the meaning to be other than how it is defined.

In chapter 7, Jesus says that the doctrine that He delivers is not His own doctrine; it is the doctrine of the Father (who again has sent Him). He really nails it down and says those who do the Father's will are those who know this doctrine and will also know from where the doctrine originates. In other words, whose doctrine it is—whether it is from God or whether Jesus is speaking on His own.

JOHN 7

> Jesus answered them and said, "My doctrine is not Mine, but His who sent Me. If anyone wills to do His will, he shall know concerning the doctrine, whether it is from God or whether I speak on My own authority." (John 7:16–17)

Sometimes as I write the comments on all of these verses, I think, *How can one not understand what is so plainly written?* Jesus next will say that He has not come of His own self, but again—you guessed it—of Him who sent Him. Jesus is about to tell us how He came to earth and that He knows the one who sent Him here.

If someone sent you on an errand to the grocery store, wouldn't you know the person who sent you? That's what Jesus is telling us when He says that He knows the Father for He came from Him and was sent by Him. In other words, Jesus is saying, "I know the one who sent me." If Jesus knew the one who sent Him, there has to be more than one in the Trinity. Here's the verse:

> Then Jesus cried out, as He taught in the temple, saying, "You both know Me, and you know where I am from; and I have not come of Myself, but He who sent Me is true, whom you do not know. But I know Him, for I am from Him, and He sent Me." (John 7:28–29)

All right, my friends, we're still here in John 7, but we told you that John would have a lot to say to us.

Now that Jesus has been with the disciples, He's about to tell them that He will leave them and who He's going to. If one was to say, "I'm going to see my father," wouldn't you understand what they were saying? That's all that Jesus is saying in this upcoming verse: "I'm going to my Father who sent me here." This is as obvious as grease in a paper sack!

> Then Jesus said to them, "I shall be with you a little while longer, and then I go to Him who sent Me. You will seek Me and not find Me, and where I am you cannot come." (John 7:33–34)

Are you ready for this? The next verse has Jesus at the festival of Hanukkah. Hanukkah was not one of the Levitical feast days; it was a celebration commemorating the deliverance of Jerusalem and the rededication of the second temple in the second century BCE. It starts on the twenty-fifth day of the Jewish month of Kislev (from late November to late December on the Gregorian calendar).

It is winter in the upcoming verse. Jesus will stand and say something that practically every Christian has heard: "If any man thirst let him come unto Me and drink and out of his heart will flow rivers of living water."

The scriptures tell us who this living water is. John will say Jesus was speaking of the Holy Spirit, which had not yet come because Jesus would have to first be glorified by ascending back to the Father. The Trinity is manifested before our very eyes:

> On the last day, that great day of the feast, Jesus stood and cried out, saying, "If anyone thirsts, let him come to Me and drink. He who believes in Me, as the Scripture has said, out of his heart will flow rivers of living water." But this He spoke concerning the Spirit, whom those believing in Him would receive; for the Holy Spirit was not yet given, because Jesus was not yet glorified. (John 7:37–39)

In chapter 8, Jesus is about to say something that is irrefutable. He is going to tell us that He is not alone, and He will tell us who he's in the company of.

We all know what it means if one is alone; it means to be all by yourself. However, if a person is not alone, someone has to be with them. I know this is simple, but we're using the KISS philosophy: "Keep it simple, scholar!" Jesus said, "Feed my sheep", not my giraffes. We're putting the cookies on the lower shelf so even the children can eat. We all know what "alone" means.

There are times the Bible says that Jesus was alone. He usually would go alone to pray, the disciples would not be with Him (Matthew 14:23; Mark 6:47; Luke 9:18, 36).

The Greek word for alone is *monos*, which means "by oneself, by himself, by myself, only, only in a single."

In the upcoming verse, Jesus says that He is not "monos." He is not alone. He is not by Himself. He is not only in a single. If one is not alone, there has to be someone with them.

JOHN 8

Now we will see Jesus getting into the mathematics of this truth. This is one of the best verses.

> And yet if I do judge, "My judgment is true; for I am not alone, but I am with the Father who sent me. It is also written in your law that the testimony of two men is true. I am one who bears witness of Myself, and the Father who sent Me bears witness of Me." (John 8:16–17)

This is so good! In the above verse, Jesus actually uses the number "two" and states that He is "one" of the two and the Father is the other. Jesus is using the Mosaic law, which says that in two or three witnesses, a matter will be established (Deuteronomy 19:15). Jesus is speaking to the Pharisees, and they were certainly aware of this law. They knew exactly what two and three meant.

When Jesus said He is the Light of the World, the Pharisees said, "You bear witness of yourself, and your witness is not true."

Jesus told them there were two! He said, "I'm one of the two, and the Father is the other!"

I read something funny recently, which said, "Five out of three people have a problem with math." My friend, before one even gets to kindergarten, they know how to count to two. If one can count to two, they can figure this out easily.

That verse should be enough to convince any sincere student. At this point each of us should be crying aloud with Jacob when he saw the wagons, "It is enough" (Genesis 45:28). In fact John is giving us way more than enough concerning our Triune God.

Many people struggle with understanding the Trinity, but it's nothing new. If one is struggling with the Trinity today, it's most likely because of the tradition in which one has been brought up (the church or family members). That person can take comfort in knowing they are not alone; they are not the first to find certain things in scripture difficult to understand.

When I decided to write this book, I determined that I would do so without any condemnation. I understand the struggle and only seek to help those who have a sincere desire to know what the scriptures teach.

During the ministry of Jesus, there were those who did not understand. Jesus again says that He does nothing of Himself, which He said in John 5:30. The things that Jesus taught were given to Him by the Father. If you are a reader and finding the Trinity hard to understand perhaps the following verse will assure you that you are not the first who had struggles.

> "I have many things to say and to judge concerning you, but He who sent Me is true; and I speak to the world those things which I heard from Him." They did not understand that He spoke to them of the Father.
>
> Then Jesus said to them, "When you lift up the Son of Man, then you will know that I am He, and that I do nothing of Myself; but as My Father taught Me, I speak these things. And He who sent Me is with Me. The Father has not left Me alone, for I always do those things that please Him." (John 8:26–29)

In the days of Christ, there were those who did not understand. They struggled with the Lord's teachings. It's very hard to break from tradition, especially things we have been taught since we were growing up.

If it helps, there are even things that this author has had to check out by looking at the scriptures. I have had to abandon things I was taught from my early years. I'm attempting to say that I understand. The verse in Romans 4:3 helped me: "What does the scripture say?" (Some translations read: "What saith the scripture?")

To me, the Word of God should be the decision-maker. Jesus told the Sadducees who didn't believe in the resurrection, "You are mistaken, not knowing the scriptures." (Some translations read: "Ye do err not knowing the scriptures").

I know it's very hard to set aside traditional teaching that we've heard all our lives. That's tough, and sometimes it even means that we are abandoned by friends, church, or family. I want the reader to know that I understand. My only advice is to go to God and ask Him to let the Holy Spirit teach us. Jesus said the Holy Spirit would guide us into all truth.

The Holy Spirit can bring the pages to life and bring the truth to the surface. I believe that is the only answer.

Solomon said, "A wise man will hear and increase learning, and a man of understanding will attain wise counsel" (Proverbs 1:5). He went on to say that we should apply our hearts to understanding (Proverbs 2:2). It is my sincere belief that if one truly desires truth, God will give it. In verse 6, Solomon said, "The Lord gives wisdom; From His mouth come knowledge and understanding." The challenge is setting aside our traditions.

In the next verse, Jesus just keeps hitting the same nail, driving it in that He came from God and not of Himself. He was sent from God. He also tells us that He gave us the truth, which He received from God Himself.

> But now you seek to kill Me, a Man who has told you the truth which I heard from God. Abraham did not do this. Jesus said to them, "If God were your Father, you would love Me, for I proceeded forth and came from God; nor have I come of Myself, but He sent Me." (John 8:40)

All of us have probably heard that Jesus said that He did not receive the honor of men. He also said that He did not honor Himself. (Many of us can learn a lesson from what He is about to say).

If Jesus received no honor from men or from Himself, where did His honor originate? Jesus will tell us that it is His Father who honors Him. He also will say, "If He did not know the Father, He would be a liar."

> Jesus answered, "If I honor Myself, My honor is nothing. It is My Father who honors Me, of whom you say that He is your God. Yet you have not known Him, but I know Him. And if I say, 'I do not know Him,' I shall be a liar like you; but I do know Him and keep His word." (John 8:54–55)

JOHN 10

The following verses will answer many questions:

- Who loves Christ?
- Where did Jesus receive His commands?
- In whose name did Jesus do His works?
- In whose hand are those who believe in Jesus?

We will also see the numeric number of "one" and define what it means.

> And when he brings out his own sheep, he goes before them; and the sheep follow him, for they know his voice.
>
> "Therefore, My Father loves Me, because I lay down My life that I may take it again. No one takes it from Me, but I lay it down of Myself. I have power to lay it down, and I have power to take it again. This command I have received from My Father."
>
> Jesus answered them, "I told you, and you do not believe. The works that I do in My Father's name, they bear witness of Me. My Father, who has given them to Me, is greater than all; and no one is able to snatch them out of My Father's hand. I and My Father are one. If I do not do the works of My Father, do not believe Me; but if I do, though you do not believe Me,

> believe the works, that you may know and believe that the Father is in Me, and I in Him." (John 10:4, 17–18, 25, 29–30, 37–38)

We have a clear distinction from Christ and the Father. Jesus has received "commands" from the Father, and He does the works of the Father. The Father has given His sheep to Him.

From our definitions in chapter 2, "one" means one in unity and agreement (not numeric in this case). This is a good place to repeat the following scriptures.

> Therefore, a man shall leave his father and mother and be joined to his wife, and they shall become one flesh. (Genesis 2:24)

> That they all may be one, as You, Father, are in Me, and I in You; that they also may be one in us, that the world may believe that You sent Me. And the glory which You gave Me I have given them, that they may be one just as we are one: I in them, and You in Me; that they may be made perfect in one, and that the world may know that You have sent Me, and have loved them as You have loved Me. (John 17:21–23)

The scripture in Genesis can only mean one in unity as it is impossible for a man and woman to be one in number. The scripture in John is also one in unity as it is impossible for multiple individuals to be one in number.

Jesus is stating that as many different believers are "one," they should be one "just as" He and the Father are one. If the Father and the Son are one in person, how can we in the church be one in person? It is impossible physically, but we can be one in harmony. We are to be one "as" Jesus and the Father are one. Remember this verse?

> And there are three that bear witness in earth, the Spirit, and the water, and the blood: and these three agree in one. (1 John 5:8)

The Father and Son are one in "agreement" (unity), not numerically.

JOHN 11

Martha knew that Jesus could ask anything of God, and God would do it for Him:

> But even now I know that whatever You ask of God, God will give You. Then they took away the stone from the place where the dead man was lying. And Jesus lifted up His eyes and said, "Father, I thank You that You have heard Me. And I know that You always hear Me, but because of the people who are standing by I said this, that they may believe that You sent Me." (John 11:22, 41–42)

There's a lot in that verse, Martha knew Jesus would not ask Himself anything; she did know that Jesus could ask the Father.

- Why did Jesus raise His eyes?
- To whom was He looking up?
- Who always hears Jesus when He prays?

The answers are found in the Lord's own prayer. He addressed the Father and said that the Father always hears Him. He goes on to say that it was the Father who had sent Him. Jesus was not looking into heaven to Himself or asking Himself to raise Lazarus.

JOHN 12

God the Father speaks three times in the four Gospels:

- He spoke at the Lord's baptism.
- He spoke on the Mount of Transfiguration.

Now we are going to see the Father speak for the third and last time.

> If anyone serves Me, let him follow Me; and where I am, there My servant will be also. If anyone serves Me, him My Father will honor.
>
> "Now My soul is troubled, and what shall I say? 'Father, save Me from this hour'? But for this purpose I came to this hour. Father, glorify Your name."
>
> Then a voice came from heaven, saying, "I have both glorified it and will glorify it again." (John 12:26–28)

These verses are self-explanatory. If we serve Christ, the Father will honor us. As the Father spoke from heaven at the Lord's baptism and the Mount of Transfiguration, the Father speaks from heaven again while Jesus is on earth. This shows a clear difference between the Father and the Son.

> Then Jesus cried out and said, "He who believes in Me, believes not in Me but in Him who sent Me. And he who sees Me sees Him who sent Me. For I have not spoken on My own authority; but the Father who sent Me gave Me a command, what I should say and what I should speak. And I know that His command is everlasting life. Therefore, whatever I speak, just as the Father has told Me, so I speak." (John 12:44–45, 49–50)

These verses are packed with the distinction between the Father and the Son. Jesus says again that He was "sent" by the Father. He does not speak of "his own" authority but the Father's. He had received a "command" from the Father, and what the Father tells Him is what He speaks.

JOHN 13

From the following verses, we determine that Jesus knew the hour had come to return "to" the Father. The Father had "given" Him all things, and He had come "from God" and was returning "to God."

> When Jesus knew that His hour had come that He should depart from this world to the Father. Jesus, knowing that the Father had given all things into His hands, and that He had come from God and was going to God, rose from supper and laid aside His garments, took a towel and girded Himself. So, when he had gone out, Jesus said, "Now the Son of Man is glorified, and God is glorified in Him." (John 13:1, 3–4, 31)

We now move on to a very popular chapter. Almost every Christian can quote from the beginning verses. The next passages from John 14 are among some of the most detailed related to the Trinity.

John was the closest to Jesus of the twelve, and He was the only disciple who dared to witness the crucifixion. He was called "the disciple whom Jesus loved." At the Last Supper, he was seen "leaning on the bosom of Jesus."

Although Jesus had other half brothers and sisters (Mark 6:3), Jesus on the cross did not give the keeping of his mother to his own half brothers who also were sons of Mary. He placed the care of his mother in the hands of John. It is believed that he was the last disciple alive who walked with Jesus, saw His miracles and heard his teachings.

It is not surprising that there are so many references about Jesus, the Father, and the Holy Spirit in the Gospel of John. Who of the twelve apostles knew Jesus the best? The answer would have to be John.

JOHN 14

Concerning the Trinity, the following verses are astonishing! There will be quite a few verses, but they are golden! While reading these verses, see if you see any of our key words (we, our etc.). Read the verses as you would read any other book, the Trinity should jump of the page.

> Let not your heart be troubled; you believe in God, believe also in Me.
>
> In My Father's house are many mansions; if it were not so, I would have told you. I go to prepare a place for you. And if I go and prepare a place for you, I will come again and receive you to Myself; that where I am, there you may be also.
>
> Jesus said to him, "I am the way, the truth, and the life. No one comes to the Father except through Me. If you had known Me, you would have known My Father also; and from now on you know Him and have seen Him."
>
> Do you not believe that I am in the Father, and the Father in Me? The words that I speak to you I do not speak on My own authority; but the Father who dwells in Me does the works.
>
> Believe Me that I am in the Father and the Father in Me, or else believe Me for the sake of the works themselves.

"Most assuredly, I say to you, he who believes in Me, the works that I do he will do also; and greater works than these he will do, because I go to My Father. And whatever you ask in My name, that I will do, that the Father may be glorified in the Son. And I will pray the Father, and He will give you another Helper, that He may abide with you forever, the Spirit of truth, whom the world cannot receive, because it neither sees Him nor knows Him; but you know Him, for He dwells with you and will be in you. At that day you will know that I am in My Father, and you in Me, and I in you. He who has My commandments and keeps them, it is he who loves Me. And he who loves Me will be loved by My Father, and I will love him and manifest Myself to him."

Judas (not Iscariot) said to Him, "Lord, how is it that You will manifest Yourself to us, and not to the world?"

Jesus answered and said to him, "If anyone loves Me, he will keep My word; and My Father will love him, and we will come to him and make our home with him. But the Helper, the Holy Spirit, whom the Father will send in My name, He will teach you all things, and bring to your remembrance all things that I said to you."

You have heard Me say to you, "I am going away and coming back to you." If you loved Me, you would rejoice because I said, "I am going to the Father," for My Father is greater than I.

But that the world may know that I love the Father, and as the Father gave Me commandment, so I do. Arise, let us go from here. (John 14:1–3, 6–7, 10–13, 16–17, 20–23, 26, 28, 31)

My friend, one cannot help but see the Trinity in what we just read. John 14 is loaded with all three persons of the Godhead, and all three are mentioned and easily defined.

While reading the upcoming verses, please try to find the key words "I," "My," "As," "Just As", "Both" and "Also." Let's push the gas pedal and drive on!

JOHN 15

> I am the true vine, and My Father is the vinedresser.
>
> As the Father loved Me, I also have loved you; abide in My love. If you keep My commandments, you will abide in My love, just as I have kept My Father's commandments and abide in His love.
>
> No longer do I call you servants, for a servant does not know what his master is doing; but I have called you friends, for all things that I heard from My Father I have made known to you.
>
> You did not choose Me, but I chose you and appointed you that you should go and bear fruit, and that your fruit should remain, that whatever you ask the Father in My name He may give you.
>
> But all these things they will do to you for My name's sake, because they do not know Him who sent Me.
>
> He who hates Me hates My Father also.
>
> If I had not done among them the works which no one else did, they would have no sin; but now they have seen and also hated "both" Me and My Father.
>
> But when the Helper comes, whom I shall send to you from the Father, the Spirit of truth who proceeds from the Father, He will testify of Me. (John 15:1, 9–10, 15–16, 24)

All three persons in the Godhead are referenced here. Did you notice the word "both" when Jesus stated that they hated "both" me and my Father? Did you see the word, "also?" Did you see that we are to keep the Lord's commandments "just as" He keeps the commandments of His Father? These key words can certainly bring the Trinity to life.

JOHN 16

Chapter 16 will be a little bit of reading, but I promise it's worth it. We'll even have a new key word: "nor."

> And these things they will do to you because they have not known the Father nor Me.
>
> But now I go away to Him who sent Me, and none of you asks Me, "Where are You going?"
>
> Nevertheless, I tell you the truth. It is to your advantage that I go away; for if I do not go away, the Helper will not come to you; but if I depart, I will send Him to you.
>
> I still have many things to say to you, but you cannot bear them now. However, when He, the Spirit of truth, has come, He will guide you into all truth; for He will not speak on His own authority, but whatever He hears He will speak; and He will tell you things to come. He will glorify Me, for He will take of what is Mine and declare it to you. All things that the Father has are Mine. Therefore I said that He will take of Mine and declare it to you.
>
> A little while, and you will not see Me; and again a little while, and you will see Me, because I go to the Father.
>
> And in that day you will ask Me nothing. Most assuredly, I say to you, whatever you ask the Father in My name He will give you.

> In that day you will ask in My name, and I do not say to you that I shall pray the Father for you; for the Father Himself loves you, because you have loved Me, and have believed that I came forth from God.
>
> I came forth from the Father and have come into the world. Again, I leave the world and go to the Father.
>
> Now we are sure that You know all things, and have no need that anyone should question You. By this we believe that You came forth from God. Indeed, the hour is coming, yes, has now come, that you will be scattered, each to his own, and will leave Me alone. And yet I am not alone, because the Father is with Me. (John 16:3, 5, 7, 12–16, 23, 26–28, 30, 32)

Once more, the Trinity in its entirety is seen in the above verses. Jesus references Himself, the Father, and the Helper the Holy Spirit.

- Jesus is returning to the Father.
- The Father has "sent" Jesus.
- The Holy Spirit will come after Jesus ascends to the Father.
- The Holy Spirit will not speak of "his own authority."
- What the Holy Spirit hears is what He will speak.
- All things the Father has belong to Christ.
- Jesus came from God the Father.
- We are to pray to the Father and ask Jesus nothing, and what we ask in His name, He will give to us.
- Jesus says He is "not alone, for the Father is with Him."

One of the most striking parts of those verses are that Jesus tells us that after His ascension, we are no longer to pray to Jesus. Jesus will not pray for us any longer. You read that correctly! That eats the lunch of many new Christians—and even some older ones. If one is to pray properly, they are not to pray to Jesus. We are to pray to the Father in the name of Jesus. Why? Because the Father loves us! Praise the

Lord! We can now go to the Father directly—with the name of Jesus of course.

When Jesus died, the veil in the temple was rent. Before it was rent, only the high priest could enter the holy of holies—where the presence of God dwelt—and then only once a year on the Day of Atonement (Yom Kippur). Now that the veil is rent, we each have access to the Father directly, and we have the promise that what we ask in the name of Jesus will be given to us. This is powerful! One of the reasons that our prayers are not always answered is that we aren't praying properly. This is one of the greatest truths that the Christian can learn as it relates to our prayer life. Jesus is telling us the proper way to pray, and we should obey Him.

JOHN 17

Buckle your seat belts! We are giving you the entire chapter 17 of the book of John, which—from beginning to end—is a prayer of Christ. This is the only time we'll post an entire chapter. This chapter is so loaded with the Trinity that we won't even leave out one verse!

In this prayer, Jesus gives reference to the Trinity many times. In the New Testament, we will see the plural pronouns "We" and "Us" that Jesus uses to reference Himself and the Father.

> Father, the hour has come. Glorify Your Son, that Your Son also may glorify You, as You have given Him authority over all flesh, that He should give eternal life to as many as You have given Him. And this is eternal life, that they may know You, the only true God, and Jesus Christ whom You have sent.
>
> I have glorified You on the earth. I have finished the work which You have given Me to do. And now, O Father, glorify Me together with Yourself, with the glory which I had with You before the world was.

I have manifested Your name to the men whom You have given Me out of the world. They were Yours, You gave them to Me, and they have kept Your word.

Now they have known that all things which You have given Me are from You.

For I have given to them the words which You have given Me; and they have received them, and have known surely that I came forth from You; and they have believed that You sent Me.

I pray for them. I do not pray for the world but for those whom You have given Me, for they are Yours.

And all Mine are Yours, and Yours are Mine, and I am glorified in them.

Now I am no longer in the world, but these are in the world, and I come to You.

Holy Father, keep through Your name those whom You have given Me, that they may be one as we are.

While I was with them in the world, I kept them in Your name. Those whom You gave Me I have kept; and none of them is lost except the son of perdition, that the Scripture might be fulfilled.

But now I come to You, and these things I speak in the world, that they may have My joy fulfilled in themselves.

I have given them Your word; and the world has hated them because they are not of the world, just as I am not of the world.

I do not pray that You should take them out of the world, but that You should keep them from the evil one.

They are not of the world, just as I am not of the world.

Sanctify them by Your truth. Your word is truth.

As You sent Me into the world, I also have sent them into the world.

> And for their sakes I sanctify Myself, that they also may be sanctified by the truth.
>
> I do not pray for these alone, but also for those who will believe in Me through their word; that they all may be one, as You, Father, are in Me, and I in You; that they also may be one in us, that the world may believe that You sent Me.
>
> And the glory which You gave Me I have given them, that they may be one just as we are one: I in them, and You in Me; that they may be made perfect in one, and that the world may know that You have sent Me, and have loved them as You have loved Me.
>
> Father, I desire that they also whom You gave Me may be with Me where I am, that they may behold My glory which You have given Me; for You loved Me before the foundation of the world.
>
> O righteous Father! The world has not known You, but I have known You; and these have known that You sent Me.
>
> And I have declared to them Your name, and will declare it, that the love with which You loved Me may be in them, and I in them. (John 17:1–26)

What a chapter! The light bulb should be on by now! If not, let's recap:

- Jesus lifts up His eyes to the Father in heaven.
- Jesus prays to the Father.
- Jesus is "sent from" God.
- Jesus finishes the work "of the Father."
- Jesus is "loved by God the Father" before the foundation of the world!
- Jesus was glorified "with" the Father before the world began.
- Jesus manifested and declared the Father's name in His ministry.

- Those who believe in Christ are "given to Him from the Father."
- Jesus says He wants the many believers to be "One as we are one" (plural)
- Jesus prays that His many believers may be "One in us" (plural)
- Jesus prays for Himself in verses 1–5.
- Jesus prays for the disciples in verses 6–19.
- Jesus prays for all believers in Christ in verses 20–26.

The entire prayer is loaded with the doctrine of the Trinity!

JOHN 18

There's a light at the end of the tunnel, and it's not a locomotive! After two more passages, we will have completed the Trinity in the book of John. Let's head to the finish line!

> Jesus said to Peter, "Put your sword into the sheath. Shall I not drink the cup which My Father has given Me?" (John 18:11)

> Jesus said to her, "Do not cling to Me, for I have not yet ascended to My Father; but go to My brethren and say to them, 'I am ascending to My Father and your Father, and to My God and your God.'"
>
> So Jesus said to them again, "Peace to you! As the Father has sent Me, I also send you."
>
> And when He had said this, He breathed on them, and said to them, "Receive the Holy Spirit. (John 20:17, 21–22)

Did you see that? Jesus breathed on them and said, "Receive the Holy Spirit." They were already believers in Christ, and Peter even declared that Jesus was the Christ the Son of the living God. Although they were believers they did not have the Holy Spirit dwelling within them, I don't think anyone would debate that if any of them died that they would have died saved.

Jesus tells these who believe in Him, "Receive the Holy Spirit." This was spoken after the resurrection and before the Day of Pentecost when the disciples were gathered on the first day of the week behind shut doors.

Jesus leaves them His peace, and He tells them, "As My Father has sent me, so I also send you." He breathes on them and says, "Receive the Holy Spirit." Jesus sends the disciples as His Father had sent Him and commissions them to receive the Holy Spirit.

These scriptures reinforce the doctrine of the Trinity. In this chapter, we toured the entire book of John's Gospel, citing 158 scriptures on the Trinity. All of them were in the book of John! John knew Jesus better than any other disciple, and he gives us 158 references. John only has twenty-four chapters, which is seven references per chapter on the Trinity. This does not include 1 John, 2 John, 3 John, and the book of Revelation, which John also wrote!

CHAPTER 18

THE TRINITY IN THE BOOK OF ACTS

Now we move to the book of action. The Acts of the Apostles was written by Dr. Luke. Luke was a physician and a very intelligent man. There has been much discussion concerning whether Luke was Jewish. If he was not Jewish, this would mean that he was the only writer in the entirety of the Word of God who was Gentile.

Those who hold to the opinion that Luke was not Jewish take it from Colossians 4:10–14 where Paul lists those who are "among the circumcision," and Luke seems to not be included in that list.

There are others who maintain that Luke was Jewish because of Romans 3:1–2: "The Jews were entrusted with the oracles of God." Therefore, Luke must be Jewish.

Others believe that Luke was among the Hellenistic Jews (biologic Jews of Greek culture) because many scholars believe that Luke was from Antioch, Syria.

Luke was not among the eyewitnesses of the resurrection, and he was not listed as an apostle appointed by Christ (pre-Pentecost) or among the other apostles listed in the New Testament (post-Pentecost). There are at least twenty-five named and unnamed apostles in the New Testament. This list includes both pre- and post-Pentecost apostles.

Pre-Pentecost Apostles

- Jesus Christ (Hebrews 3:1)
- Simon Peter (Matthew 10:2)
- Andrew (Matthew 10:2)
- James the son of Zebedee (Matthew 10:2)
- John (Matthew 10:2)
- Philip (Matthew 10:3)
- Bartholomew (Matthew 10:3)
- Thomas (Matthew 10:3)
- Matthew (Matthew 10:3)
- James the son of Alphaeus (Matthew 10:3)
- Thaddaeus (Matthew 10:3) or Judas, the son of James (Luke 6:16)
- Simon the Zealot (Matthew 10:4)
- Judas Iscariot (Matthew 10:4)
- Matthias (Acts 1:26) (Matthias was elected before the Day of Pentecost had "fully" come

Post-Pentecost Apostles

- Paul (Galatians 1:1)
- Barnabas (1 Corinthians 9:5–6, Acts 14:4, 14)
- James, the Lord's brother (Galatians 1:19)
- Silas (Silvanus) (1 Thessalonians 1:1, 2:6)
- Timothy (1 Thessalonians 1:1, 2:6)
- Epaphroditus (Philippians 2:25)
- Apollos (1 Corinthians 4:6–9 and 1 Corinthians 3:22)
- two unnamed apostles (2 Corinthians 8:23)

Possible Apostles

- Andronicus (Romans 16:7)
- Junia (Romans 16:7) (if she was an apostle, she is the only female apostle listed who was).

- Jude, the half brother of Jesus
- Mark
- the writer of Hebrews
- Titus
- other unnamed apostles (1 Corinthians 15:7)
- Dr. Luke

Andronicus and Junia are under debate because the scriptures say they were "of note among the apostles." Scholars ask, "Does this mean they were apostles or that the apostles knew about them?" It could be interpreted either way.

Notice that Luke is among the "possible" apostles. This list gives us around thirty apostles in the scripture. Twenty-three of them for certain were apostles, and some of them were not eyewitnesses of the resurrection being from Gentile regions, as the original twelve were. The names of the twelve apostles chosen by Christ will be the names in the foundations of the New Jerusalem.

Dr. Luke "may" have been an apostle. His traveling companion, Paul, called Luke "the beloved physician" (Colossians 4:14).

When Paul was in prison, he wrote to Timothy and said, "Only Luke is with me." Dr. Luke went to Jerusalem with Paul at the end of his third missionary journey.

We could stay on Luke for quite a while, there is so much that could be said for this wonderful man. He was faithful and beloved, and he wrote two books of the New Testament: Luke (the Gospel that bears his name) and the book of Acts.

Dr. Luke begins his Gospel by saying that he had a "perfect understanding of all things from the very first to write an orderly account" (Luke 1:3). That's a good thing to know as we deal with the Trinity in the book of Acts. We want to hear from a man with a "perfect understanding."

Let's begin our journey with Luke and what the book of Acts has to say concerning the Triune Godhead. Right from the opening verses of the book of Acts, the Trinity is already before us. In the first eight verses, Dr. Luke is already making reference to Jesus being taken up. He follows with the Holy Spirit and proceeds to the promise of the Father. Right off the bat, Dr. Luke has us swimming in the Trinity. Let's take a look.

ACTS 1: LUKE'S INTRODUCTION TO THEOPHILUS

> The former account I made, O Theophilus, of all that Jesus began both to do and teach, until the day in which He was taken up, after He through the Holy Spirit had given commandments to the apostles whom He had chosen, to whom He also presented Himself alive after His suffering by many infallible proofs, being seen by them during forty days and speaking of the things pertaining to the kingdom of God. And being assembled together with them, He commanded them not to depart from Jerusalem, but to wait for the Promise of the Father, "which," He said, "you have heard from Me; for John truly baptized with water, but you shall be baptized with the Holy Spirit not many days from now."
>
> Therefore, when they had come together, they asked Him, saying, "Lord, will You at this time restore the kingdom to Israel?"
>
> And He said to them, "It is not for you to know times or seasons which the Father has put in His own authority. But you shall receive power when the Holy Spirit has come upon you; and you shall be witnesses to Me in Jerusalem, and in all Judea and Samaria, and to the end of the earth." (Acts 1:1–8)

What a way to begin the book of Acts! All three persons of the Godhead are referenced by Dr. Luke:

- Jesus is who was taken up.
- Through the Holy Spirit Jesus gave commandments.

- He presented Himself alive (before the Holy Spirit came in Acts 2).
- The promise of the Father is what they were to wait for.
- Jesus said that they heard this from "Me."
- The Holy Spirit is who Jesus will baptize them with.
- Only the Father knows "times and seasons."
- The Holy Spirit is what will bring the disciples power.

Now we go to the apostle Peter's message on the day of Pentecost after they were baptized with the Holy Spirit on the birthday of the church.

In Peter's message, we'll see our key word "My." Please look for who says the word "My." Peter will be quoting from Joel 2:28. Peter will then go into the prophecies of the tribulation, which the scriptures call "The Day of the Lord." Peter will end the message by telling us who can be saved and how to be saved. After Peter gives this altar call, three thousand will be added to the church.

Acts 2

> And it shall come to pass in the last days, says God, That I will pour out of My Spirit on all flesh; Your sons and your daughters shall prophesy, Your young men shall see visions, Your old men shall dream dreams. And on My menservants and on My maidservants I will pour out My Spirit in those days; And they shall prophesy. I will show wonders in heaven above And signs in the earth beneath: Blood and fire and vapor of smoke. The sun shall be turned into darkness, And the moon into blood, Before the coming of the great and awesome day of the Lord. And it shall come to pass That whoever calls on the name of the Lord shall be saved. (Acts 2:17–21)

- God is speaking through the Old Testament prophet to Joel.
- "My Spirit" is who God says "I" will pour out.
- Whosoever shall call on the name of The Lord shall be saved.

There's the Trinity in Peter's inaugural message!

But Peter isn't finished; that was only part of his message. Peter has more!

> Men of Israel, hear these words: Jesus of Nazareth, a Man attested by God to you by miracles, wonders, and signs which God did through Him in your midst, as you yourselves also know.
>
> Him, being delivered by the determined purpose and foreknowledge of God, you have taken by lawless hands, have crucified, and put to death; whom God raised up, having loosed the pains of death, because it was not possible that He should be held by it.
>
> For David says concerning Him: "I foresaw the LORD always before my face, For He is at my right hand. For You will not leave my soul in Hades, Nor will You allow Your Holy One to see corruption."
>
> This Jesus God has raised up, of which we are all witnesses.
>
> Therefore, being exalted to the right hand of God, and having received from the Father the promise of the Holy Spirit, He poured out this which you now see and hear.
>
> For You will not leave my soul in Hades, Nor will You allow Your Holy One to see corruption.
>
> For David did not ascend into the heavens, but he says himself: "The Lord said to my Lord, 'Sit at My right hand, Till I make Your enemies Your footstool.'"
>
> Then Peter said to them, "Repent, and let every one of you be baptized in the name of Jesus Christ for

the remission of sins; and you shall receive the gift of the Holy Spirit." (Acts 2:22–24, 27, 32–35, 38)

Jesus was attested by God. The Greek word for attested is *apodeiknymi*, which means "to display, exhibit, proclaim, prove, to be accredited." Now all this concerning Jesus was done by who? Peter says Jesus was attested by God! Jesus was put on display, exhibited, proclaimed, proven, and accredited. According to Peter, it was God who did all of this.

If one receives a degree from a college or university and the degree is "accredited," the accreditation would have to come from some authoritative body. Jesus was accredited, but where did His accreditation come from? It came from God!

Peter says that all the miracles, signs, and wonders were done by God through Jesus, Jesus was delivered by the foreknowledge of God, and God raised Jesus from the dead. Peter is on a roll! Could this be the same Peter who denied the Lord three times? It's amazing what boldness the Holy Spirit can bring! Peter is known for putting his foot in his mouth and repeatedly receiving rebukes for the things he would say. But on the Day of Pentecost, Peter is right on the mark and hitting the nail on the head!

He says that Jesus has been exalted to the right hand of God. He says God will not leave Jesus in Hades (paradise in the heart of the earth where He went for three days). God will not let the Lord's body see corruption.

Peter declares that receiving the Holy Spirit is a promise of the Father. He goes on to the conversation between the Father and Son while they both are in heaven. I love this verse! "The Lord said unto my Lord, 'Sit at my right hand.'"

Peter ends by saying the Holy Spirit is a "gift." There must be a giver. The Holy Spirit is not the giver but the gift itself. My friend, the Holy Spirit is the promise of the Father. Peter's message in Acts 2 is consumed with the doctrine of the Trinity.

ACTS 3

In chapter 3, Peter and John are about to enter the temple at three o'clock in the afternoon. A man who had been lame since birth would be healed. Peter takes him by the hand and says, "I'm a preacher, and I'm as broke as Moses's Ten Commandments." OK, we know Peter really said, "Silver and gold have I none, but what I have I give to you." The lame man gets up and enters the temple, leaping and walking and praising God!

Peter will now preach from Solomon's porch. What will Peter's message be—and will it contain the Trinity? Peter begins by saying that God calls Jesus "God's servant." In fact, Jesus will be called "God's servant" twice in these verses, which is quite a statement. Jesus taught His disciples that a servant was never greater than his master (John 13:16; John 15:20). To be a servant, one would need to have a master. Jesus is God's servant, and the Father was the Master who Jesus served.

When Jesus came to earth, He was made a little lower than "Elohim" (God). Paul said that God is the "head of Christ" (1 Corinthians 11:3). Jesus was God's servant, which validates the doctrine of the Trinity. Peter reminds us that it was God that raised Jesus from the dead, glorified Him, foretold that Jesus would suffer, and sent Jesus to us."

> The God of Abraham, Isaac, and Jacob, the God of our fathers, glorified His Servant Jesus, whom you delivered up and denied in the presence of Pilate, when he was determined to let Him go. And killed the Prince of life, whom God raised from the dead, of which we are witnesses. But those things which God foretold by the mouth of all His prophets, that the Christ would suffer, He has thus fulfilled.
>
> And that He may send Jesus Christ, who was preached to you before, whom heaven must receive until the times of restoration of all things, which God

> has spoken by the mouth of all His holy prophets since the world began. For Moses truly said to the fathers, "The Lord your God will raise up for you a Prophet like me from your brethren. Him you shall hear in all things, whatever He says to you. To you first, God, having raised up His Servant Jesus, sent Him to bless you, in turning away every one of you from your iniquities." (Acts 3:13, 15, 18, 20–22, 26)

ACTS 4

In chapter 4, we see that the miracle of the healing of the lame man has caused some concerns with the Sanhedrin. The Sanhedrin, a supreme council (or tribunal) of the Jews, was headed by the high priest and made up of seventy-one elders in the Great Sanhedrin or twenty-three elders in the Lesser Sanhedrin, which was in all the cities in Israel. The Great Sanhedrin was in Jerusalem, and this is where the lame man was healed (at the temple in Jerusalem).

While recently visiting Jerusalem, I visited the Temple Mount. The second temple was expanded to the size of 37 acres (twenty-six football fields) by Herod. As I sat there, I pictured Peter preaching from Solomon's porch and the lame man leaping and walking in the temple. What an event that had to be! The healing of this lame man was so big that it caught the attention of the Sanhedrin.

> Then Peter, filled with the Holy Spirit, said to them, "Rulers of the people and elders of Israel: If we this day are judged for a good deed done to a helpless man, by what means he has been made well, let it be known to you all, and to all the people of Israel, that by the name of Jesus Christ of Nazareth, whom you crucified, whom God raised from the dead, by Him this man stands here before you whole." (Acts 4:8–10)

All three persons of the Godhead were acknowledged in Peter's message:

- Peter is filled with the Holy Spirit.
- The lame man was healed by the name of Jesus.
- God raised Jesus from the dead.
- Jesus made the lame man whole.

ACTS 5

After this miracle, great things were happening in the church at Jerusalem. Many people were believing in Christ, which eventually led to a trial of Peter and the apostles. They each declared the Trinity at the trial.

> The God of our fathers raised up Jesus whom you murdered by hanging on a tree. Him God has exalted to His right hand to be Prince and Savior, to give repentance to Israel and forgiveness of sins. And we are His witnesses to these things, and so also is the Holy Spirit whom God has given to those who obey Him. (Acts 5:30–32)

All of the apostles, along with Peter, declare these things:

- God raised Jesus from the dead.
- Jesus was exalted to God's right hand.
- The Holy Spirit is who God has given.
- The Holy Spirit also bore witness of the death, resurrection, and exaltation of Jesus.

As we digest these verses, there's no other way to interpret the passage without the Trinity.

ACTS 6

In chapter 6, we have the first martyr recorded in the early church. Stephen, a deacon, was elected by the church in Jerusalem. Stephen was full of faith and the Holy Spirit. Although he was not an apostle, God did great wonders and signs through him. Isn't it wonderful that God doesn't just use preachers? This means God can use any member of the body of Christ.

Stephen was later accused of blasphemy against God and Moses, and he was brought before the council.

We won't be finished with Stephen in chapter 6, but we certainly can see the Trinity in the following verses. I encourage you to read verses 1–15, but I will only list the verses that relate to the Trinity below.

> Then the twelve summoned the multitude of the disciples and said, "It is not desirable that we should leave the word of God and serve tables. Therefore, brethren, seek out from among you seven men of good reputation, full of the Holy Spirit and wisdom, whom we may appoint over this business."
>
> And the saying pleased the whole multitude. And they chose Stephen, a man full of faith and the Holy Spirit, and Philip, Prochorus, Nicanor, Timon, Parmenas, and Nicolas, a proselyte from Antioch,
>
> Then the word of God spread, and the number of the disciples multiplied greatly in Jerusalem, and a great many of the priests were obedient to the faith.
>
> And Stephen, full of faith and power, did great wonders and signs among the people.
>
> Then they secretly induced men to say, "We have heard him speak blasphemous words against Moses and God. For we have heard him say that this Jesus of Nazareth will destroy this place and change the

> customs which Moses delivered to us." (Acts 6:2–3, 5, 7, 11, 14)

The above passage calls attention to God, Jesus of Nazareth, and the Holy Spirit.

ACTS 7

In chapter 7, we have Stephen's message before the Sanhedrin council, which followed with his death.

We will not type the entire message (Acts 7 is quite lengthy at more than fifty verses). We will only list the main passages of what Stephen saw at the time of his stoning that relate to the Trinity.

Stephen speaks of the God of the patriarchs (Abraham, Isaac, and Jacob). He speaks of God and His glory and mentions God speaking and God being pleased with Moses. This "preaching deacon" tells them that they resist the Holy Spirit and killed the "Just One" (Christ). Then it gets very interesting in verses 55–56:

> But he, being full of the Holy Spirit, gazed into heaven and saw the glory of God, and Jesus standing at the right hand of God, and said, "Look! I see the heavens opened and the Son of Man standing at the right hand of God!" (Acts 7:55–56)

Stephen was full of the Holy Spirit and saw two in heaven. He first saw the glory of God and next saw Jesus standing at the right hand of God:

- the Holy Spirit is indwelling Stephen on earth
- God and His glory is in heaven
- Jesus is at the right hand of God

ACTS 8

In chapter eight, we will see the Trinity concerning Philip and the Ethiopian. We will even see that the Holy Spirit can speak.

We all know there was a Philip who was one of the original twelve disciples; this Philip in Acts chapter 8 is a different Philip, and he's known as Philip the Evangelist.

He lived in Caesarea, about seventy miles northwest of Jerusalem, on the Mediterranean Sea. Paul actually stayed once in the home of Philip (Acts 21:8), and Philip had four daughters who were prophetesses in the New Testament church (Acts 21:9). Philip was one of the original seven deacons chosen in Acts (Acts 6:5). Like Stephen, Philip is a "preaching deacon." This shows that a person can have more than one calling. Philip was both an evangelist and a deacon.

The following records one of the first Gentiles to be saved. This is great! This happens even before Cornelius receives Christ in Acts 10. (Cornelius also lived in Caesarea).

Philip will be sent to an Ethiopian eunuch who was under Candace, the queen of the Ethiopians, and took care of all her treasury. The eunuch had a high rank in Ethiopia. He was reading passages from Isaiah chapter 53 in his chariot. I mentioned earlier that the Holy Spirit can speak, and the Holy Spirit commands Philip to go and preach to this non-Jewish man. If you take the time to read the story, this Gentile will receive Christ—and Philip ends up baptizing him. The following verses give us the Trinity:

> Then the Spirit said to Philip, "Go near and overtake this chariot."
>
> Then Philip opened his mouth, and beginning at this Scripture, preached Jesus to him.
>
> Now when they came up out of the water, the Spirit of the Lord caught Philip away, so that the eunuch saw him no more; and he went on his way rejoicing. (Acts 8:29, 35, 39)

We see here a clear difference between the Holy Spirit and Jesus. The Holy Spirit is called the "Spirit of the Lord," and the Trinity is represented.

- The Holy Spirit speaks to Philip.
- Jesus is who Philip preaches to a congregation of one man.
- The Holy Spirit "of the Lord" caught Philip away.

ACTS 9

Almost every believer has heard of what just may be the greatest conversion that has ever happened. We speak of the conversion of Saul. Saul, a Pharisee, persecuted Christians and even consented to the death of Stephen and stood by and watched. Saul is about to have the transformation of his life in Acts 9. Again, we will let the reader read how Jesus saved Saul who would later be known by the name of Paul.

He was traveling from Jerusalem to Damascus, which is in Syria. His assignment was to have Christians bound and returned to Jerusalem to be persecuted. While on the road to Damascus, he falls to the ground, most likely from a horse, and sees a light. Jesus appears to him and says "Saul, Saul, why are you persecuting me?"

Jesus knew Saul's name, and He knows our names too! He knows our names before we are saved. Zacchaeus was saved while sitting on a limb in a Sycamore tree in Jericho. Jesus stopped and called him by name. When we receive Jesus, He takes our names and records them in the Lamb's book of life in heaven. I'll never forget the day Jesus called me to Himself. My friend, Jesus knows your name.

I love what happens next. Saul asked, "Who are you, Lord?" Saul didn't know who he saw, but he still called him "Lord." It was like Saul was saying, "I don't know who you are, but from now on, you are my Lord." Saul made Jesus the Lord of his life while flat on his back on a dusty road. Someone said, "Man was made from the dust of the ground and has been dirty ever since." Regardless of how dirty one has been in sin, Jesus can save that person. Jesus doesn't say, "Go clean up first, and then I'll receive you." He saves us while we're lying in the dirt! It was while we were sinners that Jesus died for us, and it is through His precious blood that we are washed and cleansed.

As Saul was asking who was speaking to him, Jesus used the name that Saul hated more than any other name. He said, "I am Jesus, whom you are persecuting. It is hard for you to kick against the goads?"

A goad was a sharp stick used to drive livestock. Sometimes the ox would "kick against the goads" while trying to resist. That's what Saul had been doing. This lets me know that God had been dealing with Saul. I don't think he ever forgot the day he stood by at the stoning of Stephen. As he watched, Stephen asked God to forgive those who were killing him. Stephen's death remained with Saul from then on, and I don't think he ever forgot it.

After Saul was saved he went by the name of Paul, he was arrested in Jerusalem. He gave his defense in Acts 21:22. In that discourse, he confessed that he stood by guarding the clothes of those who were killing Stephen, consenting to his death. I believe Saul had been feeling conviction by the Holy Spirit and was "kicking against the goads," resisting God's dealing with his heart.

Saul was saved that day on the road to Damascus. After meeting Jesus, he went into the city of Damascus, blinded by the light he had seen. He would be blind for three days and later be healed by the laying on of hands of Ananias, a believer in Christ. We are on the subject of the Trinity, let's take a look at the words of Ananias.

Ananias and Saul

And Ananias went his way and entered the house; and laying his hands on him he said, "Brother Saul, the Lord Jesus, who appeared to you on the road as you came, has sent me that you may receive your sight and be filled with the Holy Spirit." (Acts 9:17)

- Who appeared to Saul on the road to Damascus?
- Who sent Ananias to Saul?
- Who was Saul to be filled with?

Ananias tells us all the answers. He says it was Jesus who appeared to Him. Ananias says it was "the Lord Jesus" who sent him to Saul. According to Ananias, Jesus (the second person of the Godhead) told him that Saul would be filled with the Holy Spirit (the third person of the Godhead).

ACTS 10

We are about to see another Gentile—along with all his family and friends—receiving Christ and being baptized with the Holy Spirit.

Cornelius lived in Caesarea. If you ever are privileged to visit the Holy Land, make sure you visit Caesarea. Many wonderful and biblical things happened there.

Cornelius was a centurion of the Italian Regiment. He was a Gentile, but the Bible tells us quite a bit about him. Cornelius, in spite of all of his good works, still was not saved.

Acts 10:2–3 describes Cornelius:

- devout
- feared God
- gave Alms (money)
- prayed
- saw a vision of an angel of God
- had a good reputation among the Jews

Is a man saved if he is devout, fears God, gives money, prays to God, sees visions, has a good reputation and speaks with angels of God? Most people would say, "Yes, that man is saved." However, the sad news is that—in spite of all these good works—Cornelius was lost.

A man can be a good man with many good works, but he can still be lost. It certainly is a thought to ponder.

Do we see the Trinity in the record of Cornelius? An angel commands Cornelius to send for Peter who was just south in Joppa (now Jaffa). Peter is living at Simon the Tanner's home. I've been to this home; it's right on the Mediterranean Sea, a little more than thirty miles from Caesarea. It was at this home where Peter, up on the roof, saw a vision from God. He saw a sheet lowered with all types of unclean animals that the Jews were forbidden to eat. God showed him this vision three times and told Peter to arise, kill, and eat.

Peter, as a Jew, had never even had a ham sandwich. He told God he had never eaten anything unclean. God told Peter not to call common what God had cleansed. God was prepping Peter to get some Gentiles saved and filled with the Holy Spirit. Peter was sent for by Cornelius.

When Peter arrived at the home of Cornelius, Cornelius was not alone; his family and friends were there too. Peter entered this Gentile's home and began to preach. Peter doesn't even get to finish his sermon before the Holy Spirit falls on every last one of those Gentiles.

Cornelius and his family were the first Gentiles who were baptized with the Holy Spirit. This is a historical event! Did Peter mention anything about the Trinity in his sermon? Let's read his message. We won't type the entire sermon—just the passages related to the Trinity—but Peter's sermon starts in Acts 10:34.

> God anointed Jesus of Nazareth with the Holy Spirit and with power, who went about doing good and healing all who were oppressed by the devil, for God was with Him.
>
> And He commanded us to preach to the people, and to testify that it is He who was ordained by God to be Judge of the living and the dead. While Peter was still speaking these words, the Holy Spirit fell upon all those who heard the word.

> "Can anyone forbid water, that these should not be baptized who have received the Holy Spirit just as we have?" (Acts 10:38, 42, 44, 47)

- Who anointed Jesus?
- With whom did God anoint Jesus?
- Who was with Jesus?
- Who fell on the hearers of the Word?
- Who ordained Jesus so that He would be judge of the living and the dead?

The answers are simple and straightforward. God anointed Jesus with the Holy Spirit. (All three persons in the Trinity are in that one line)! God was with Jesus, and the Holy Spirit fell on Cornelius, his family, and his friends.

ACTS 11

Peter, after God saves and fills the Gentiles, returns to Jerusalem and meets some very unhappy "Christian Jews." (I know that no one was called a Christian until Antioch in verse 26, but I just had to throw that in). They were Jews who had received Christ.

The church in Jerusalem had some problems with Peter entering the home of a Gentile. Yes, although they had received Christ, they were still struggling with the works of the law. Before we come down on them too hard, there are many today who still believe one must do good works in order to be saved. We, like these Jews, have our own traditions (man-made laws) to overcome.

These believing Jews thought salvation was only for them, and they still thought they were saved by keeping the Mosaic law. They accused Peter of entering the home of a Gentile and eating a ham sandwich!

What would be Peter's reply—and will we see the Trinity in his response?

And as I began to speak, the Holy Spirit fell upon them, as upon us at the beginning.

Then I remembered the word of the Lord, how He said, "John indeed baptized with water, but you shall be baptized with the Holy Spirit. If therefore God gave them the same gift as He gave us when we believed on the Lord Jesus Christ, who was I that I could withstand God?"

When they heard these things they became silent; and they glorified God, saying, "Then God has also granted to the Gentiles repentance to life."

Now those who were scattered after the persecution that arose over Stephen traveled as far as Phoenicia, Cyprus, and Antioch, preaching the word to no one but the Jews only.

But some of them were men from Cyprus and Cyrene, who, when they had come to Antioch, spoke to the Hellenists, preaching the Lord Jesus.

And the hand of the Lord was with them, and a great number believed and turned to the Lord.

Then news of these things came to the ears of the church in Jerusalem, and they sent out Barnabas to go as far as Antioch.

When he came and had seen the grace of God, he was glad, and encouraged them all that with purpose of heart they should continue with the Lord.

For he was a good man, full of the Holy Spirit and of faith. And a great many people were added to the Lord. (Acts 11:15–24)

Well folks, there it all is!

- It was God who gave the gift—and what was that gift? The Holy Spirit.
- In whom did they believe? Jesus!

- Who granted repentance to the Gentiles? God!
- Whose hand was upon them? The hand of the Lord.
- Whose grace was seen? God's grace!
- Who did they continue with? The Lord!
- With whom were they filled? The Holy Spirit!
- To whom were they added? To the Lord!
- Whom did John the Baptist say would fill us with the Holy Spirit? Jesus!

ACTS 13

In this chapter, we travel northward into Syria to a city that would become a very important one to the New Testament church: Antioch! We could write quite a bit about Antioch since some critical things happened here, especially on the subject of "law versus grace." When I say "critical," I'm not exaggerating.

Paul and Barnabas founded the church in Antioch. Paul's first missionary journey began in Antioch, and he had a good church going. Since law versus grace is not the topic of this book, we won't deal with it here except to say that Galatians 2:11–16 records a very interesting event that Paul had to correct.

After Paul established the church in Antioch, "certain men came from James (the Lord's half brother) from Jerusalem. They are known as "Judaizers." They told these Gentiles in Antioch that they had to be circumcised to be saved. Paul had to quickly fix this problem, and even Peter and Barnabas were carried away with what Luke calls "hypocrisy." Paul had to rebuke Peter publicly because he wouldn't eat with the Gentiles. (Yes, that same Peter we saw eating with Cornelius was turning back to the law). Paul had to remind these "apostles" that no flesh shall be justified by the works of the law.

An apostle like James, Peter, and Barnabas could still fall off the track. Regardless of how much any minister is exalted in the eyes of the people, none are ever beyond error. It's very important to remember that.

Here in Antioch, the Holy Spirit is about to speak. The Holy Spirit can speak, and He's been giving utterance since the Day of Pentecost. Let's notice what the Spirit is going to say.

> As they ministered to the Lord and fasted, the Holy Spirit said, "Now separate to Me Barnabas and Saul for the work to which I have called them." Then, having fasted and prayed, and laid hands on them, they sent them away.
>
> So, being sent out by the Holy Spirit, they went down to Seleucia, and from there they sailed to Cyprus. And when they arrived in Salamis, they preached the word of God in the synagogues of the Jews. They also had John as their assistant.
>
> Now when they had gone through the island to Paphos, they found a certain sorcerer, a false prophet, a Jew whose name was Bar-Jesus, who was with the proconsul, Sergius Paulus, an intelligent man. This man called for Barnabas and Saul and sought to hear the word of God.
>
> But Elymas the sorcerer (for so his name is translated) withstood them, seeking to turn the proconsul away from the faith.
>
> Then Saul, who also is called Paul, filled with the Holy Spirit, looked intently at him and said, "O full of all deceit and all fraud, you son of the devil, you enemy of all righteousness, will you not cease perverting the straight ways of the Lord?
>
> And now, indeed, the hand of the Lord is upon you, and you shall be blind, not seeing the sun for a time." And immediately a dark mist fell on him, and he went around seeking someone to lead him by the hand. Then the proconsul believed, when he saw what

> had been done, being astonished at the teaching of the Lord. (Acts 13:2–12)

From the above verses, we see that the Holy Spirit spoke. We had an earlier chapter showing that God the Father spoke in the Old Testament, and Jesus spoke during the Gospels. The Holy Spirit speaks today in the age of grace. The scripture does not say, "God said or that Jesus spoke as He did to Saul on the Damascus road." It was the Holy Spirit who "said" to separate Barnabas and Saul for the work He (the Holy Spirit) had called them.

The scripture says they preached the Word of God being filled with the Holy Spirit. What did they teach? They taught the teaching "of the Lord." Jesus said the Holy Spirit would speak about "the Lord." Jesus said the Holy Spirit would not speak of Himself, but He would testify "of Me." The work of the Holy Spirit is to speak the Word of God and the teachings of the Lord.

- The Holy Spirit called Paul and Barnabas. (third person of the Godhead)
- The Word of God is what they preached. (first person of the Godhead)
- The teachings of the Lord are what they preached. (second person of the Godhead)

Paul and Barnabas, on their first missionary journey, arrived at Antioch in Pisidia (not the Antioch in Syria).

The verses confirm that God raised Jesus from the dead. The following verses confirm a dialogue that occurred between God and His Son in eternity past. God declares, "You are my Son. I have begotten You." God will raise His Son from the dead not to see corruption.

The key words of "I," "Him" "You," and "He" also give confirmation of the Trinity. The fact that God and the Son are engaging in a conversation is proof enough for the doctrine of the Trinity.

> But God raised Him from the dead.
>
> God has fulfilled this for us their children, in that He has raised up Jesus. As it is also written in the second Psalm: "You are My Son, Today I have begotten You."
>
> And that He raised Him from the dead, no more to return to corruption, He has spoken thus:
>
> "I will give you the sure mercies of David."
>
> Therefore He also says in another Psalm:
>
> "You will not allow Your Holy One to see corruption."
>
> But He whom God raised up saw no corruption. (Acts 13:30, 33–35, 37)

ACTS 15

Due to salvation now reaching the Gentiles, concerns arose concerning whether the Gentiles had to keep Mosaic law. There was division, and the Jews in Jerusalem who had accepted Christ as their Savior were still zealous for Mosaic law.

We must keep in mind that salvation through the price Jesus paid on Calvary was still new to many of them. The Jews in Jerusalem had been raised with Mosaic law from birth. If one places themselves in the shoes of these Jews, one might be a little more understanding with their error. Some were insisting that the Gentiles go through circumcision to be saved (Acts 15:1).

A council meeting with the mother church at Jerusalem had to be called to settle the matter. Paul, Barnabas, and some others made the trip to Jerusalem. They were received well, and they gave a report concerning how salvation had now reached the Gentiles.

The scripture says there was much dispute, especially from a sect of the Pharisees (of course). After a dispute, Peter finally takes the podium. The following verse is just one line from his speech, and it verifies the distinction between God and the Holy Spirit:

> God, who knows the heart, acknowledged them by giving them the Holy Spirit, just as He did to us. (Acts 15:8)

This is another scripture stating that the Holy Spirit is a gift that comes from God. If the Holy Spirit is a gift, there has to be a "giver." God is the giver, the Holy Spirit is the gift, and you and I are the recipients.

ACTS 20

Now we set our sails to Ephesus. The church at Ephesus was founded by Paul on his third missionary journey. Paul stayed in Ephesus longer than he did any other church that he established. Paul spent more than two years in Ephesus, and this church was very special to him. Paul wrote one of the prison epistles to Ephesus (the book of Ephesians).

There were many challenges in Ephesus for Paul. Ephesus worshipped a pagan god by the name of Artemis (called Diana by the Romans). Actually, Paul came close to losing his life in Ephesus in Acts 19.

After the apostle John left Patmos, he went to Ephesus to pastor there—and he is believed to be buried there. Mary, the mother of Jesus, is believed by many to have spent her last years in Ephesus.

In the following verses, Paul was at Miletus (thirty-six miles south of Ephesus in Turkey) and had decided to go to Jerusalem for the feast of Pentecost. Because he was in a hurry, he decides to sail past Ephesus, but from Miletus, he called for the elders of the church in Ephesus to meet with him. They came to Paul, and this is a part of Paul's discourse to them:

> Testifying to Jews, and also to Greeks, repentance toward God and faith toward our Lord Jesus Christ. And see, now I go bound in the spirit to Jerusalem,

> not knowing the things that will happen to me there, except that the Holy Spirit testifies in every city, saying that chains and tribulations await me.
>
> But none of these things move me; nor do I count my life dear to myself, so that I may finish my race with joy, and the ministry which I received from the Lord Jesus, to testify to the Gospel of the grace of God.
>
> "And indeed, now I know that you all, among whom I have gone preaching the kingdom of God, will see my face no more." (Acts 20:21–25)

- Repentance is toward God.
- Faith is toward our Lord Jesus Christ.
- The Holy Spirit spoke to Paul concerning bonds and afflictions.
- The ministry Paul received was "of the Lord Jesus."
- The Gospel testifies to the grace of God.

In these verses, Paul references all three persons of the Godhead.

CHAPTER 19

THE TRINITY IN THE BOOK OF ROMANS

When we read Paul's salutation to the church at Rome, it's easy to see that the apostle Paul believed in the Trinity as it is substantiated greatly in the book of Romans.

Paul confirms that he is the author in Romans 1:1 and that it was written to the church in Rome in verse 7. The book of Romans is the sixth book of the New Testament, and during the life of Paul, Rome was considered the center of the world. It is believed to have been written in AD 57–59.

Among Protestants, Paul is considered the founder of the church in Rome—even though he had never been to Rome. The thought by some is that Paul, through his journeys, had led many to Christ, and some of them went to Rome and established a church.

In the corporate world today, a lot of work is done remotely. Software programs make it easy for many to work from home without going into the office. Virtual meetings are now the norm, and individuals attend meetings remotely from anywhere in the world. In our day, remoting is a big deal. Paul is credited as the founder of the church in Rome because he founded it remotely. He led people to Christ, and they later traveled to Rome. The church there was established through the work of his ministry.

When Paul wrote the book of Romans, a church was already in existence, but he had never been there. As Protestants, we do not accept that Peter was the first pope or bishop in Rome. If one would take the time to research, they would find no evidence that Peter ever visited Rome. I know that ruffles some feathers since many have been taught differently in our traditions.

It is my opinion that Peter never went to Rome. We have record of him visiting Babylon (1 Peter 5:13), Antioch, Syria (Galatians 2:11), Caesarea, Joppa (Acts 10:23–24), and regions he traveled as a disciple with Jesus, but there is no solid proof that Peter ever went to Rome. I wish we could deal with this much more, there's much that can be said about the subject, but we'll have to save the full discussion for another day. We hold to the belief that Paul founded the church in Rome.

It is believed by many that Romans was written when Paul was in Corinth after he had left Athens (Acts 18:1–2). This is where Paul met Aquila and Priscilla after they were excommunicated from Rome. Most likely, he met this couple because they were tentmakers.

The theme of the book of Romans is "justification by faith." Paul even quotes Habakkuk 2:4 and says, "The Just shall live by faith."

A preacher I greatly respected who has gone to heaven said, "If I was placed on a deserted island and could only have one book of the Bible left with me, I would say, 'Give me Romans.'"

Romans 1

Paul wastes no time in diving right into the doctrine of the Trinity. Paul begins the great book of Romans with a distinction between the Father and the Son.

> To all who are in Rome, beloved of God, called to be saints: Grace to you and peace from God our Father and the Lord Jesus Christ.

> First, I thank my God through Jesus Christ for you all, that your faith is spoken of throughout the whole world.
>
> For God is my witness, whom I serve with my spirit in the Gospel of His Son, that without ceasing I make mention of you always in my prayers. (Romans 1:7–9, 16)

Did you notice the little conjunction "and" in verse 7? Now let's look at verse 16 where the Gospel of Christ and the power of God are used in the same verse.

> For I am not ashamed of the Gospel of Christ, for it is the power of God to salvation for everyone who believes, for the Jew first and also for the Greek. (Romans 1:16)

In chapter 2, Paul tells us the details of how we will be judged. He tells us how God will judge the secrets of men.

ROMANS 2

> In the day when God will judge the secrets of men by Jesus Christ, according to my Gospel. (Romans 2:16)

That was self-explanatory using our key word "by."

ROMANS 3

Paul tells us how the child of God receives justification in the sight of God. We can all be thankful for this verse. He tells us that Christ Jesus is the channel through which God's grace is given to us. He also tells us that the Holy Spirit has been given to us. A gift must have a giver; God is the giver, and the Holy Spirit is the gift.

> Being justified freely by His grace through the redemption that is in Christ Jesus. (Romans 3:24)

Romans 5

Paul tells us the channel through which we receive peace with God and access to God. It will be through our Lord Jesus Christ. He will tell us how the love of God is shed abroad in our hearts by the Holy Spirit. He gives us the assurance that God proves His love because Christ died for us, and we are reconciled to God through the Lord Jesus Christ. The Trinity is clear in all these verses.

> Therefore, having been justified by faith, we have peace with God through our Lord Jesus Christ, through whom also we have access by faith into this grace in which we stand, and rejoice in hope of the glory of God.
>
> And not only that, but we also glory in tribulations, knowing that tribulation produces perseverance; and perseverance, character; and character, hope.
>
> Now hope does not disappoint, because the love of God has been poured out in our hearts by the Holy Spirit who was given to us.
>
> But God demonstrates His own love toward us, in that while we were still sinners, Christ died for us.
>
> Or if when we were enemies we were reconciled to God through the death of His Son, much more, having been reconciled, we shall be saved by His life.
>
> And not only that, but we also rejoice in God through our Lord Jesus Christ, through whom we have now received the reconciliation. (Romans 5:1–5, 8, 10–11)

We are traveling through Romans quite quickly. Paul is about to talk about life and death in our Christian walk. We are alive to God by being in Christ Jesus.

Romans 6

> For the death that He died, He died to sin once for all; but the life that He lives, He lives to God. Likewise you also, reckon yourselves to be dead indeed to sin, but alive to God in Christ Jesus our Lord. (Romans 6:10–11)

That was quite a verse, very powerful, I hope we absorbed that; the life that Jesus lives He lives to God! Paul goes on to say it's the same way with us; we are alive to God in Christ Jesus our Lord.

Romans 7

In this masterful chapter, Paul shows the world his vulnerabilities. He tells us a lot about ourselves when he admits that he cannot live the Christian life within himself. He says that not one good thing dwells in his flesh. He's already been saved and filled with the Holy Spirit. He is preaching the Gospel and holding the office of an apostle, and he tells us that nothing good at all dwells in his flesh. He even uses present tense and says that he *is* wretched. He cries out in desperation.

> O wretched man that I am! Who will deliver me from this body of death? I thank God—through Jesus Christ our Lord! (Romans 7:24–25)

Praise the name of the Lord, folks. Paul found the answer to his problem, and he gave thanks to God that his victory was through Jesus Christ! He realizes that the life he lives for God is through faith in Christ and not himself. Paul gave thanks to God through Christ!

I have met people who were quite proud of how they live for God. Some foolishly even feel they have attained perfection.

> Not that I have already attained, or am already perfected; but I press on, that I may lay hold of that for which Christ Jesus has also laid hold of me. (Philippians 3:12)

My friends, if Paul couldn't say he could live the Christian life in his own efforts, what gives us the idea that any of us can? If Paul had not attained perfection, what makes us think we have? No, like Paul, we "press on." When the trumpet of the Lord sounds, we will be like Him—and that's when we will attain perfection. Let us not be like some Christians who say, "I can do all things" without finishing the verse. We can do all things "through Christ" that give us strength (Philippians 4:13). Jesus told us that we could do nothing without Him (John 15:5).

Paul shouts, "I thank God through Jesus Christ our Lord." How did Paul give thanks to God? He gave thanks through Jesus Christ. That's more than one person in the Trinity.

ROMANS 8

There's not a chance that we will leave out Romans 8. The Trinity is massive in this chapter. We won't post the entire chapter, but I strongly suggest taking the time to read all of it. In Romans 8 we will discover the following truths about the Triune God:

- No condemnation to those in Christ who walk after the Spirit.
- The law of the Spirit of life is in Christ Jesus.
- God sends His Son to condemn sin in the flesh.
- We are not in the flesh but in the Spirit if the Spirit of God dwells in us.
- If we have not the Holy Spirit, we are none of His.

- When Christ dwells in us, the body becomes dead to sin because the Spirit is life.
- But if the Spirit of Him that raised up Jesus from the dead dwells in you, He who raised up Christ from the dead shall also quicken your mortal bodies by his Spirit that dwelleth in you.
- If we are led by the Spirit of God, we are the sons of God.
- We have received the Spirit of adoption and cry, "Abba Father."
- The Holy Spirit bears witness that we are the children of God.
- We are heirs of God and joint heirs with Christ.
- The Holy Spirit helps our infirmities, making intercessions to God for us.
- The Holy Spirit intercedes for us according to the will of God.
- If God did not spare His own Son, He will also freely give us all things.
- Christ died and is at the right hand of God.
- Nothing can separate us from the love of God, which is in Christ Jesus our Lord.

What a masterpiece! I hope you'll take time to read the entire chapter.

If I could only have one chapter with me on a deserted island, I'd say, "Give me Romans 8."

Romans 9

In verse 1, Paul calls attention to Christ and the Holy Spirit:

> I tell the truth in Christ, I am not lying, my conscience also bearing me witness in the Holy Spirit. (Romans 9:1)

Isn't that wonderful? How do we know we are "in Christ?" We know it because the Holy Spirit who dwells in us bears witness.

Romans 10

Paul is going to give us instructions for how to be born again, how to be saved, and what to do to be saved. Those who have learned about winning souls or leading someone to salvation have probably heard about the "Roman Road." The Roman Road is a group of scriptures that shows we all have sinned and come short (missed the mark). We all need a Savior. In Romans, Paul tells us how to pray to receive Christ.

I get weary sometimes when people say we shouldn't teach "the sinner's prayer." My friends, there are many people who don't know what to pray for—or even what to say—to receive the Lord. To be saved is easy and there's no probation period that one has to go through to finally have a confirmation of salvation. One can be saved in a moment's time.

The dying thief on the cross was saved by saying, "Lord, remember me," and the publican went home justified by saying, "God, be merciful to me a sinner." Those prayers are what we could call "one-liners." Paul was aware that many didn't know what to say to be saved, and he told them what to confess with their mouths. He was leading them in what to say.

It's simple. We admit we are sinners, we exercise faith in that Jesus died for us and shed His blood on Calvary for our sins, we confess that Jesus is Lord and believe in our hearts that God raised Jesus from the dead, and we call on the Lord to save us. "Whosoever calls on the name of the Lord shall be saved" (Romans 10:13).

We tell others how to be saved by doing the same thing we did when we received Christ. I heard someone a few weeks ago say, "Receiving Christ is not in the Bible." I wanted to tell him that John 1:12 is still in the scriptures: "But as many as received Him, to them He gave the right to become children of God, to those who believe in His name." That verse says, "Receive and believe," and you become a child of God. Jesus says that He is "standing at the door and knocking" and that if anyone would "open the door," He would "come in." I fear many have made the plan of salvation way too hard. Jesus went to the cross. He was spat on, mocked, flogged, nailed, and pierced on His brow, hands, feet, and side. Jesus did the hard part. He got the hard part over with, and He did it to make it easy to receive and believe!

That's the theme of the book of Romans; it's justified by faith!

It matters little what men say concerning the plan of salvation. What do the scriptures say? To be saved, this is what we confess with our mouths and believe in our hearts. This is the Trinity:

> If you confess with your mouth the Lord Jesus and believe in your heart that God has raised Him from the dead, you will be saved. (Romans 10:9)

What a promise! One must believe and confess two things in order to be saved. The first is that we confess that Jesus is Lord (that's one in the Godhead) and within our very hearts, we must believe that God (that's two in the Godhead) raised Jesus from the dead. Based on those two requirements, the promise is "you will be saved," and it is for "whosoever."

When Paul and Silas were in jail and the earthquake shook the jailhouse, the Philippian jailer cried, "What must I do to be saved?" Paul and Silas both said, "Believe on the Lord Jesus Christ and you will be saved."

In chapter 1, Paul said, "I am not ashamed of the Gospel of the Lord Jesus Christ for it is the power of God to everyone who believes."

My friend, can we say that we truly are believers? From the depths of our hearts, do we believe it? Do we believe that Jesus came and was born of a virgin, lived a sinless and spotless life, went to the cross and shed His blood for our redemption, rose again on the third day, and is alive right now and seated at the right hand of God? Do we believe it?

I'm so glad there's not even the shadow of a doubt in my mind. I'm so thankful that He found me and brought me unto Himself and has written my name in the Lamb's book of life in heaven!

Jesus told his seventy disciples, "Do not rejoice in this, that the spirits are subject to you, but rather rejoice because your names are written in heaven" (Luke 10:20).

I'm glad that I know today, beyond any doubt whatsoever, that if I died today, if my heart quit beating, if I drew my last breath, I would awake in His presence being absent from the body and present with my Lord!

It's so easy to be saved. Let's declare, "If we confess with our mouth the Lord Jesus, and believe in our hearts that God has raised Jesus from the dead, we will be saved." That's the Trinity right there, my friend. We must believe that God raised Jesus from the dead to be saved.

Romans 14

In Romans 14, we find two verses where Paul displays the Trinity so simply. In fact, it would be difficult to write it any simpler than Paul did.

Each of us should want to be acceptable to God. Paul uses the word "acceptable" ten times in his epistles, and five of those times are in Romans. Paul told us to present our bodies as a living sacrifice, holy and acceptable to God and prove the perfect will of God. That's in Romans. Paul is going to tell us how to be acceptable to God. Here's the secret.

Paul is about to give us the definition of the kingdom of God and how to be acceptable to God. He will reference the Holy Spirit and then exhort us to serve Christ in righteousness, peace, and joy. The results will be that we have God's acceptance.

> For the kingdom of God is not eating and drinking, but righteousness and peace and joy in the Holy Spirit. For he who serves Christ in these things is acceptable to God and approved by men. (Romans 14:17–18)

Can you see the Trinity in those two verses? Did you see the terms, "of God", "the Holy Spirit", "Christ" and acceptable "to God?"

ROMANS 15

I suggest you to read verses 5–30 on your own. For easier and less reading, we will only present the verses pertaining to the Trinity. All three persons of the Godhead are listed in these scriptures.

God the Father is mentioned ten times, Jesus Christ is mentioned eleven times, and the Holy Spirit is mentioned four times, which totals twenty-five times in these verses. The last verse in the list references all the persons of the Trinity in one verse.

> Now may the God of patience and comfort grant you to be like-minded toward one another, according to Christ Jesus, that you may with one mind and one mouth glorify the God and Father of our Lord Jesus Christ. Receive one another, just as Christ also received us, to the glory of God.
>
> Jesus Christ has become a servant to the circumcision for the truth of God that the Gentiles might glorify God for His mercy.
>
> Now may the God of hope fill you with all joy and peace in believing, that you may abound in hope by the power of the Holy Spirit.
>
> Because of the grace given to me by God, that I might be a minister of Jesus Christ to the Gentiles, ministering the Gospel of God, that the offering of the Gentiles might be acceptable, sanctified by the Holy Spirit.
>
> Therefore, I have reason to glory in Christ Jesus in the things which pertain to God.
>
> For I will not dare to speak of any of those things which Christ has not accomplished through me, in mighty signs and wonders, by the power of the Spirit of God, so that from Jerusalem and round about to Illyricum I have fully preached the Gospel of Christ.

> And so I have made it my aim to preach the Gospel, not where Christ was named.
>
> But I know that when I come to you, I shall come in the fullness of the blessing of the Gospel of Christ. Now I beg you, brethren, through the Lord Jesus Christ, and through the love of the Spirit, that you strive together with me in prayers to God for me. (Romans 15:5–30)

Romans 16

We have now arrived at the last chapter of Romans, meaning we have come to Paul's salutation to the church at Rome. What a journey it has been seeing our Thrice Holy God through this masterpiece of Paul. Just as Paul opened Romans with the Trinity, he will close bringing attention to the glory of God that comes to us through (one of our key words) Jesus Christ:

> To God, alone wise, be glory through Jesus Christ. (Romans 16:27)

CHAPTER 20

THE TRINITY IN 1 AND 2 CORINTHIANS

The book of Corinthians has often been called the book of correction. This church was founded by Paul on his second missionary journey around AD 50. Corinthians was probably written around AD 57 or a little earlier.

Corinth was a city that worshipped false gods. Idolatry was rampant, morals were degraded, and sexual immorality was prevalent. A temple was built there for the worship of Aphrodite (Venus). It was also a city of great commerce. A few hundred thousand people from different regions of the Roman Empire lived there.

It would probably be easier to preach to the people in the days of Noah than to take the Gospel to Corinth since they took sin about as far as anyone could ever take it.

There would only be one answer for reaching the people in Corinth, and that would be "Christ and Him crucified," which Paul determined he would know nothing else among them (1 Corinthians 2:2)

When one studies the book of Acts and reads the sermons preached by the apostles, they usually focused on preaching the resurrection. Paul's focus was to preach Christ crucified (1 Corinthians 1:7, 18, 23; 2:2; Galatians 6:14; Philippians 3:18; Colossians 1:20, 2:14; Hebrews 12:2). Yes, they all peached both, but we're speaking of the main focus of their messages. There would only be one message that would work in Corinth, and that would be the preaching of the cross.

During the three missionary journeys of Paul, when he would enter a city, he always started preaching in the Jewish synagogues if they had one. In Philippi, since there was no synagogue, Paul preached to women by the river. Preaching Christ crucified in the Jewish places of worship sometimes caused Paul a lot of problems and opposition, but this was Paul's message.

Why did Paul always go to the Jewish synagogues first? In Romans 1, Paul said, "For I am not ashamed of the Gospel of Christ, for it is the power of God to salvation for everyone who believes, for the Jew first and also for the Greek." After Paul was saved on the road to Damascus, he headed straight to the Jewish synagogue and started preaching Christ to them. In Acts 20:26, Paul said that he declared first to those in Damascus (where he was saved), then Jerusalem, then to Judea, and lastly to the Gentiles. My friend, it was to the Jews first!

Remember the command of our Lord in Acts 1:8? "And you shall be witnesses to Me in Jerusalem, and in all Judea and Samaria, and to the end of the earth." Paul obeyed this command. Going to the synagogues first was his custom.

Paul founded the church in Corinth after leaving Athens. In Athens Paul had very little success. Corinth is about 50 miles west of Athens in south central Greece. Paul wrote the book of Romans while in Corinth. He also met Aquila and Priscilla in Corinth (a married couple who had to leave Rome because all Jews had been expelled).

The church at Corinth had a lot of problems, and they were not good representatives of Christian character. They were taking communion improperly, taking each other to court, abusing the gifts of the Spirit, and permitting sexual sin among its membership, which wasn't even done by pagans. Paul had to face opposition from false teachers, and he had to defend his apostleship. We've all heard the term "carnal Christians." The Corinthian Christians were completely carnal! This is why the book of Corinthians is sometimes called the book of corrections; it was to correct their carnality.

Now that we have the setting of the Corinthians, the purpose of our book is the Trinity.

The apostle Paul repeatedly made references concerning the Trinity to the church at Corinth. Paul made most of his statements concerning the Trinity in his first letter (most verses on the Trinity come from 1 Corinthians). In addition, Paul uses some of the terms we used in earlier definitions such as "and" and "by." On that note, let's see the Trinity in 1 Corinthians. Of course, Paul will begin in his salutation. He begins by showing the believer that the grace of God is given to us by Christ and the cross. Don't miss our key words of "and" and "by."

1 CORINTHIANS 1

> Grace be unto you, and peace, from God our Father, "and" from the Lord Jesus Christ.
>
> I thank my God always concerning you for the grace of God which was given to you by Christ Jesus
>
> But of Him you are in Christ Jesus, who became for us wisdom from God and righteousness and sanctification and redemption. (1 Corinthians 1:3–4, 30)

We see that the grace of God comes to us by way of Christ Jesus. Next, Paul gives insight to God and the Holy Spirit. These are certainly beautiful verses.

1 CORINTHIANS 2

The following verses really do a breakdown of the Trinity by mentioning the "testimony of God." Paul determines to know nothing among the Corinthians except "Jesus Christ crucified." His preaching would be in a demonstration of "the Spirit," and the Holy Spirit would be our teacher. Paul plainly tells us that no one knows the things of God except the Spirit of God. All three persons of the Trinity are referenced. This is too good not to take the time to read.

> And I, brethren, when I came to you, did not come with excellence of speech or of wisdom declaring to you the testimony of God. For I determined not to know anything among you except Jesus Christ and Him crucified.
>
> I was with you in weakness, in fear, and in much trembling. And my speech and my preaching were not with persuasive words of human wisdom, but in demonstration of the Spirit and of power that your faith should not be in the wisdom of men but in the power of God.
>
> However, we speak wisdom among those who are mature, yet not the wisdom of this age, nor of the rulers of this age, who are coming to nothing. But we speak the wisdom of God in a mystery, the hidden wisdom which God ordained before the ages for our glory, which none of the rulers of this age knew; for had they known, they would not have crucified the Lord of glory.
>
> But as it is written: "Eye has not seen, nor ear heard, Nor have entered into the heart of the things which God has prepared for those who love Him."
>
> But God has revealed them to us through His Spirit. For the Spirit searches all things, yes, the deep things of God.
>
> For what man knows the things of a man except the spirit of the man which is in him? Even so no one knows the things of God except the Spirit of God.
>
> Now we have received, not the spirit of the world, but the Spirit who is from God, that we might know the things that have been freely given to us by God.

> These things we also speak, not in words which man's wisdom teaches but which the Holy Spirit teaches, comparing spiritual things with spiritual.
>
> But the natural man does not receive the things of the Spirit of God, for they are foolishness to him; nor can he know them, because they are spiritually discerned. (1 Corinthians 2:1–14)

- How does God reveal to us about the things He has prepared for us?
- Who searches and knows the "deep things of God?"
- Who knows the things of God?

The doctrine of the Trinity is easy to understand in those verses with a clear distinction between God and the Holy Spirit.

1 Corinthians 6

In chapter 6, we notice the importance of our key words. We're about to see "and" and "by" bumped right up against each other to show the distinction between Christ and the Holy Spirit.

I love this passage because it also uses past tense concerning the Christians washing, sanctification, and justification. Paul is going to tell believers that all of that has already been done.

We are about to see how when a person comes to Jesus, they are washed, sanctified, and justified (all past tense).

One might ask, "How am I already sanctified? Isn't that a progressive thing in the Christian walk?" Yes, it is, in our own sight and in the sight of others, like family members and church members, and so on. However, in God's sight, when He looks down at us through the cleansing blood of His Son, God says, "You're already sanctified." I told you this was a beautiful passage!

Don't get your position (in Christ) mixed up with your condition of presently growing in the grace and knowledge of the Lord. Our position in Christ is that we are already sanctified. However, for our condition of growing to be more like Jesus, we all have some growing to do—and we will until the trumpet of the Lord sounds.

In this very moment, right now, we are justified and sanctified, but when Jesus takes us out of this world, we will be "glorified." John told us when we see Him, we will finally be like Him (1 John 3:2).

Let's go for a swim in this passage! I know we're looking for the Trinity, but we shouldn't miss the past tense word "were (which is used 4 times)!"

> And such were some of you. But you were washed, but you were sanctified, but you were justified in the name of the Lord Jesus "and by" the Spirit of our God.
>
> And God both raised up the Lord and will also raise us up by His power.
>
> Or do you not know that your body is the temple of the Holy Spirit who is in you, whom you have from God, and you are not your own? 1 (Corinthians 6:11, 14, 19)

These are some wonderful verses. We are justified in the name of Christ and by the Spirit of God, and we are told that God raised the Lord, that our bodies are temples of the Holy Spirit, and that the Holy Spirit is given to us from God. All three persons in the Godhead are acknowledged.

In the next verse, we'll see our conjunction "and" differentiating between God the Father "and" the Lord Jesus Christ.

1 Corinthians 8

> Yet for us there is one God, the Father, of whom are all things, and we for Him; "and" one Lord Jesus Christ, through whom are all things, and through whom we live. (1 Corinthians 8:6)

No more comments need to be added to that verse. The Trinity is obvious: "one God who is the Father and one Lord who is Jesus Christ."

1 Corinthians 12

Paul is going to take the ball and run with it! He says that no one can say, "Jesus is Lord" except "by" the Holy Spirit.

He uses terms such as "same Spirit," "same Lord," and "same God." We'll explain more on this later in Ephesians. For now, we are baptized into the body of Christ by the Holy Spirit.

> Therefore, I make known to you that no one speaking by the Spirit of God calls Jesus accursed, and no one can say that Jesus is Lord except "by" the Holy Spirit.
>
> There are diversities of gifts, but the same Spirit.
>
> There are differences of ministries, but the same Lord.
>
> And there are diversities of activities, but it is the same God who works all in all.
>
> For as the body is one and has many members, but all the members of that one body, being many, are one body, so also is Christ.
>
> For by one Spirit we were all baptized into one body—whether Jews or Greeks, whether slaves or free—and have all been made to drink into one Spirit.
>
> For in fact the body is not one member but many.
>
> But now God has set the members, each one of them, in the body just as He pleased.
>
> And if they were all one member, where would the body be?
>
> But now indeed there are many members, yet one body. (1 Corinthians 12:3–6, 12–14, 18–20)

As we can see from the above verses, "one" spoken of in the singular can have "many members" spoken of in the plural.

The fact that the one Godhead can include multiple persons is clearly seen in scripture. We emphasize there is only one God (not three) and that the one Godhead includes three persons.

Once one understands the above scriptures, and "that one can contain many," they will see how John makes complete sense when he says the three who bear witness in heaven and earth are one. Just as one Bible may contain many books and verses, one can contain multiples.

> For there are three that bear witness in heaven: the Father, the Word, and the Holy Spirit; and these three are one. (1 John 5:7)

1 CORINTHIANS 15

The discussion of the Trinity in Corinthians would not be complete without the following verses. Everyone at some time has quoted from this great chapter concerning the resurrection of our bodies. There are a couple of verses in this chapter that are too good to miss. Let's take a look at what Paul will tell us.

> Then comes the end, when He delivers the kingdom to God the Father, when He puts an end to all rule and all authority and power.
>
> Now when all things are made subject to Him, then the Son Himself will also be subject to Him who put all things under Him, that God may be all in all. (1 Corinthians 15:24, 28)

I told you that passage was too good to miss! What a beautiful set of verses! Paul says that Jesus will deliver the kingdom (don't miss the next word) "to" God the Father.

Paul goes on to say that when all things are made subject to Christ, the Son Himself will also be subject to Him who put all things under him that God may be all in all! Verse 28 is powerful, it describes the time when Christ will turn "everything" over to the Father. Let's break down the verse.

> Now when all things are made subject to Him (Jesus), then the Son Himself (Jesus) will also be subject to Him (the Father) who put all things under Him (Jesus), that God (the Father) may be all in all. (1 Corinthians 15:24, 28)

The phrase "that God may be all in all" is referring to the time after He returns to the earth and reigns for 1000 years until He humbles all of His enemies beneath His feet, then Jesus Himself will have everything under His authority. Then, the Jesus will place Himself under God (the Father) so that God (the Father) who gave us His Son (Jesus) will be "all in all", in other words "supreme over all things everywhere!"

The Trinity is undeniable in the above verses and yet we're still not done with 1 Corinthians 15. There is one more verse from this tremendous chapter. Verse 57 tells us "who" and "through" the believer obtains victory.

> But thanks be to God, who gives us the victory through our Lord Jesus Christ. (1 Corinthians 15:57)

How does God give victory to us? Through the Lord Jesus Christ! If someone gave you a gift through someone else, you could still receive it. If someone sent a gift through the postal service, you could still be the recipient, right?

That's how God the Father gives us the gift of eternal life and a victorious life at that! It is given to us through what His Son did on Calvary's cross! Salvation is a gift of God delivered through the sacrifice of Jesus Christ. All we have to do is receive it! Salvation is a gift we receive.

Many have a problem with this, and many believe they have to work for salvation. I guess they feel that the terrible price Jesus paid on the cross just wasn't enough to save them—and that when Jesus cried, "It is finished," it really wasn't. Many believe they have to add to what Jesus did on the cross with good works. If we could have saved ourselves, Jesus would never have had to come in the first place. If we could have gotten our own selves to heaven with our own efforts, don't you believe that God would have said, "They can get here on their own. I don't need to send my Son to go through the horrors of Golgotha?"

If you're still struggling with salvation being a free gift that we simply receive by faith in Jesus Christ, here are a couple of words from the Word of God that may help:

> But the free gift is not like the offense. For if by the one man's offense many died, much more the grace of God and the gift by the grace of the one Man, Jesus Christ, abounded to many. (Romans 5:15)

> But as many as received Him, to them He gave the right to become children of God, to those who believe in His name. (John 1:12)

My friend, eternal life is a free gift. We can't earn it with works or purchase it with money; it is believe and receive!

It's my personal observation that those who deny the Trinity also have a problem with justification by faith. They also believe we are saved by works that we do (believing that one must be baptized to be saved, be baptized by a certain formula, join a church, or wear their hair or clothes in a certain way, etc.).

When it comes to salvation, Jesus took care of the hard part at Calvary. Today, it's believe and receive! Now, most certainly, out of our hearts of love for Him, we will perform good works not to be saved by them—but because we love Him and live to please Him.

I'd like to give us a scripture on this because many don't think it's in the Bible that we work for Christ because we love Him. This scripture will come right out and say that "righteousness comes by faith." Paul says that circumcision or uncircumcision avails nothing at all. He's trying to tell us that works avail nothing at all! Works do not produce salvation. Works will avail when it comes to receiving rewards once we reach heaven. When it comes to the new birth, works avail nothing at all!

Paul also tells us how our faith works; it's all through love! We work for Him because we love Him!

> For we through the Spirit eagerly wait for the hope of righteousness by faith. For in Christ Jesus neither circumcision nor uncircumcision avails anything, but faith working through love. (Galatians 5:5–6)

This is very important. If we miss this truth, we might end up missing heaven because we have misplaced our faith. Instead of believing in the blood of Jesus and the price He paid on Calvary, we place our faith in our own efforts, which cannot save us. If our faith is not in the Lord's payment for the penalty of sin, our faith is in the wrong place. Faith in the cross of Christ is the only saving faith.

None of us can ever live a good enough life to get ourselves to heaven. If we could save ourselves by our own good works, why would God the Father send His only Son into this world to go through the horrors of the crucifixion? If we could get to heaven ourselves, why did Jesus even have to come to die at all?

I've heard people say, "Well, if that person is going to heaven, then I'm surely going to make it." That statement shows that they are placing their faith in their own works. Are not they comparing their good life to another's life? The scripture says that all have sinned and come short of the glory of God. It says that there is none righteous, no not one (Romans 3:10).

I need a Savior, the minister needs a Savior, and every church member needs a Savior. We cannot save ourselves. None of us can live a life that is good enough to go to heaven. This is why Jesus told the Pharisees who trusted in their good works that prostitutes and tax collectors would enter the kingdom of God ahead of them (Matthew 21:31).

All of us should take a self-examination to ensure that our faith is properly placed in Christ. Our faith must be in Jesus alone (plus nothing and minus nothing).

> Examine yourselves as to whether you are in the faith. Test yourselves. Do you not know yourselves, that Jesus Christ is in you? Unless indeed you are disqualified. (2 Corinthians 13:5)

This wraps up the Trinity in 1 Corinthians. Let's move into the second letter to the church at Corinth. In 2 Corinthians, Paul gives us five more passages related to our Holy God. As always, we begin with Paul's greeting.

2 CORINTHIANS 1

> Blessed be the God and Father of our Lord Jesus Christ, the Father of mercies and God of all comfort. Now, He, who establishes us with you in Christ and has anointed us is God, who also has sealed us and given us the Spirit in our hearts as a guarantee. (2 Corinthians 1:3, 21–22)

As common in Paul's greetings, he opens with grace from God the Father of (in some epistles, Paul uses "and") the Lord Jesus Christ.

Paul addresses all three members of the Godhead by telling us that it is God who has established us "in Christ." God has given us the Holy Spirit in our hearts as a guarantee. God also has "sealed" us. We've all seen seals that have the word "guaranteed." God places His seal "in our hearts" as God's guarantee that He has established us in Christ.

First Paul gives thanks to God who leads him into a triumphant life in Christ. I have a sermon that covers all the sufferings that Paul endured, he endured a lot. When he was first saved Jesus told Ananias that Saul would suffer much for the sake of Christ, and suffer he did. (2 Corinthians 2)

From the time he was saved to the time he was beheaded in Rome, he suffered—but never do we hear Paul say he was ever defeated. We hear him say he was "hindered," but he never said he was defeated. No outside force ever conquered him.

> Now thanks be to God who always leads us in triumph in Christ. (2 Corinthians 2:14)

Did you see the word "always?" Paul didn't say sometimes, when the sun is shining, or when all is well. He says "always." God always leads us to victory, but it's always "in Christ."

Doesn't that remind you of how he finally found victory of his own flesh in Romans 7? He cried out, "O wretched man that I am! Who will deliver me from this body of death? I thank God through Jesus Christ our Lord."

The victory that God gave to Paul was a victory that came through Jesus Christ. The faith that saved him was the faith that would keep Paul and give him a victorious and triumphant life.

2 Corinthians 3

It would be good to read this chapter on your own. Paul tells us that the Spirit gives life, and our sufficiency is from God. He also tells us that where the Spirit of the Lord is the Lord is, there is liberty." We will only list verses 2–4 here.

> You are our epistle written in our hearts, known and read by all men; clearly you are an epistle of Christ, ministered by us, written not with ink but by the Spirit

> of the living God, not on tablets of stone but on tablets of flesh, that is, of the heart. And we have such trust through Christ toward God. (2 Corinthians 3:2–4)

Our lives are epistles, and others who know us are reading our books. We are Christ's epistles. Christ is the pen, and the Holy Spirit is the ink that flows through Him into our hearts. Paul says we trust in this through "Christ toward God", and he also calls the Holy Spirit the "Spirit of the living God."

2 Corinthians 5

In the following passage, Paul portrays the Trinity in the first verse. First, he tells us that God has prepared us and given us the Holy Spirit. God has reconciled us to Himself through Jesus Christ. He then tells us who made Jesus sin for us. According to this verse, Jesus did not make Himself sin. Paul says God made Jesus sin for us. That's a powerful word. God the Father "made" Jesus sin on our behalf.

Why did the Father make Jesus sin? It was so that we might become the righteousness of God in Him. We might be made the children of God because Jesus was made to be sin for you and me—and Jesus was made so by the Father.

> Now He who has prepared us for this very thing is God, who also has given us the Spirit as a guarantee.
>
> Now all things are of God, who has reconciled us to Himself through Jesus Christ, and has given us the ministry of reconciliation,
>
> For He made Him who knew no sin to be sin for us, that we might become the righteousness of God in Him. (2 Corinthians 5:5, 18, 21)

For anything to be made there has to be a "maker." God the Father "made" Jesus to be sin for us. The passage also tells us that God has given us the Spirit. If a gift is given there has to be a "giver." God is both the "maker" and the "giver" in those verses and it is Jesus who was "made" and the Holy Spirit which was "given."

One more passage, and we will have finished both 1 and 2 Corinthians. We finish with Paul's last words written to the church at Corinth.

> For though He was crucified in weakness, yet He lives by the power of God. For we also are weak in Him, but we shall live with Him by the power of God toward you.
>
> The grace of the Lord Jesus Christ, and the love of God, and the communion of the Holy Spirit be with you all. Amen. (2 Corinthians 13:4–14)

What a way to cross the finish line!

- the grace of the Lord
- the love of God
- the communion of the Holy Spirit

What a book! It confirms the Trinity. Paul tells us that Christ lives by the power of God. The Trinity couldn't have been made more obvious.

CHAPTER 21

THE TRINITY IN THE BOOK OF GALATIANS

There seems to be some controversy as to when Galatians was written. The debate comes down to whether it was written before or after the Jerusalem council, which took place around AD 48–50. If Galatians was written before the council, it would have to have been written before that date. Others suggest that it was around AD 55–57 from Corinth on Paul's third missionary journey. This would mean Galatians was written after the council. There are also arguments that Galatians was written from Corinth on the second missionary journey or the third journey.

In Acts 16:6 and 18:23, we see that Paul made trips to Galatia on both his second and third journeys. Most scholars agree the book was written between AD 55 and AD 57 in Ephesus or Corinth.

GALATIANS 1

As in Paul's other epistles, his salutation opens with a distinction between God the Father and the Son. Yes, we're back to our conjunction word "and," which is used twice. Paul will make it clear that God raised Jesus from the dead and Jesus gave Himself for our sins, according to the will of God the Father.

> Paul, an apostle (not from men nor through man, but through Jesus Christ and God the Father who raised Him from the dead), Grace to you and peace from God the Father and our Lord Jesus Christ, who gave Himself for our sins so that He might rescue us from this present evil age, according to the will of our God and Father. (Galatians 1:1, 3–4)

Galatians 3

In the following verses, Paul explains that it is through faith in Jesus Christ that we received the Holy Spirit and that it is God who justifies the Gentiles. All three persons in the Godhead are recognized in these verses, and the passage makes it clear that the Holy Spirit is provided to us from God. If the Holy Spirit is "provided" to us from God, that certainly implies that they are two separate persons.

> You foolish Galatians, who has bewitched you, before whose eyes Jesus Christ was publicly portrayed as crucified?
>
> This is the only thing I want to find out from you: did you receive the Spirit by works of the law, or by hearing with faith?
>
> Are you so foolish? Having begun by the Spirit, are you now being perfected by the flesh?
>
> So then, does He who provides you with the Spirit and works miracles among you, do it by works of the law, or by hearing with faith?
>
> Just as Abraham believed God, and it was credited to Him as righteousness. (Galatians 3:1–3, 5–11)

Again, Paul is saying that God is who "provides" the Holy Spirit to us.

Next, Paul explains that it is through faith in Christ Jesus that we are made children of God. One of our key words, "through" will be seen again:

> For you are all sons and daughters of God through faith in Christ Jesus. (Galatians 3:26)

Paul then goes on to state that we are made heirs to God through Christ. In this verse, in one line Paul will say that it is "God" who sent "the Spirit" of "His Son" into our hearts.

> But when the fullness of the time came, God sent His Son, born of a woman, born under the law, so that He might redeem those who were under the law, that we might receive the adoption as sons and daughters. Because you are sons, God has sent the Spirit of His Son into our hearts, crying out, "Abba! Father!" Therefore, you are no longer a slave, but a son; and if a son, then an heir through God. (Galatians 4:4–7)

- God sent his Son into the world.
- God also sent the Spirit of His Son who lives in our hearts, giving us the ability to call God our Father.

As we conclude Galatians, did you notice the Trinity in that one simple phrase? "God has sent the Spirit of His Son?" Did you see the capital letters in the verse for all three persons proving that God, Spirit and Son are names of each person in the Godhead? Did you also see that the Spirit of the Son gives us the ability to call our God "Abba Father?"

CHAPTER 22

THE TRINITY IN THE BOOK OF EPHESIANS

When one reads the title of the book of Ephesians, almost every Bible titles it "The Epistle of Paul to the Ephesians."

> Paul, an apostle of Christ Jesus by the will of God, to the saints who are at Ephesus. (Ephesians 1:1)

So, from both the title and the first verse, one immediately believes this book was written to the church at Ephesus.

The Greek word for Ephesus is *Ephesos*. However, if one reads some of the early Greek manuscripts, the word Ephesos is not found in them. When researching your Greek translations, you will either see *Ephesos* completely omitted or at least a footnote acknowledging that some of the earliest manuscripts leave out the word.

Among scholars, the reason for the omission is that the book was written to be widely circulated—and the distribution of the book was to go out from Ephesus. Ephesus, a very large city, was close to the Aegean Sea. Some say it was second only to Rome. It was a great city of commerce, and many travelers went through Ephesus, which greatly contributed to the city's wealth. Ephesus was the banking center of Asia Minor. The city today is in ruins, yet it is one of the most visited places in Turkey.

Paul established this church on his third missionary journey around AD 52. He spent more time in Ephesus than in any of the other churches on his missionary journeys. In Acts 20, Paul talked to the elders of Ephesus at Miletus, which was south of Ephesus:

> Therefore, watch and remember that for three years I did not cease to warn everyone night and day with tears. (Acts 20:31)

When Paul first went to Ephesus, he taught in the Jewish synagogue for three months. After that was completed, he stayed in Ephesus and taught in the school of Tyrannus for another two years:

> And he went into the synagogue and spoke boldly for three months, reasoning and persuading concerning the things of the kingdom of God.
>
> But when some were hardened and did not believe, but spoke evil of the Way before the multitude, he departed from them and withdrew the disciples, reasoning daily in the school of Tyrannus.
>
> And this continued for two years, so that all who dwelt in Asia heard the word of the Lord Jesus, both Jews and Greeks. (Acts 19:8–10)

God was giving Paul great results in Ephesus, and Paul told the church in Corinth that he was going to remain in Ephesus because God had opened a great and effective door for him there.

> But I will tarry in Ephesus until Pentecost. For a great and effective door has opened to me, and there are many adversaries. (1 Corinthians 16:8–9)

After leaving Patmos, the apostle John returned to Ephesus and pastored there. He is buried in Ephesus. Ephesus was the first of the churches of Asia Minor to be mentioned in Revelation 2. Jesus commended them for their works, labor, patience, not bearing evil, testing, and finding false apostles who claimed apostleship. He commended them for their perseverance. They were working without being weary and hated the works of the Nicolaitans. They were eating things sacrificed to idols (in Greek, *Nicolah* means "Let us eat"). They were also involved in adultery and sexual immorality.

Some believe that this false teaching came from one of the first deacons, Nicolas, who was chosen in Acts 6. In spite of all the wonderful things Jesus said about Ephesus, the Lord still had something against them. They had left their first love.

How easy it is for a church to get wrapped up in the mechanics and programs to keep a church going forward, yet lose that which is most important: our love for Christ. We should always remember that we work for Christ because we love Him!

As I have traveled and spoken in churches across our great country, I have seen many Christians who work and labor tirelessly in the work of the Lord. Like the Ephesians, they work without being weary, yet they have become cold in their love for the Lord. If we aren't careful, it could happen to us; it's so easy to do.

Of the four prison epistles written by Paul, Ephesians, Philippians, Colossians, and Philemon, only Ephesians was written in Rome. The major theme in Ephesians is "the church." Since we are on the subject of the Trinity, we will see the church referenced as a single building, a single bride, and a single body that is made up of multiple members. One single unit with multiple members gives validity that there can be one Godhead comprised of three persons.

The book of Ephesians was written by Paul, but since he was in prison, it was delivered by Tychicus (Ephesians 6:21). Tychicus is listed as one of the men who waited for Paul in Troas (Acts 20:4). He was a man who Paul loved. In Colossians 4:7, Paul says Tychicus was a beloved brother, a faithful minister, and a fellow servant in the Lord. In Paul's second letter to Timothy, Paul says he sent Tychicus to Ephesus (2 Timothy 4:12). Lastly, Paul wrote to Titus and said Tychicus was in the consideration—along with Artemis —to be sent to Crete (Titus 3:12). Not many in the church today know about Tychicus; he's pretty much an unsung hero of Paul's companionship. It would be Tychicus who would deliver the book of Ephesians to Ephesus.

Ephesus was one of the seven wonders of the world, and it had a temple built for Artemis (Diana is her Roman name). This magnificent temple was originally built by Croesus, the king of Lydia, around 550 BCE. It was majestic in size. Artemis was the goddess of fertility, a multi-breasted image that stood in the temple.

The main theme of Ephesians is the church. The church was a mystery in the Old Testament, the word "church" was not even mentioned one time in the Old Testament. The church was one of the mysteries that God gave to Paul.

> This is a great mystery, but I speak concerning Christ and the church. (Ephesians 5:32)

This is why the Rapture of the church was not mentioned in the Old Testament. The church will be raptured when we rise to meet Jesus in the air (2 Thessalonians 4:13–18). If the church was unknown in the Old Testament, how could the Rapture of the church be known as well?

Ephesians is an epistle about the church, and Paul will say later that the church is a single body with many members. This is important, please remember that.

Now that we have the setting for Ephesus, let's go on to how Paul declares the Trinity here.

EPHESIANS 1

By now, one can see Paul's pattern in his greetings to each church he addresses. He begins each letter with a greeting regarding the Trinity.

If that seems repetitive, remember that it brings to the forefront the importance of the Trinity being emphasized to each church by Paul. We begin in chapter one and are expecting the conjunction word "and" in the salutation.

Paul also uses the term "the God of our Lord Jesus Christ" (don't forget in Colossians we are told that the Head of Christ is God). The verse then states that he is God the Father of Glory who "worked in Christ" and that God "raised Jesus from the dead." It goes on to say that God "seated Jesus at His right hand."

> Grace to you and peace from God our Father and the Lord Jesus Christ. That the God "of" our Lord Jesus Christ, the Father of glory, may give to you the spirit of wisdom and revelation in the knowledge of Him, which He worked in Christ when He raised Him from the dead and seated Him at His right hand in the heavenly places. (Ephesians 1:2, 17, 20)

Paul opens the great book of Ephesians with the Trinity. In chapter 2, Paul continues with the Godhead in one single verse below.

Ephesians 2

> For through Him we both have access by one Spirit to the Father. (Ephesians 2:18)

How much clearer can it be? Through Him (Christ) By One Spirit access is given to The Father.

Another way we could say it is this: "We have access to God the Father through Christ by the Spirit."

EPHESIANS 3

Again, we have the Father of our Lord Jesus strengthening us through His Holy Spirit. The Ephesians were made aware of the Trinity!

> And to make all see what is the fellowship of the mystery, which from the beginning of the ages has been hidden in God who created all things through Jesus Christ; For this reason I bow my knees to the Father of our Lord Jesus Christ, that He would grant you, according to the riches of His glory, to be strengthened with might through His Spirit in the inner man, to Him be glory in the church by Christ Jesus to all generations, forever and ever. Amen. (Ephesians 3:9, 14, 16, 21)

EPHESIANS 4

Paul will now begin using the terminology of "One Spirit, One Lord, and One God and Father of all." He then tells us how God gives us forgiveness; it will be as God in Christ has forgiven us.

> There is one body and one Spirit, just as you were called in one hope of your calling; One Lord, one faith, one baptism; One God and Father of all, who is above all, and through all, and in you all. And be kind to one another, tenderhearted, forgiving one another, even as God in Christ forgave you. (Ephesians 4:4–6, 32)

Plainly written by Paul, there is one Spirit, one Lord, and one Father of all. Did you get the last verse? It is only because of Christ and what He did on Calvary that we have God giving us forgiveness. God in Christ is forgiving us. It reminds us of how the Lord on the cross prayed to His Father for the forgiveness of those who were crucifying Him. He prayed to the Father, "Father, forgive them." Forgiveness from God comes to us through Christ!

EPHESIANS 5

In the following verse, we have the conjunction "and."

> For this you know, that no fornicator, unclean person, nor covetous man, who is an idolater, has any inheritance in the kingdom of Christ and God. (Ephesians 5:5)

CHAPTER 23

THE TRINITY IN THE BOOK OF PHILIPPIANS

As we have mentioned, Philippians is one of the four prison epistles written by the apostle Paul (along with Ephesians, Colossians, and Philemon).

We know that Paul had three missionary journeys. The first Paul and Barnabas worked together. John Mark was also with them.

In Acts 13, Paul and Barnabas went to Galatia to Perga in Pamphylia. John Mark out of fear of robbers and wild beasts decided, "I think I'll go home to Mommy." Paul and Barnabas continued without John Mark and entered the synagogue at Pisidian Antioch, and God gave them success.

We mentioned that Paul had a custom of going straight to the Jewish synagogues to preach because salvation was to the Jew first and then to the Greeks (we covered that in Romans). They always began preaching in the synagogues. This custom of going first to the synagogues started with Paul in Damascus right after his conversion, this custom he continued in all of his journeys. I took the time to record Paul's synagogue visits listed in scripture for you.

Damascus

Immediately he preached the Christ in the synagogues, that He is the Son of God. (Acts 9:20)

Salamis

And when they arrived in Salamis, they preached the word of God in the synagogues of the Jews. They also had John as their assistant. (Acts 13:5)

Perga

But when they departed from Perga, they came to Antioch in Pisidia, and went into the synagogue on the Sabbath day and sat down. (Acts 13:14)

Iconium

Now it happened in Iconium that they went together to the synagogue of the Jews, and so spoke that a great multitude both of the Jews and of the Greeks believed. (Acts 14:1)

Thessalonica

Now when they had passed through Amphipolis and Apollonia, they came to Thessalonica, where there was a synagogue of the Jews. (Acts 17:1)

Berea

Then the brethren immediately sent Paul and Silas away by night to Berea. When they arrived, they went into the synagogue of the Jews. (Acts 17:10)

Athens

Therefore, he reasoned in the synagogue with the Jews and with the Gentile worshipers, and in the marketplace daily with those who happened to be there. (Acts 17:17)

Corinth

And he departed from there and entered the house of a certain man named Justus, one who worshipped God, whose house was next door to the synagogue. Then Crispus, the ruler of the synagogue, believed on the Lord with all his household. And many of the Corinthians, hearing, believed and were baptized. (Acts 18:7–8)

Ephesus

And he came to Ephesus and left them there; but he himself entered the synagogue and reasoned with the Jews. (Acts 18:19)

And he went into the synagogue and spoke boldly for three months, reasoning and persuading concerning the things of the kingdom of God. (Acts 19:8)

In the above scriptures, Paul first went to the Jewish synagogues because salvation was first to the Jews and secondly to the Gentiles (see Romans 1:16; 2:9–10; Acts 1:8; 10:37; 13:46).

Now we come to the church at Philippi, and this city had no Jewish synagogue. This is important—Paul is now in Europe! All of us have heard the old saying from Horace Greeley: "Go west, young man." Paul had thought about going east into Asia, but the Holy Spirit said, "No" (Acts 16:6). The Holy Spirit forbade him to go south into Bithynia (Acts 16:7). He has already traveled into the north in the regions of Galatia, and through process of elimination, there's only one way left to go. All who live in the West should be eternally grateful to the Holy Spirit for sending Paul to Philippi because the Gospel went to Europe, and from Europe, the Gospel came to the West.

God gave Paul a vision that has become known as the *Macedonian Call*, and even songs have been written about it. In Paul's vision, he saw a man from Macedonia who said, "Come over into Macedonia and help us" (Acts 16:9).

It is so important to listen to the voice of the Holy Spirit. Had Paul not listened, we may have never received the good news of the Gospel in the West. Paul made his way to Philippi. Philippi was named after Philip II, the Macedonian king and father of Alexander the Great.

There was no Jewish synagogue in Philippi, but Paul found some women praying on a riverbank. One of the women, Lydia, was a businesswoman who had come from Thyatira.

Paul preached, and God "opened her heart" to Paul's message. Her entire household received Christ, and all of them were baptized. She and her husband persuaded Paul to stay in their home. I hope the reader sees that Lydia was the first European convert to Christ. A church was started in Europe in her home. May God bless women who love the Lord!

The Gospel in Philippi would not be without opposition; Satan would surely fight it. Paul cast a demon out of a damsel who had made a lot of money for her masters. Once the girl was delivered and her master's wallet was getting hit, Paul and Silas would be cast into the Philippian jail after being beaten.

Most of us know what happens next. Paul and Silas are in prison with their feet fastened in stocks. At midnight—when things are darkest—Paul and Silas begin to pray and sing hymns to God. God sent an earthquake, and the foundations of the jail began to rock. Talk about the jailhouse rock! Paul and Silas were rejoicing in their persecution. Talk about rock and roll! Paul and Silas, had their feet on the rock, and in heaven, their name was on the roll!

The jailer asked, "What must I do to be saved?"

Paul gave him the message of justification by faith and said, "Believe on the Lord Jesus Christ, and you will be saved."

The jailer and his whole family ended up getting saved. That jailer took Paul and Silas home with him and bound up their wounds and bruises. I've sometimes wondered if this is the same jailer that placed the stripes on their backs, now he was binding up their wounds and feeding them.

In Corinth, Paul worked with his own hands as a tentmaker. He was not funded in any way from the church at Corinth. One might say that the church at Corinth "muzzled the ox that treaded the corn," they did not support Paul financially. How was Paul supported other than working as a tentmaker? The following is what Paul wrote to the church at Corinth.

> Did I commit sin in humbling myself that you might be exalted, because I preached the Gospel of God to you free of charge? I robbed other churches, taking wages from them to minister to you. And when I was present with you, and in need, I was a burden to no one, for what I lacked the brethren from Macedonia supplied. And in everything I kept myself from being burdensome to you, and so I will keep myself. (2 Corinthians 11:7–9)

Paul was writing Philippians in a prison in Rome. The church at Philippi had raised funds for Paul and sent them by way of Epaphroditus (who most likely was now their pastor).

In Paul's letter to the Philippian church, he thanked them. If a pastor is reading this book, I hope we learn a lesson from Paul concerning this. Like Paul, we should say, "Thank you for your support." I have seen some pastors who never thanked their people for their giving. My father was a pastor, and he taught me a lot about ministerial ethics. He taught me many things. He would say, "Remember to tell the people thank you and let the people know that all they are doing is appreciated." Paul certainly did!

I know this is a given, but every pastor should know proper ministerial behavior. As an evangelist, I have spoken in churches all across America. I have sometimes been disappointed in what I've seen concerning ministerial ethics. I know pastors who couldn't organize a two-car funeral—much less give honor where honor is due (Romans 13:7). Paul wrote the letter of Philippians and expressed his gratitude. He wasn't their responsibility when they blessed him financially in Corinth, but those at Philippi went the second mile. Ministers today should have good "pulpit manners." One of which is remembering to say "thank you."

In the chapter about Galatians, I mentioned some of my personal disappointments in James, and this is another one of them. Paul brought an offering to the suffering Jewish Christians when he came to Jerusalem. When Paul first met with the apostles, they told him that he should remember the poor:

> And when James, Cephas, and John, who seemed to be pillars, perceived the grace that had been given to me, they gave me and Barnabas the right hand of fellowship, that we should go to the Gentiles, and they to the circumcised. They desired only that we should remember the poor, the very thing which I also was eager to do. (Galatians 2:9–10)

They ask Paul to remember the poor. You might not think much of that request, but there's something pretty big here. The Jewish Christians in Jerusalem were being persecuted. They were being expelled from the temple and synagogues, losing their jobs, and losing their homes. So many of them were going without because of their trust in Christ.

Paul received an offering for the poor in Jerusalem, the very place he was told to "remember the poor."

> For it pleased those from Macedonia and Achaia to make a certain contribution for the poor among the saints who are in Jerusalem. (Romans 15:26)

Paul is receiving funds in the Grecian world for the saints in Jerusalem. He returns to Jerusalem with the funds from Christians in Macedonia and Achaia (provinces of the Roman Empire).

> And when we had come to Jerusalem, the brethren received us gladly. On the following day Paul went in with us to James, and all the elders were present. When he had greeted them, he told in detail those things which God had done among the Gentiles through his ministry. And when they heard it, they glorified the Lord. And they said to him, "You see, brother, how many myriads of Jews there are who have believed, and they are all zealous for the law; but they have been informed about you that you teach all the Jews who are among the Gentiles to forsake Moses, saying that they ought not to circumcise their children nor to walk according to the customs. (Acts 21:17–22)

Scholars often ask, "Where is the thank you from James for the contribution?" Dr. Luke here gives no record of any gratefulness to Paul, but he immediately claims that the Jerusalem Christians are still zealous for the law. James, without a thank you, asks, "What then?"

James gave the decree in Acts 15 that the Gentiles did not have to be circumcised. Had he forgotten his own decree? There was no thank you recorded. Some scholars think the elders at Jerusalem refused the funds, but I don't think that's likely. Even if they did, they still should have said thank you.

From a Roman prison, Paul thanked the church at Philippi. He told them that God would meet all of their needs, according to His riches in glory by Christ Jesus.

The lack of gratitude from many pastors these days astounds me, and many lack even the basics in ministerial ethics. It's OK to let the people know—as Paul did—that their support is appreciated.

Here it is in Paul's own words:

> Indeed, I have all and abound. I am full, having received from Epaphroditus the things sent from you, a sweet-smelling aroma, an acceptable sacrifice, well pleasing to God. And my God shall supply all your need according to His riches in glory by Christ Jesus. (Philippians 4:18–19)

When Epaphroditus was sick unto death, Paul was ill at the same time. Paul certainly thought greatly of this man; he called him his brother, fellow worker, and fellow soldier who ministered to Paul's needs.

Not everyone Paul prayed for was healed. There are times when we as believers go through illnesses and wonder why that happens to good people—and so it was with Epaphroditus. Paul was sick right along with him (Philippians 2:25–30).

I don't know if you've ever noticed, but when Paul wrote the book of Galatians, he wrote it in frustration and holy anger. When he wrote 1 and 2 Corinthians, he held back no punches. He strongly rebuked them. In the letter to the church of Philippi, Paul has nothing but praise for this church.

The only small hint of problems at Philippi was that there were two women who were having some differences. Paul told them to be of the same mind (Philippians 4:2). If that's all the problems a church is having, I would gladly pastor that church! Now that we know a little about this church, let's see what Paul tells the Philippians about God. By now, we know how Paul greets the churches in his letters, he usually begins confirming the Trinity. We would be so disappointed if Paul had not given us this salutation to the church at Philippi. This is our first reference to the Trinity in Philippians.

> Grace to you and peace from God our Father and the Lord Jesus Christ. (Philippians 1:2)

The Trinity in Jesus Receiving His Name and Exaltation

In Philippians 2, Paul is going to tell us that it wasn't Joseph, Mary, or the angels who gave Jesus His name. God will be the one who gives Jesus His name. Paul will also tell us that it was God who exalted Jesus. If a name is "given," there has to be a "giver." The giver is God the Father, and Jesus is the recipient of the name. Christ will be exalted by the Father. Lastly, he says that Jesus is Lord "to" the glory of God the Father.

> Therefore, God also has highly exalted Him and given Him the name, which is above every name, that at the name of Jesus every knee should bow, of those in heaven, and of those on earth, and of those under the earth, and that every tongue should confess that Jesus Christ is Lord, "to" the glory of God the Father. (Philippians 2:9–11)

From these verses, one must ask the following questions:

- Who exalted Jesus?
- Who gave Jesus His name?
- When every tongue confesses that Christ is Lord to whom will the glory be given?

Simple common sense answers these questions, and we only need to read the verses as Paul wrote them. God exalted Christ gave Jesus His name. When every knee bows and every tongue confesses that Jesus is Lord, it will be to the glory of God the Father.

CHAPTER 24

THE TRINITY IN THE BOOK OF COLOSSIANS

If you've been reading along with us through all of Paul's epistles, you know by now what is coming first: the salutation to the church as Colossae (a prison epistle).

Colossians 1

We are expecting the "and" conjunction to be there, will Paul let us down? Let's find out.

> Grace to you and peace from God our Father and the Lord Jesus Christ. (Colossians 1:2)

Paul continues his pattern of greetings by saying that peace comes from God the Father and the Lord Jesus Christ.

The Son of His Love

> Giving thanks to the Father who has qualified us to be partakers of the inheritance of the saints in the light.

> He has delivered us from the power of darkness and conveyed us into the kingdom of the Son of His love. (Colossians 1:12–13)

- The Father qualified us to partake of the inheritance.
- The Father delivered us from the power of darkness.
- The Father conveyed us into the kingdom of the "Son of His love."

If it is God the Father who does all of the above, who then is the Son of his love? If any earthly father on the earth stands next to his son and declares, "This is the son of my love," we know this father is not stating that he is loving himself! Jesus told us that He was this "Son of His love."

> The Father loves the Son, and has given all things into His hand. (John 3:35)

> For the Father loves the Son, and shows Him all things that He Himself does; and He will show Him greater works than these, that you may marvel. (John 5:20)

This next verse will overwhelm you. Would you believe it if I told you that God loves you and me just as He loves Jesus? Get ready to get happy and excited! Jesus Himself says:

> I in them, and You in Me; that they may be made perfect in one, and that the world may know that You have sent Me, and have loved them as You have loved Me! (John 17:23)

If anybody ever wonders how God loves them, the answer is right there. God the Father loves you and me just the same as He loves his own Son! That means we are loved a lot! Jesus said it Himself!

We know who the "Son of His love" is, and the apostle Paul says we have been conveyed into the kingdom "of the Son of His love."

If Jesus is loved by the Father there must be more than one in the Godhead.

Colossians 2

The next verse is too good not to include in this book:

> That their hearts may be encouraged, being knit together in love, and attaining to all riches of the full assurance of understanding, to the knowledge of the mystery of God, "both" of the Father and of Christ. (Colossians 2:2)

Anyone with even a basic knowledge of English understands the word "both." It means "the one as well as the other," "affecting or involving the one and the other, or "two people or things regarded and identified together."

The Holy Spirit guided the hands of Paul as he wrote, using the word "both," and refers to the mystery of God including "both" the Father and Christ.

Colossians 3

> If then you were raised with Christ, seek those things which are above, where Christ is, sitting at the right hand of God. And whatever you do in word or deed, do all in the name of the Lord Jesus, giving thanks to God the Father through Him. (Colossians 3:1, 17)

Here Paul tells the church at Colossae where Christ is currently seated. Many scriptures validate where Jesus sits, both in the Old and New Testaments.

> The Lord said to my Lord, "Sit at My right hand, Till I make Your enemies Your footstool." (Psalm 110:1)

I believe Paul is the writer of Hebrews, I understand there are some debates concerning that.

> But to which of the angels has He ever said: "Sit at My right hand, Till I make Your enemies Your footstool?" (Hebrews 1:13)

> But this Man, after He had offered one sacrifice for sins forever, sat down at the right hand of God (Hebrews 10:12)

> Looking unto Jesus, the author and finisher of our faith, who for the joy that was set before Him endured the cross, despising the shame, and has sat down at the right hand of the throne of God. (Hebrews 12:2)

> This Jesus God has raised up, of which we are all witnesses. Therefore being exalted to the right hand of God, and having received from the Father the promise of the Holy Spirit, He poured out this which you now see and hear. "For David did not ascend into the heavens, but he says himself: 'The Lord said to my Lord, "Sit at My right hand, Till I make Your enemies Your footstool."' (Acts 2:32–35)

> So then, after the Lord had spoken to them, He was received up into heaven, and sat down at the right hand of God. (Mark 16:19)

> Hereafter the Son of Man will sit on the right hand of the power of God. (Luke 22:69)

> But he, being full of the Holy Spirit, gazed into heaven and saw the glory of God, and Jesus standing at the right hand of God, and said, "Look! I see the heavens opened and the Son of Man standing at the right hand of God." (Acts 7:55–56)

> Who is he who condemns? It is Christ who died, and furthermore is also risen, who is even at the right hand of God, who also makes intercession for us. (Romans 8:34)

> Who has gone into heaven and is at the right hand of God, angels and authorities and powers having been made subject to Him. (1 Peter 3:22)

Jesus is at the right hand of the throne of God, and there is a conversation that takes place between the Father and Son. For a conversation to happen, there have to be at least two in the conversation. Someone is speaking, and another is being spoken to.

> The Lord said to my Lord, "Sit at My right hand, Till I make Your enemies Your footstool." (Psalm 110:1)

I love this next verse so much. This is the verse that Jesus used to permanently silence the Pharisees. Jesus reinforces the conversation between the Father and the Son.

> While the Pharisees were gathered together, Jesus asked them, saying, "What do you think about the Christ? Whose Son is He?" They said to Him, "The Son of David." He said to them, "How then does David in the Spirit call Him 'Lord,' saying: The Lord said to my Lord, "Sit at My right hand, Till I make Your enemies Your footstool?" If David then calls Him 'Lord,' how is He his Son?" And no one was able to

> answer Him a word, nor from that day on did anyone dare question Him anymore. (Matthew 22:41–46)

I can't help but laughing at these Pharisees every time I read this, but it's sad that there are many churches today, much like the Pharisees, that deny the Trinity and think their good works will get them to heaven. As Paul said in Romans 1, they profess to be wise, but they have become fools. These ministers, like the Pharisees, hold to their traditions.

Jesus condemned the traditions made by man in Matthew's Gospel:

> "Why do Your disciples transgress the tradition of the elders? For they do not wash their hands when they eat bread." He answered and said to them, "Why do you also transgress the commandment of God because of your tradition?" Thus, you have made the commandment of God of no effect by your tradition. (Matthew 15:2–3, 6)

I feel it important to emphasize that denominations today that deny the Trinity also incorporate into their beliefs the doctrines of man, bringing in rules and regulations and adding to the finished work of Christ.

They cause their followers to believe in their works for salvation. It is nothing more than legalism, claiming their holiness and righteousness is in their works (hairstyles, dress codes, baptisms, formulas for baptisms, belonging only to their churches, etc.).

There are three that bear witness in heaven (plainly stated in scripture as we have seen), not four by claiming Mary the mother of Christ is deity. To verify my above statements, notice that each of these (deniers of the Trinity) I am listing will either deny the Trinity or add works to the finished work of Christ on Calvary. Through their works, they add to the finished work of Christ on Calvary—as if to say the price Jesus paid on Calvary was not enough or that His sacrifice was not sufficient for man's redemption—and claim we must "add" to what Jesus did on the cross by our good deeds.

These beliefs are right there with the Pharisees who pride themselves in their good works. I am speaking of the story Jesus mentioned concerning the Pharisee and publican (tax collector). The Pharisee believed in his good works and said, "God, I thank you I am not as this man." The publican in humbleness wouldn't as much lift his head toward heaven and simply said, "God be merciful to me a sinner." Jesus said it was the publican who left "justified."

With the destination of our eternal souls at stake, this is a matter that we must get right. Are we coming to salvation God's way or in ways which are developed by man? All of us are responsible for the eternal destiny of our souls, and we must get this right. The traditions of man can bring eternal destruction.

It is faith in what Jesus did on Calvary's cross (plus nothing, minus nothing) that brings forgiveness of sins. It is justification by faith! We are saved by believing in the price Jesus paid on Calvary for the forgiveness of our sins.

In these three letters to the churches in Crete, Ephesus, and Galatia, Paul confirmed that it is not by works that reconciles us to God. In these passages, Paul says it's not "we" but "He." He clearly lays it out that it is not anything "we have done," salvation is "not of ourselves," and a person is "not saved by works of the law."

> Not by works of righteousness which we have done, but according to His mercy He saved us, through the washing of regeneration and renewing of the Holy Spirit, whom He poured out on us abundantly through Jesus Christ our Savior, that having been justified by His grace we should become heirs according to the hope of eternal life. (Titus 3:5–7)

Did you see the "Not We but He" in that first line ? It is by His mercy we are washed through the Holy Spirit poured out abundantly through Jesus Christ our Savior and justified by God's grace.

> For by grace you have been saved, through faith, and that not of yourselves; it is the gift of God. For we are His workmanship, created in Christ Jesus "for" good works. (Ephesians 2:8, 10)

The believer isn't saved "by" good works, we were brought to salvation "for" good works. (Note: Some translations use the word "unto" good works). Salvation is God's gift and a gift cannot be earned or paid for, then it would become wages. I trust we also saw that we are not saved "of yourselves." In the past two verses we see the word, "not" twice. In Titus it was "not of works of righteousness which we have done" and in Ephesians we are saved "not of yourselves."

So far we have seen two "nots". Here's a third and fourth.

> Knowing that a man is "not" justified by the works of the law but by faith in Jesus Christ, even we have believed in Christ Jesus, that we might be justified by faith in Christ and "not" by the works of the law; for by the works of the law no flesh shall be justified. (Galatians 2:16)

Four "nots"! Not of works of righteousness, not of ourselves and now a man is "not" justified by the works of the law and that last "not" is repeated twice in that one verse! The last line in that verse is quite powerful, "for by the works of the law NO flesh shall be justified."

My dear friends, is our faith in our own efforts, our own works or in the work that Jesus did on Calvary's cross? Our eternal soul's destiny rests in how we answer this question. Everyone should ask, "Has there been a time in my life when I went to the Father and placed my faith in the sacrifice that Jesus made on the cross?" I can't get to heaven because of my church membership, my giving, my church attendance, my baptism, my being a good person to others and so on. It is not "we" but "He" and us placing our faith in what "He" did when He died for us.

CHAPTER 25

THE TRINITY IN THE BOOK OF 1 AND 2 THESSALONIANS

The church at Thessalonica was founded by Paul on his first missionary journey around AD 50. This church also had false teachers who troubled the saints.

Paul, the founder of the church, teaches them the Trinity. The following scripture is straightforward. It confirms how the Christian receives the Holy Spirit who is "given" to us from God. The word "also" is our key word, which shows that the believer has God and the Holy Spirit:

> Therefore he who rejects this does not reject man, but God, who has "also" given us His Holy Spirit. (1 Thessalonians 4:8)

Paul to the church at Thessalonica says that if a person rejects God, they are "also" rejecting the Holy Spirit.

The Holy Spirit is God and not some "force" from God. In the scriptures the Holy Spirit is called a "He" and is referenced as the "eternal Spirit" in Hebrews. He has always been in eternity past.

He was there in Genesis 1, in the beginning, and we saw Him as He moved on the face of the waters:

> In the beginning God created the heavens and the earth. The earth was without form, and void; and darkness was on the face of the deep. And the Spirit of God was hovering over the face of the waters. (Genesis 1:1–2)

The Holy Spirit is the third person in the Triune Godhead and God's gift to the believer. He dwells within the heart of every believer. The scriptures teach us that if one does not have the Holy Spirit, he is none of His. The Bible tells us that our bodies are the temples of the Holy Spirit, which is in you, whom you have from God (1 Corinthians 6:19).

The Holy Spirit does not live within the heart of the unbeliever, one must first be saved (receive Christ) for the Holy Spirit to live within their heart. Jesus clearly told us that the world (the unsaved) cannot receive the Holy Spirit (John 14:17). The Holy Spirit enters the heart of a person when they are saved. At that very moment when we place our faith in the finished work of Christ on Calvary's cross is when the Holy Spirit comes to live in the heart of a person.

Again,

> Now if anyone does not have the Spirit of Christ he is not His (Romans 8:9).

The scriptures also teach that the Spirit of God that is "within" us will be the same Spirit that raises the believer from the dead when we are resurrected to meet the Lord (Romans 8:11). The point we are making is that the Holy Spirit lives within the heart of every believer and we are His temple where He now dwells. Let's repeat a few verses we have already seen concerning the Holy Spirit.

The Holy Spirit Was Present at the Incarnation of Christ

> Now the birth of Jesus Christ was as follows: After His mother Mary was betrothed to Joseph, before they came together, she was found with child of the Holy Spirit. (Matthew 1:18)

> And the angel answered and said to her, "The Holy Spirit will come upon you, and the power of the Highest will overshadow you; therefore, also, that Holy One who is to be born will be called the Son of God. (Luke 1:35)

The Holy Spirit Anointed Jesus for His Ministry

> He came to Nazareth, where He had been brought up. And as His custom was, He went into the synagogue on the Sabbath day, and stood up to read. And He was handed the book of the prophet Isaiah. And when He had opened the book, He found the place where it was written: "The Spirit of the Lord is upon Me, Because He has anointed Me To preach the Gospel to the poor; He has sent Me to heal the brokenhearted, To proclaim liberty to the captives And recovery of sight to the blind, To set at liberty those who are oppressed; To proclaim the acceptable year of the Lord." Then He closed the book, and gave it back to the attendant and sat down. And the eyes of all who were in the synagogue were fixed on Him. And He began to say to them, "Today this Scripture is fulfilled in your hearing." (Luke 4:16–21)

The Holy Spirit superintended the crucifixion. Please remember that the crucifixion was not an assassination; it was a sacrifice.

> How much more shall the blood of Christ, who through the eternal Spirit offered Himself without spot to God, cleanse your conscience from dead works to serve the living God? (Hebrews 9:14)

Notice that the Holy Spirit is called the "eternal Spirit."

The Holy Spirit Raised Jesus from the Dead

> But if the Spirit of him that raised up Jesus from the dead dwell in you, he that raised up Christ from the dead shall also quicken your mortal bodies by his Spirit that dwelleth in you. (Romans 8:11)

The Holy Spirit was sent from heaven by God the Father, resulting from the prayers of Christ after His ascension.

> And I will pray the Father, and he shall give you "another" Comforter, that he may abide with you forever. (John 14:16)

The Holy Spirit gives the last invitation for salvation in the scripture:

> And the Spirit and the bride say, Come. And let him that heareth say, Come. And let him that is athirst come. And whosoever will, let him take the water of life freely. (Revelation 22:17)

The Holy Spirit is God, the third person in the Godhead. The Holy Spirit was in the beginning in Genesis, and is still giving invitations for salvation in Revelation.

CHAPTER 26

THE TRINITY IN THE BOOK OF 1 TIMOTHY

In Paul's letter to Timothy, we find some of the most wonderful verses related to the Godhead, and the verses even use numbers. Paul tells us there is one God and one mediator between God and man: Christ Jesus.

1 TIMOTHY 2

> For there is one God and one Mediator between God and men, the Man Christ Jesus. (1 Timothy 2:5)

How much clearer could it be? There is one God and one mediator "between God and man." Someone once said it was appropriate that Jesus was crucified and suspended between heaven and earth because He is our "go-between" to bring man to God. For Jesus to be "between" God and man, He could not be God the Father. He is between us and the Father.

The definition of a Mediator is "one who attempts to make people involved in a conflict come to an agreement, a go-between, or one who facilitates discussions between parties in order to negotiate a resolution to a dispute."

Jesus is man's go-between; we have access to God the Father because of Christ our mediator.

1 TIMOTHY 5

In chapter 5, Paul uses our conjunction "and."

> I charge you before God and the Lord Jesus Christ and the elect angels that you observe these things without prejudice, doing nothing with partiality. (1 Timothy 5:21)

Paul concludes 1 Timothy by exhorting them in the presence of God "and" of Christ Jesus.

CHAPTER 27

THE TRINITY IN THE BOOK OF TITUS

Titus has always been one of my favorite books; it's sometimes called one of the pastoral epistles (1 and 2 Timothy and Titus). Paul left a young man who he had called one of his sons in Crete (Titus 1:4). He also called Timothy a son (1 Timothy 1:2). Apparently, Paul had to think quite a lot of these two young preachers. I love that Paul calls both of them his "true sons." This means they were led to Christ by Paul himself.

For such a small book, Titus certainly has a lot of good information. Someone said dynamite comes in little packages. This little book has information about entering the ministry, setting up a church in an orderly fashion, and performing good works for the Lord.

The island of Crete didn't have the best reputation in the world. I can't help but chuckle a little at how Paul said there was a prophet among them who called the Cretans liars, evil beasts, and lazy gluttons. Some translations use the term "slow bellies." In Titus 1:13, Paul told Titus that it was true and that he should rebuke them and to do it sharply. I would have loved to have been a fly on the wall and watched Titus tell them these things. Some have said this might be why Paul left; maybe he didn't want to be around such people.

Paul leaves Crete and tells Titus to stay, and he'd have to stay a good while to do all the things Paul commissioned Titus to do. He had to appoint elders in every city, set the church in order, and get these lying and lazy slow bellies doing good works. Apparently, they eventually got up and went to do good works. Today, there are more than three hundred churches in Crete!

It is believed that Titus was written by Paul around AD 64–67. We know that Paul took Titus to Jerusalem with him, but as a Gentile, Paul refused to circumcise him (Galatians 2:3). It's interesting that Paul did circumcise his other spiritual son Timothy. Timothy had a Jewish mother, but his father was Greek. Paul met Timothy in Lystra (Acts 16:1–3).

In the book of Galatians, Paul made the statement that if we are in Christ, neither circumcision nor uncircumcision avails anything. The only thing that matters is our faith that works through love (Galatians 5:6). If there ever was a clear example of that, it's with Timothy and Titus. Paul circumcised Timothy, but he refused to circumcise Titus—and both were leaders in the churches.

That's a little history about Titus. I wish we knew a lot more about these two young men. Not a lot is said concerning them, but they were special enough to Paul for him to write two letters to Timothy and one to Titus.

Did Paul mention the Trinity in the epistle to Titus?

Titus 3

Paul calls attention to the kindness and love of God and then states that we were saved by His mercy. He explains that we were regenerated and renewed by the Holy Spirit and that the Holy Spirit is poured out on us through Jesus Christ:

> But when the kindness and the love of God our Savior toward man appeared, not by works of righteousness which we have done, but according to His mercy He saved us, through the washing of regeneration and

> renewing of the Holy Spirit, whom He poured out on us abundantly through Jesus Christ our Savior, that having been justified by His grace we should become heirs according to the hope of eternal life. (Titus 3:4–7)

In these four simple verses, Paul addresses all three persons of the Trinity:

- love of God and His mercy
- renewing of the Holy Spirit
- God pouring out the Holy Spirit through Jesus Christ

CHAPTER 28

THE TRINITY IN THE BOOK OF HEBREWS

The book of Hebrews was written to Jews who had received Christ and become partakers of the heavenly gift, but some were now considering returning into the works of Mosaic law.

There has been a tremendous amount of debate concerning the author of Hebrews. I have seen opinions ranging from Apollos to Dr. Luke, and some say it was Barnabas or Silas. It is my opinion that the author is none other than Paul. Why was there no salutation or greeting to these Jewish Christians?

Paul was hated by the Jews in Jerusalem. They had him arrested in the temple, falsely accused him, and even traveled to Caesarea to charge him. Paul was a Jew, but he was looked upon as one who had betrayed his Jewish traditions. We discussed how the Jews in Jerusalem had been spreading rumors that Paul was teaching to abandon the law of Moses. James asked Paul, "What then?"

If Paul had placed his signature on this epistle, it is most likely the Book of Hebrews would have been rejected immediately by the Jews. We do know that whoever wrote Hebrews was in chains in Italy, knew of Timothy's release, and was expecting to see Timothy in the near future. This is proven by the next three verses:

> Greet all those who rule over you, and all the saints. Those from Italy greet you. (Hebrews 13:24)

> For you had compassion on me in my chains, and joyfully accepted the plundering of your goods, knowing that you have a better and an enduring possession for yourselves in heaven. (Hebrews 10:34)

> Know that our brother Timothy has been set free, with whom I shall see you if he comes shortly. (Hebrews 13:23)

That pretty much tells us that Paul wrote the book of Hebrews. Let's pile on more evidence.

Let's take a look at the salutations of Peter's two epistles. This will give us much more clarity on the topic about who wrote Hebrews. Follow along closely because we're about to round the bases. We have to go to first, then second, on to third, and then go home. Let's all stay on our toes!

Peter is going to tell us that Paul wrote a book to the Jews. Not one of Paul's epistles that has his name attached is written to Jews. Peter tells us there's a book out there somewhere that Paul has written to the Jews, but where is this book?

As we step up to the plate, we first establish who Peter is writing to:

> Peter, an apostle of Jesus Christ, To the pilgrims of the Dispersion in Pontus, Galatia, Cappadocia, Asia, and Bithynia, elect according to the foreknowledge of God the Father. (1 Peter 1:1–2)

The Greek is going to help us here. The word *pilgrims* comes from the Greek word *eklektos* ("elect" or "chosen"). The Greek word for *dispersion* is *parepidēmos* ("exiles").

Peter is writing to the "elect" (Jews) who were in "exile" in Pontus, Galatia, Cappadocia, Asia, and Bithynia. The apostle Peter was writing to the Jews in exile in these areas. We're going somewhere with this, and it's about to get good!

Peter tells us he has written a book to the Jews in 2 Peter. Let's establish that he is still writing to the Jews in 2 Peter:

> Simon Peter, a bondservant and apostle of Jesus Christ, To those who have obtained like precious faith with us by the righteousness of our God and Savior Jesus Christ. (2 Peter 1:1)

This time in II Peter, there was no salutation at all other than "to those who have obtained like faith with us." Since this is not addressed to anyone else, 2 Peter is a continuation of 1 Peter, which means he's speaking to Jews of "like faith." In other words, he was speaking to Jews who had received Christ.

Peter is now going to tell us that Paul also has written a book to these Jews. None of the other thirteen epistles of Paul were written to Jews. Here's the magic verse:

> And consider that the longsuffering of our Lord is salvation as also our beloved brother Paul, according to the wisdom given to him, has written to you, as also in all his epistles, speaking in them of these things, in which are some things hard to understand, which untaught and unstable people twist to their own destruction, as they do also the rest of the Scriptures. (2 Peter 3:15–16)

Peter says Paul has written a book to the Jews. When we look at Paul's epistles, which one was written to the Jews?

- Romans was written to Rome.
- Corinthians was written to Corinth.
- Galatians was written to the churches in the Galatian region.

- Ephesians was written to Ephesus and the churches in that region.
- Philippians was written to Philippi in Europe.
- Colossians was written to Colossae.
- Thessalonians was written to Thessalonica.
- Timothy was most likely in Ephesus.
- Titus was on the Cretan Island.
- Philemon was written to Philemon in Colossae.

That's all of them. Where in the world is this book Paul wrote to the Jews? Hebrews comes to our rescue because it was written to Hebrews (Jews). My dear friend, Paul wrote Hebrews.

Even the very nature of the letter of Hebrews corresponds with Paul, the epistle ends the same as all of other Paul's letters: "Grace be with you all. Amen." In all of Paul's other books, he quotes from the Old Testament—and so does Hebrews. Whoever wrote it had to have great knowledge about temple worship, the sacrificial system, and the priesthood.

Hebrews was written in the same era as Paul, but how do we know that? The temple was still up and operational when Hebrews was written. It references the temple, the priests, and the offerings, which means Hebrews had to have been written before the destruction of Jerusalem by Titus in AD 70. Paul being a Pharisee and the son of a Pharisee would know all about the Temple and the sacrificial system in detail! (Acts 23:6)

The key word in Hebrews is the word "better."

- a better county (11:16)
- a better hope (7:19)
- better promises (8:6)
- a better resurrection (11:35)
- better sacrifices (9:23)
- a better substance (10:34)
- better things (6:9; 11:40; 12:24)
- a better covenant (7:22; 8:6)

As always, we try to give the setting of the book. As we dive into this masterpiece, let's see what he tells the Christian Jews about the Trinity.

HEBREWS 2

> How will we escape if we neglect so great a salvation? After it was at first spoken through the Lord, it was confirmed to us by those who heard, God also testifying with them, both by signs and wonders, and by various miracles and by gifts of the Holy Spirit according to His own will. (Hebrews 2:3–4)

There we have it, we see the three persons in the Godhead in the above verses:

- the Lord is addressed
- God "also" testifying
- the Holy Spirit and His gifts are referenced

HEBREWS 3

Paul now calls to attention the faithfulness of Jesus to His heavenly Father who Paul says "appointed Him." Jesus did not appoint Himself to the crucifixion; in Gethsemane, we even saw that Jesus submitted to the will of the Father in going to the cross. The appointment for Christ to go to the cross was made by the Father and not the Son.

The scripture also says that Jesus was faithful to the Father. Being faithful to someone else would require two: the one being faithful and the one being faithful to.

> Therefore, holy brethren, partakers of the heavenly calling, consider the Apostle and High Priest of our

> confession, Christ Jesus, who was faithful to Him who appointed Him, as Moses also was faithful in all His house. (Hebrews 3:1–2)

When it comes to mankind, appointments are not always kept. Some are interrupted, delayed, or even canceled. Jesus however, was faithful to His Father and kept His appointment. I've had people make appointments before, and they never showed up or made excuses. On the cross Jesus showed up for His appointment, and no excuses were made. He was on time for every one of His appointments. He was born on time. He lived on time. He slept on time. He ate on time. He healed on time. He performed miracles on time. He died on time. He was buried on time. He arose on time. He ascended on time and my friends, He's coming back on time!

Who made this appointment for Christ? The scripture is plainly written that it was not Jesus who made this appointment. The verse says that Jesus was faithful "to" the one who appointed Him. This definitely supports the doctrine of the Trinity. To be faithful to someone, there has to be someone who is faithful and someone to whom the faithfulness is given.

If someone who is married is faithful to their spouse, there would have to be two for this to be possible. A person can't marry themselves and be faithful to themselves; there has to be at least two people. This verse is telling us that Jesus was faithful to His Father who made an appointment for Him to go to the cross.

HEBREWS 5

The next verse has been controversial for decades. The controversy has been within the Trinitarians. Regardless of which side one takes in the debate, the verse declares the truth of the Trinity. The way the verse is worded, it cannot be done by a single person. Let's look at the passage first, and then I'll explain the debate.

> So also, Christ did not glorify Himself to become High Priest, but it was He who said to Him: "You are My Son, Today I have begotten You." (Hebrews 5:5)

The controversy is around this question: "Was Jesus always the Son of God—or was there a day in which He was begotten and became the Son of God?" Scholars have debated this for years, and it's a great question. This question can sizzle one's brain.

When did the Father make this statement? When was the *today* in this verse? When was Jesus *begotten*? Was it when the Father made the statement (sometime in eternity past before the foundation of the world) or when He was born in Bethlehem? Was Jesus always the Son of God in eternity past—or was there a day when He became the Son of God?

Regardless of which position one holds, it does not affect one's salvation at all. What does matter is that we do believe He is the Son of God. Whether we believe Jesus was the Son of God always in eternity past, that He became the Son of God when this statement was made, or that He became the Son of God in Bethlehem is not the deciding factor concerning our salvation. We must believe that Jesus is the Son of God:

- John the Baptist believed it (John 1:34).
- Peter believed it (Matthew 16:16).
- John believed it (1 John 5:20).
- Gabriel believed it (Luke 1:35).
- Demons believed it (Luke 4:41; Mark 3:11).
- All of the disciples believed it (Matthew 14:33).
- The Centurion at the cross believed it (Mark 15:39).
- Jesus said He was the Son of God (Mark 14:61–62)
- God the Father proclaimed it (Matthew 3:16; Matthew 17:5).

I certainly believe it beyond any doubt. Regardless of one's position on the debate, it does not matter regarding one's salvation. What does matter is that one must believe that Jesus is the Son of God.

When Paul made the statement in Hebrews, he was quoting David from the Book of Psalms:

> I will declare the decree: "The Lord has said to Me, 'You are My Son. Today I have begotten You.'" (Psalm 2:7)

Staying with the subject of the Trinity, we see that one is speaking to another. In this passage, there is a conversation where the Father is speaking to Christ. This is similar to what we saw when the Father said to the Son, "Sit at my right hand." This is another example of the Father speaking directly to the Son. God also said, "You are my Son. Today I have begotten you." We see the words "I" and "You," and one has been "begotten."

There must be two in this conversation: one doing the speaking and the other being spoken to. This is certain proof of more than one person in the Godhead: "I" have "begotten" "You."

Hebrews 9

Let's continue on to Hebrews 9. Paul tells the Hebrews that the blood of Christ was offered through the eternal Spirit without spot to God. He even returns to the topic of Christ as our mediator. It's difficult to understand how one cannot see the Trinity in this verse. It couldn't be said better than the way Paul (or the Holy Spirit) writes it:

> How much more shall the blood of Christ, who through the eternal Spirit offered Himself without spot to God, cleanse your conscience from dead works to serve the living God? And for this reason He is the Mediator of the new covenant, by means of death, for the redemption of the transgressions under the first covenant, that those who are called may receive the promise of the eternal inheritance. (Hebrews 9:14–15)

The eternal Spirit is through whom Jesus offered Himself. To God is to whom Jesus was offered through the eternal Spirit. Jesus again is called "the Mediator" (capital "M"), let us not forget for there to be a mediator there must be at least three in the equation, two parties with the mediator as the go-between.

HEBREWS 10

In chapter 10, we see all three persons of the Trinity once more. Christ will offer one sacrifice on the cross. He will then sit down at the right hand of the Father, and the Holy Spirit will bear witness within our hearts.

> But this Man, after He had offered one sacrifice for sins forever, sat down at the right hand of God, But the Holy Spirit also witnesses to us; for after He had said before, "This is the covenant that I will make with them after those days, says the Lord: I will put My laws into their hearts, and in their minds I will write them. Their sins and their lawless deeds I will remember no more." Now where there is remission of these, there is no longer an offering for sin. (Hebrews 10:12, 15–18)

Jesus was offered once and has sat down at the right hand of God. The Holy Spirit also bears witness to us. God is the one who said, "This is the covenant I will make" (See Jeremiah 31:31)

We have one more verse in Hebrews where Jesus is called the author and finisher of our faith and has sat down at the right hand of God's throne.

HEBREWS 12

> Looking unto Jesus, the author and finisher of our faith, who for the joy that was set before Him endured the cross, despising the shame, and has sat down at the right hand of the throne of God. (Hebrews 12:2)

If your father was sitting in his favorite chair and you sat down next to him, wouldn't there be two of you? When we were children, we might have even climbed up in the same chair with him.

Jesus told the mother of the sons of Zebedee that only God the Father will make the decision about who sits next to Him in the kingdom. I have such good news; even if we're not the ones who get to sit right next to Him, Jesus made a promise that if we are overcomers, He will allow us to sit down with Him in his throne as He overcame and sits with His Father on His throne!

Journey with me for a minute into the throne room of God. Someday Jesus will motion for us to come. He'll scoot over to make us some room, and we will sit with Him on His throne. Like John, we'll lean our heads on His chest and be that close to Him (Revelation 3:21).

The Trinity seems to be a never-ending topic. This concludes all the writings of Paul from Romans through Hebrews and his references in Acts.

CHAPTER 29

THE TRINITY IN 1 AND 2 PETER

Now let's turn our attention to one whom we all love: the apostle Peter. We all love Peter. He's so much like the rest of us. He is so human, yet he was a "water walker." While the other eleven didn't even attempt to get out of the boat it was Peter who took that step of faith. When Peter began to sink Jesus took him by the hand and kept him from going under. I also believe that Peter walked back to the boat as well.

Peter was the orator of the early church. He was sometimes valiant, and every once in a while, he was victorious. When Jesus told him, "Follow me, and I will make you fishers of men," he dropped his nets, left his occupation, and forsook all to follow Christ.

Everyone enjoys talking about him sinking, but until we can duplicate his accomplishments, we shouldn't criticize his defeats. I also want to remind us that he didn't sink! There were eleven others in the boat who never even attempted to get out. I can see him with his arm around the mast—his beard anointed with the foam of the sea—and thinking it would be safer on the waves during a storm and being close to Jesus than staying in the boat. He cuffs his hands over his mouth and cries, "Lord if it is you, bid me come to you." Jesus said, "Come." Peter pushes the boat out from under his feet and "walked on the water." Up to this point, Peter had been doing everything he could on the raging sea to stay in the boat, but now he was ready to leave the boat and go to Jesus.

I bet his brother Andrew said, "Peter, I've seen you do some ridiculous things, but this exceeds them all." Thomas, known for his doubting, probably said, "Peter, no one has ever done this—and here you are trying to make history."

In the scriptures Jesus never discouraged anyone's faith.

I love a daring man! When Jesus said, "Come," my friends I would have wanted more than that. I would have probably asked, "How?"

But Peter steps out and walks on the water.

Andrew probably said, "Watch out, Peter. Here comes a big one!" When a courageous man takes a big step of faith, the deacons and church members usually say, "Watch out for the big one. There's waves out there that can take us under."

Yes, when he put his eyes on his circumstances and began to sink, and Peter cried out, "Lord, save me." This is the shortest prayer recorded in the Bible, it is even shorter than that of the dying thief who prayed nine words: "Lord, remember me when you enter into your kingdom." It is shorter than the publican's prayer of seven words: "God, be merciful to me a sinner." If he had to pray a long prayer for Jesus to rescue him, he would have drowned for sure! In emergencies, I'm so glad we can cry out, "Lord, save me!" His hand is always ready to catch us and lift us back up. Peter walked back to the boat!

On the Mount of Transfiguration, Peter did get a little too excited about entering a building program. He wanted to stay on that mountain forever. Like many of us, when we're basking in the Lord's presence, we want to stay there and never leave. But there are others in need at the foot of the mountain. Peter bit off more than he could chew, and God had to correct him—but I love a man with zeal more than those who attempt to do nothing.

On the Day of Pentecost, Peter was preaching the inaugural message on the birthday of the church. Peter—who once denied Jesus before a damsel—was preaching Jesus to a hostile and unbelieving crowd, and three thousand people walked the isle to accept Christ.

In Acts 3, Peter and John were going to the temple at three o'clock in the afternoon. A lame man was at the gate called Beautiful. Peter said, "I'm a preacher who is more broke than Moses's Ten Commandments. I don't have any silver or gold, but what I do have I give unto you." Peter took this man by the hand and lifted him to his feet! On the sea Jesus took Peter by the hand and lifted him to his feet, now Peter is taking a man by the hand and getting him up on his feet!

Everyone was hearing what God was doing through Peter. One day the word got out that Peter was going to take his morning stroll. People brought the sick, the lame, the blind, and the deaf. They were leaning on their canes as they lined up on the west side of the street. They had faith that they would be made whole if even the shadow of Peter touched them.

Peter walks to the end of the street, turns, and looks over his shoulder. Canes are hurling in the air, and beds are being picked up. The lame are walking, the blind are seeing, and the deaf are hearing. This is Peter! This man knows about God, let's see what he will tell us about the Trinity.

We have already heard Peter's declaration: "Thou art the Christ the Son of the Living God." Jesus told Peter that flesh and blood had not revealed it unto him but the Father of Christ who was in heaven, which shows two members of the Trinity: Christ, the Son of the Living God on earth, and the Father of Jesus in heaven.

In Acts, Jesus gave his great sermon on the day of Pentecost and said that God has raised Jesus from the dead.

1 Peter 1

> Peter, an apostle of Jesus Christ, To the pilgrims of the Dispersion in Pontus, Galatia, Cappadocia, Asia, and Bithynia, elect according to the foreknowledge of God the Father, in sanctification of the Spirit, for

> obedience and sprinkling of the blood of Jesus Christ: Grace to you and peace be multiplied. (1 Peter 1:1–2)

Peter wastes no time; in the first two verses, he's addressing the Trinity. First, he is speaking of the foreknowledge of God, second, the sanctification of the Spirit, and lastly, the blood of Jesus Christ. That's the Trinity! Next, Peter will give us the Trinity in one single verse:

> For Christ also suffered once for sins, the just for the unjust, that He might bring us to God, being put to death in the flesh but made alive by the Spirit, who has gone into heaven and is at the right hand of God, angels and authorities and powers having been made subject to Him. (1 Peter 3:18, 22)

Peter embeds the three persons of the Godhead in a single verse. He tells us that Jesus suffered to bring us to God. Peter also shows us who raised Jesus from the dead, saying Jesus was "made alive by the Spirit."

In verse 22, Peter tells us where Jesus is today. He has gone into heaven and is now at the right hand of God with all things being made subject to Him.

Next, Peter uses another one of our key words: "through." Even though we've seen many verses using this key word, we see Peter doing the same:

> If anyone speaks, let him speak as the oracles of God. If anyone ministers, let him do it as with the ability which God supplies, that in all things God may be glorified through Jesus Christ, to whom belong the glory and the dominion forever and ever. Amen. (1 Peter 4:11)

How is God glorified? Through Jesus Christ.

People sometimes ask how we have access to the grace of God, and here's the answer. We see another key word: "by." God calls us into His grace "by" Christ Jesus and what He did on the cross:

> But may the God of all grace, who called us to His eternal glory by Christ Jesus, after you have suffered a while, perfect, establish, strengthen, and settle you. (1 Peter 5:10)

Peter next recalls his experience on the Mount of Transfiguration, which many believe to be Mount Tabor. Peter spoke out of order, and God the Father—from a thick cloud—had to correct him.

If there's any verse in the Word of God that teaches us that no matter how great a man of God may be, our focus should always be to Christ and Christ alone, this is the verse. Elijah came down from heaven, Moses came up from paradise (the heart of the earth), and they met in the middle on the Mount of Transfiguration.

Peter said, "Lord let us build three tabernacles: one for Moses, one for Elijah, and one for You." God would do the speaking to correct Peter.

I find it amazing that the Holy Spirit had the writers of the Bible write about their own failures. Moses wrote about how he murdered a man and ran from the will of God and then smote the rock and was denied access to Canaan. Jonah had to write about his voyage to Tarsus. Jeremiah wrote about how he wanted to quit the ministry and never again make mention of the Lord's name. Isaiah told us he was a man of unclean lips. In Revelation, John wrote how he bowed before a man and was corrected and was told to stand up. David wrote Psalm 51, which is a reminder forever of his failure with Bathsheba. If the Bible was written by man, these men would probably have left all of this out of their books! You don't see many authors today writing about how they dropped the ball.

Luke and Mark record the story of how Jesus healed the woman with the issue of blood when she reached out and touched the hem of his garment. Mark said that she suffered at the hands of the physicians, but Luke wouldn't say that:

> Mark wrote:
>
> > Now a certain woman had a flow of blood for twelve years, and had suffered many things from many physicians. She had spent all that she had and was no better, but rather grew worse. (Mark 5:25–26)
>
> Dr. Luke wrote:
>
> > Now a woman, having a flow of blood for twelve years, who had spent all her livelihood on physicians and could not be healed by any, came from behind and touched the border of His garment. And immediately her flow of blood stopped. (Luke 8:43–48)

Luke was a doctor, and he wasn't about to say she suffered at the hands of the physicians! I find that kind of humorous. God did use the writers' own personalities when they wrote the Bible.

The holy men of God spoke as they were moved by the Holy Spirit. These men were the pens that God used to write the scriptures, and the Holy Spirit was the ink that filled those pens as they wrote!

> For He received from God the Father honor and glory when such a voice came "to" Him from the Excellent Glory: "This is My beloved Son, in whom I am well pleased." And we heard this voice which came from heaven when we were with Him on the holy mountain. (2 Peter 1:17–18)

Peter would never forget that day. Christ is on the mountain as the voice comes from the cloud. The honor and glory of Christ were "received from" God, and the voice came "to" Jesus. If we receive something or are speaking "to" someone, there must be at least two persons.

Whose voice did they hear? It certainly was not the voice of Jesus. If it wasn't Jesus making this statement, then who was it? It was none other than the Father who had spoken from the cloud—just like He did at the Lord's baptism when the Father spoke from heaven. This certainly gives weight to the doctrine of the Trinity.

CHAPTER 30

THE TRINITY IN 1 AND 2 JOHN

As we said before, if anyone would have known the Lord the best, it would have been John. He was closer to Jesus than any of the other disciples.

Some of the most magnificent verses relating to the Trinity come to surface as we journey through 1 and 2 John. Two of our key words are "and" and "with." John, in this next verse, gives us three "withs."

First, John says that Christ (here called the Word of life and eternal life) was "with" the Father. Second, John says that you and I may have fellowship "with" the Father and "with" the Son. Jesus has promised us that He will be with us always—even to the end of the age. We have fellowship with Him.

I once preached a sermon on "Bible Ships." The points were sonship, godship, stewardship, etc. My favorite was fellowship:

> But if we walk in the light as He is in the light, we have fellowship with one another, and the blood of Jesus Christ His Son cleanses us from all sin. (1 John 1:7)

Now, I've visited churches where I thought I was the "fellow they wanted to ship!" Jesus will never set sail to leave us or send us away

(John 6:37). If you go to your concordance, you will see that the phrase "cast out" is used fifty times in scripture, but when it comes to those who have believed in Him, He has promised to never cast us out. In other words, we have eternal fellowship with Him.

When we rise to meet the Lord in the air the Bible says, "and so shall we ever be with the Lord." My friend, that is eternal fellowship. There will never be a time in all of eternity future that we will not be in His presence. However, the scripture does not say that our fellowship is only with Jesus; it is also with the Father! We see that in verse 3 of the next passage:

> That which was from the beginning, which we have heard, which we have seen with our eyes, which we have looked upon, and our hands have handled, concerning the Word of life— the life was manifested, and we have seen, and bear witness, and declare to you that eternal life which was with the Father and was manifested to us that which we have seen and heard we declare to you, that you also may have fellowship with us; and truly our fellowship is with the Father and with His Son Jesus Christ. (1 John 1:1–3)

Yes, we have fellowship with both the Father and the Son. Jesus taught us the proper way to pray after He ascended. In John 16:23, Jesus said that we will no longer ask Him about anything. He goes on to say that what we ask "the Father" in His name, He will give to us. We can now ask the Father for ourselves because we have "fellowship" with the Father. We no longer need an earthly priest to go into the holy of holies on our behalf. The veil has been rent, and we can go to the Father directly! That's fellowship!

This was special for the apostle John. He fellowshipped closer to Jesus than any of the others. John was found leaning on the bosom of Jesus, and he was the only disciple who followed Jesus all the way to the cross. When Jesus told the disciples that one of the twelve would betray Him, Peter looked over at John and said, "John, I can't ask Him—you ask Him." That's something that many people just read over and never notice. John wrote about this himself in John 13:21–25.

Peter didn't feel close enough to Jesus to ask Him who it was that would betray Him, but John was leaning on the chest of Jesus. He was close to Him, he had the best seat at the table. If any apostle would want to write about fellowship with Jesus, it would be John. John, in that wonderful passage above, says we have fellowship with both the Father and the Son. How wonderful is that?

We don't pray directly to Jesus now; we pray to the Father. Jesus told us we are to no longer ask Him anything but to make our request to the Father. If we don't ask Jesus for anything, how do we have fellowship with Him? Folks, we can love Him, we can thank Him, and we can worship Him.

Fellowship with Jesus is more than just asking for things. I fear that's the sum total of many Christians' prayer lives. I personally have made it a habit—when I go to God in prayer—to never ask anything without first giving thanks and worshipping Him and telling Him all that He means to me.

In our earthly relationships, it would not make us happy if those who called us their friends or family only spoke to us to ask us for things. It would be an unhealthy marriage if one's spouse was always asking for something without saying, "I love you." One would not be happy if they were always on the giving end and never hearing any "thank you's."

There would be something wrong if the person one was engaged to never wanted to spend time with them. Paul said that the church has been "betrothed to Christ," which means we've been promised to Him, engaged to Him, and espoused to Him. Jesus wants the fellowship of those who are promised to Him and will be presented unto Him one day as His bride at the Marriage Supper of the Lamb.

> God is faithful, by whom you were called into the fellowship of His Son, Jesus Christ our Lord. (1 Corinthians 1:9)

I've heard people say, "I wish I knew what God has called me to do." Well, that verse just told us our "calling." God has "called" us into fellowship with His Son. Are we fulfilling that calling? By the way, did you see the Trinity in that verse? God is faithful and called us into fellowship with Christ.

We have seen the scripture tell us we have fellowship with God and fellowship with the Son, but does the Bible mention fellowship with the Holy Spirit?

> Therefore, if there is any consolation in Christ, if any comfort of love, if any "fellowship of the Spirit", if any affection and mercy, fulfill my joy by being like-minded, having the same love, being of one accord, of one mind. (Philippians 2:1)

Yes, we have fellowship with the Trinity! We are in fellowship with our Holy, Triune, Thrice Holy God!

We are like Isaiah when he saw the Lord high and lifted up and his robe filling the temple. He saw the seraphim crying, "Holy, holy, holy!" Also, along with the living creatures of Revelation chapter four we too can cry aloud our three "Holy's!" "Holy, holy, holy is the Lord God, the Almighty, who was and who is and who is to come."

Holy is the Father, Holy is the Son, and Holy is the Holy Spirit!

The next passage we'll see makes it practically impossible to deny the Trinity. John tells us that if we sin, we have an advocate. The Greek word for *advocate* is *parakletos*, which means "one who pleads another's cause or helps another by defending them or comforting them."

It is the same word that Jesus used to refer to the Holy Spirit three times in John 14:16, John 15:26, and John 16:7. Jesus said that when He ascended, He would pray to the Father to send us "another Helper" or another "parakletos."

John uses the same word in 1 John 2:1 in regard to comforting the believer when they sin. If we sin, we have a parakletos who will plead our cause and be a helper and comforter.

John tells us who our parakletos is. In the Gospel of John, Jesus used the term for the relationship with the Holy Spirit who would come after Jesus ascends. However, in 1 John, our parakletos when we sin is Jesus Christ rather than the Holy Spirit.

We know who our parakletos is when we sin, and we also know the where He is. John tells us that our advocate is "with" the Father. The Holy Spirit today dwells with us, we are the temple of the Holy Spirit, and Jesus said the Holy Spirit would abide with us forever.

Our parakletos that is with us is the Holy Spirit, and the parakletos we need when we sin is "with the Father!" It was not the Holy Spirit who died on the cross to take care of the sin problem; in fact, we saw in Hebrews that Jesus was offered on the cross through the eternal Spirit.

Jesus paid the price for the sin problem, and Jesus is now at the Father's right hand. When we sin, he is our advocate. He pleads our case to the Father. Jesus is the parakletos for the sin problem. The Holy Spirit is our parakletos (helper, comforter) when we need power for service (Acts 1:8).

> My little children, these things I write to you, so that you may not sin. And if anyone sins, we have an Advocate with the Father, Jesus Christ the righteous. (1 John 2:1)

That is quite comforting. In the next verse, John gives an alarming warning to anyone who denies the Father and the Son. He calls such an individual an "Antichrist." The next verse is not for comfort; it is for caution.

When the Father and Son are referenced, they are referenced using the words "either" and the word "also." We also have our conjunction "and" again twice.

This is a stern warning that anyone who denies the Father and the Son is antichrist.

> Who is a liar, but he who denies that Jesus is the Christ? He is antichrist who denies the Father and the Son. Whoever denies the Son does not have the Father either; he who acknowledges the Son has the Father also. Therefore, let that abide in you which you heard from the beginning. If what you heard from the beginning abides in you, you also will abide in the Son and in the Father. (1 John 2:22, 24)

In chapter 3, John tells us how we know that "Christ abides in us and us in Him." He tells us that it is by "the Spirit" that is "given" to us that we have this assurance.

In this passage, God has given us the commandment to believe in his Son. John says that if we keep His commandments, we abide in Him and He in us. How do we know for sure that Jesus abides in us? By the Spirit who He has given us. God is the one giving the commandment to believe in His Son, and we know we are in Christ by the Holy Spirit given to us by God. Here's the verse.

> And this is His commandment: that we should believe on the name of His Son Jesus Christ and love one another, as He gave us commandment. Now he who keeps His commandments abides in Him, and He in him. And by this we know that He abides in us, by the Spirit whom He has given us. (1 John 3:23–24)

In chapter 4, the Trinity is completely evident. All one must do is read these verses as written by John. As you read note the little word "of." All three persons of the Godhead are referenced using that little word "of":

- Spirit of God
- Jesus Christ come in the flesh is of God
- The love of God

John won't be finished either, After using the word "of" five times, he will then use the word "sent" three times, removing all doubt that Christ was sent by the Father.

He also will tell us that we receive the Love of God "through" Christ and that the Holy Spirit has been "given" to us.

> By this you know the Spirit of God: Every spirit that confesses that Jesus Christ has come in the flesh is of God. In this the love of God was manifested toward us, that God has sent His only begotten Son into the world, that we might live through Him. In this is love, not that we loved God, but that He loved us and sent His Son to be the propitiation for our sins. By this we know that we abide in Him, and He in us, because He has given us of His Spirit. And we have seen and testify that the Father has sent the Son as Savior of the world. Whoever confesses that Jesus is the Son of God, God abides in him, and he in God. (1 John 4:2, 9–10, 13–15)

In the next passage, anyone who can count to three should be able to understand what John is telling us. John will give us the number of persons in the Godhead and then explain that the word "one" means one in "agreement." John continues speaking of God the Father, the Son, and the Holy Spirit.

> Whoever believes that Jesus is the Christ is born of God, and everyone who loves Him who begot also loves him who is begotten of Him. This is He who came by water and blood—Jesus Christ; not only by water, but by water and blood. And it is the Spirit who bears witness, because the Spirit is truth. For there are three that bear witness in heaven: the Father, the Word, and the Holy Spirit; and these three are one. And there are three that bear witness on earth: the

> Spirit, the water, and the blood; and these three agree as one. If we receive the witness of men, the witness of God is greater; for this is the witness of God which He has testified of His Son. He who believes in the Son of God has the witness in himself; he who does not believe God has made Him a liar, because he has not believed the testimony that God has given of His Son. And this is the testimony: that God has given us eternal life, and this life is in His Son. He who has the Son has life; he who does not have the Son of God does not have life. (1 John 5:1, 5–12)

Let's talk a little about agreements. John tells us there are three that bear witness in the earth—and these three agree as one. What does that mean?

For there to be an "agreement," there has to be at least two. When anyone is in agreement, they must have another to agree with. Jesus used numbers when He spoke about agreements. In fact, He did it more than once. Consider these verses:

> Again I say to you that if two of you agree on earth concerning anything that they ask, it will be done for them by My Father in heaven. (Matthew 18:19)

> Agree with your adversary quickly, while you are on the way with him. (Matthew 5:25)

> Did you not agree with me for a denarius? (Matthew 20:13)

In every instance where Jesus spoke of agreements, there were always multiples in His teachings. The same is true in the Old Testament:

> Can two walk together, unless they are agreed? (Amos 3:3)

In Numbers 30, the word "agreement" is found ten times. In every case, there were always two in the agreements. Here's one example, but I would encourage you to read the verses on your own:

> If a man makes a vow to the Lord, or swears an oath to bind himself by some agreement, he shall not break his word. (Numbers 30:2)

I know this is simple common sense—and everyone understands this—but we prove all things by scripture.

In this chapter, there are agreements between:

- a man and the Lord
- a woman and the Lord

In these verses, we also learn more about agreements:

- A father could overrule an agreement made by his daughter.
- A husband could overrule an agreement made by his wife.
- An agreement is binding, however God made certain provisions for agreements to be made void.
- Agreements can be confirmed.

For there to be an agreement, there must be a minimum of two persons.

When John said in 1 John 5:8 that there are three that bear witness on earth—the Father, the Son, and the Holy Spirit—this is an example of three being in agreement. They are "one" in what they agreed upon.

What did they agree upon? Do we know when the agreement was made? This will bless us. Before the world was founded—sometime in eternity past—the Father, Son, and Holy Spirit agreed that Jesus would come and die on Calvary's cross for the forgiveness of our sins and to reconcile fallen man back to God.

> He indeed was foreordained before the foundation of the world. (1 Peter 1:20)

In the corporate world, when two people or two corporations decide to work together on a project, they draw up a professional agreement. It's a contract. This agreement is not valid until all parties sign it. There is no need for an agreement if one person is working alone; there must be at least two people.

Before the foundation of the word, all persons of the Trinity "signed off" on this decision that Jesus would come and die for our sins. Before the world was ever created they all "agreed as one."

In every instance of Old Testament agreements, there was always more than one party in the agreements:

- Jacob had an agreement with Laban.
- Pharaoh agreed with Moses to let Israel leave Egypt.
- Esther agreed with Mordecai to help the Jews.
- Israel entered an agreement with God at Mount Sinai.
- Israel and the Antichrist will sign a seven-year agreement.

Agreements require multiple parties. The scripture is plain; there are three who bear witness in the earth, and these three "agree in one."

This concludes the Trinity in 1 John. I sometimes shake my head at the thought that anyone could deny the Trinity.

The next verse is in II John, the Triune God just jumps right from the pages. John uses the word "both" to call attention to the persons of the Father and Son:

> Grace, mercy, and peace will be with you from God the Father and from the Lord Jesus Christ, the Son of the Father, in truth and love. Whoever transgresses and does not abide in the doctrine of Christ does not have God. He who abides in the doctrine of Christ has "both" the Father and the Son. (2 John 1:3, 9)

My friend, are you abiding in the doctrine of Christ? If the answer to that question is no, John says those who do not abide do not have God. If we abide, we have "both" the Father and the Son.

What a wonderful collection of verses we have seen in this chapter. They were penned by the disciple who knew Jesus better than any of the other eleven. If anyone knew Christ the best of all of the disciples, it would have to be John. At the Last Supper, he was leaning on the bosom of Jesus. Of the twelve, he was "that disciple whom Jesus loved." Of the twelve, Jesus had an inner circle of three—Peter, James, and John—and of those three, the one who knew Him the best was John.

When a new convert comes to salvation, they sometimes ask, "Where should I start reading in my Bible?" I always recommend beginning with John.

CHAPTER 31

THE TRINITY IN THE BOOK OF JUDE

The book of Jude only has one chapter, but Jude seizes the opportunity to mention the Trinity.

There has been some controversy about which Jude wrote this epistle. In verse 1, Jude claims authorship and states that he is the brother of James. Which James? There are at least three men named James in the New Testament—and three who are named Judas. Which James and which Judas?

Some commentaries state that this Jude is "not to be confused with the Jude who is the half brother of Jesus." Others claim that the writer is the half-brother of Christ. Those who take the position that the writer is not the half-brother of Jesus believe him to be "Judas, also known as Thaddaeus," who was one of the twelve.

In Jude 1, the author claims no blood relationship with Jesus. Instead, he references himself as "Jude, a bondservant of Jesus and the brother of James."

> Jude, a bondservant of Jesus Christ, and brother of James. (Jude 1:1)

Those who hold this view provide this as their evidence that he certainly would claim that he was "in the family."

However, James does the same. The book of James begins with "James, a servant of God and of the Lord Jesus Christ."

> James, a bondservant of God and of the Lord Jesus Christ. (James 1:1)

Why didn't James or Jude claim blood relation with Jesus? The answer is actually quite obvious. If they had claimed that their writings were "holy written" based on family status, people would question whether their books were inspired. Neither James nor Jude would take that risk. Therefore, they claim their authorship and identify themselves as "servants of God" and "bondservants of Jesus Christ."

I believe the writers of James and Jude were the half-brothers of the Lord. The brothers of Jesus are recorded in Matthew's Gospel:

> Is this not the carpenter's son? Is not His mother called Mary? And His brothers James, Joseph, Simon, and Judas? (Matthew 13:55)

There are two others by the name of Judas, and both were among the twelve disciples Jesus chose. One was Judas Iscariot. When he is mentioned in scripture, it usually distinguishes him with terms such as "Judas who also betrayed him" (see Matthew 10:4; Mark 3:19; Luke 6:16; John 6:71; John 12:4; John 13:2; John 14:22). In these verses, we see that all the Gospel writers made sure Judas Iscariot was distinguished from the other Judas.

The second Judas of the twelve is the one who asked this question in John's Gospel:

> Judas (not Iscariot) said to Him, "Lord, how is it that You will manifest Yourself to us, and not to the world?" (John 14:22)

The way the scripture speaks of him simply says that he is not Judas Iscariot who betrayed Jesus, and nowhere is it recorded that this Judas has a brother named James.

After eliminating Judas Iscariot and the other Judas of the twelve disciples, we conclude that the writer of Jude is the half-brother of Christ. Jude, the half-brother of Jesus, would have grown up hearing his mother tell the story of the virgin birth. He would have heard that Jesus was conceived of the Holy Spirit and that Jesus was the Son of God. In other words, Jude would have been aware of the Trinity:

> Jude, a bondservant of Jesus Christ, and brother of James, to those who are called, sanctified by God the Father, and preserved in Jesus Christ. But you, beloved, building yourselves up on your most holy faith, praying in the Holy Spirit, keep yourselves in the love of God, looking for the mercy of our Lord Jesus Christ unto eternal life. (Jude 1:1, 20–21)

How glorious are these verses? Jude states the following:

- We are sanctified by God the Father.
- We are preserved in Jesus Christ.
- We should pray in the Holy Spirit.
- We should keep ourselves in the love of God.
- We should look for the mercy of the Lord Jesus Christ.

This is a gold mine of invaluable nuggets; it's like diving into the sea and bringing up pearls. Jude doesn't even make us have to dig! In two simple verses (20 and 21), he delivers the Triune God, not missing one person, and he calls them all by name: God the Father, the Lord Jesus Christ, and the Holy Spirit.

In the book of Jude, he was telling us to guard against apostasy. He even told us how they would show up. He said they would "creep in."

> For certain men have crept in unnoticed, who long ago were marked out for this condemnation, ungodly men, who turn the grace of our God into lewdness and deny the only Lord God "and" our Lord Jesus Christ. (Jude 1:4)

To put it bluntly, Jude says they are creeps! Did you notice our conjunction *and*? Jude says they deny the only Lord God "and" our Lord Jesus Christ.

Concerning these who would creep in, Jude tells us in verse 3 that we should "contend for the faith which had be delivered to the saints."

Jude concludes the book in verses 24 and 25:

> Now to Him who is able to keep you from stumbling, And to present you faultless before the presence of His glory with exceeding joy. (Jude 1:24–25)

Who will Jesus present us to? I hope you didn't just skim over that. Jesus is going to present us. To whom is Jesus going to present us? Matthew records the answer from the words of Jesus Himself:

> Therefore, everyone who confesses Me before people, I will also confess him before My Father who is in heaven. (Matthew 10:32)

And for those who believe Jesus will only confess us before angels, we read again the words of Jesus Himself, written by John:

> The one who overcomes will be clothed the same way, in white garments; and I will not erase his name from the book of life, and I will confess his name before My Father and before His angels. (Revelation 3:5)

The little book of Jude also records the prophecy of Enoch. This prophecy is not found anywhere in the Old Testament, but the Holy Spirit told Jude that Enoch prophesied this:

> Now Enoch, the seventh from Adam, prophesied about these men also, saying, "Behold, the Lord comes with ten thousands of His saints." (Jude 1:14)

It is appropriate that the book of Jude ends with the prophecy of Enoch regarding the Second Coming of Christ since it comes right before the book of Revelation!

As I write these words, my heart swells up with joy, and we will end this chapter with the words of Jude himself:

> To God our Savior, Who alone is wise, Be glory and majesty, dominion and power, both now and forever. Amen. (Jude 1:25)

CHAPTER 32

THE TRINITY IN THE BOOK OF REVELATION

John the Beloved wrote the book of Revelation on Patmos, a Greek island in the Aegean Sea. John had been placed there by Domitian. Revelation was written in AD 96. Just as Genesis is known as the book of beginnings, Revelation is known as the book of conclusions. Genesis tells us how things began, and Revelation tells us how things will end.

The doctrine of the Trinity will thread its way through the entirety of this book, beginning in Revelation 1 and ending in Revelation 22 (the last chapter).

Revelation 1

Let's examine John's record of the Trinity. Immediately upon opening the book of Revelation, the Trinity is already obvious with an acknowledgment of all three persons of the Godhead:

> John, to the seven churches which are in Asia: Grace to you and peace from Him who is and who was and

> who is to come, and from the seven Spirits who are before His throne, and from Jesus Christ, the faithful witness, the firstborn from the dead, and the ruler over the kings of the earth. To Him who loved us and washed us from our sins in His own blood, and has made us kings and priests to His God and Father, to Him be glory and dominion forever and ever. Amen. (Revelation 1:4–6)

Revelation opens with a reference to God the Father, Jesus Christ, and the seven Spirits of God.

Seven, in scripture, is the number of completeness and perfection. We all know there are not seven Holy Spirits. The scripture makes that clear saying there is only one Spirit:

> Or by one Spirit are we all baptized into one body, whether we be Jews or Gentiles, whether we be bond or free; and have been all made to drink into one Spirit. (1 Corinthians 12:13)

The number seven here refers to the completeness, fullness, and perfection of the Holy Spirit. Some believe the seven Spirits represent the seven attributes or characteristics of the Holy Spirit, and they usually refer to the following scripture:

> And the spirit of the Lord shall rest upon him, the spirit of wisdom and understanding, the spirit of counsel and might, the spirit of knowledge and of the fear of the Lord. (Isaiah 11:1–2)

Some believe this scripture is a definite list of the Holy Spirit's attributes (many commentaries accept these as the attributes of the seven Spirits). Others believe they are examples of "some" of the many characteristics of the Holy Spirit. We will leave that to the interpretation of the reader.

For certain, we know there is only one Holy Spirit, and in Revelation 1:4, He is seen before the throne of God.

The passage says, "And from Jesus Christ who has made us priests unto God." If Jesus makes us priests unto God, doesn't that imply more than one person in the Godhead?

As we can see, the book of Revelation opens with the doctrine of the Trinity:

> I, John, both your brother and companion in the tribulation and kingdom and patience of Jesus Christ, was on the island that is called Patmos for the word of God And for the testimony of Jesus Christ. I was in the Spirit on the Lord's Day, and I heard behind me a loud voice, as of a trumpet. (Revelation 1:9–10)

John reinforces the Trinity by calling attention to the patience and testimony of Jesus, the Word of God, and the Spirit (capital "S") in which John was in on the Lord's Day.

All Bible translations—both word-for-word translations and thought-for-thought translations—spell Spirit here with a capital "S" which shows "Spirit" to be one of the names of the Holy Spirit.

The Hebrew Bible even translates Spirit as "*Ruach*," which is referred to more than one hundred times in the Hebrew scriptures as the "Spirit of God," the "Spirit of the Lord (YHWH)," and simply "the Spirit."

The Greek word here is *Pneuma,* which refers to the Holy Spirit 328 times in scripture.

Revelation 2

The Church of Thyatira (The Sinful Church)

In chapter 2, beginning with the church at Thyatira, we see reference to Jesus speaking with the word "I," God the Father referred to as

"My Father," and the Holy Spirit acknowledged with "Hear what the Spirit says to the churches."

> As I also have received from My Father; and I will give him the morning star. "He who has an ear, let him hear what the Spirit says to the churches."' (Revelation 2:27–29)

With the Trinity being evident in that verse, let's go to the message to the church at Sardis. In chapter 3, the message of the Trinity is "hammered" into this church:

The Seven Spirits of God (the Holy Spirit)

- Jesus promises to confess the overcomers name to the Lord's Father.
- We will be told again to hear what "the Spirit" says.
- Jesus will promise to make the overcomer a pillar in the temple of the Lord's God and to write on him "the name of My God."
- With Jesus speaking, we see a reference to the City of God.
- We are told the New Jerusalem will come down from God.
- Jesus promises to write my new name.

Revelation 3

The Church of Sardis (The Lifeless Church)

> And to the angel of the church in Sardis write, "These things says He who has the seven Spirits of God and the seven stars: 'I know your works, that you have a name that you are alive, but you are dead. Be watchful, and strengthen the things which remain, that are ready to die, for I have not found your works perfect before God. He who overcomes shall be clothed in white

> garments, and I will not blot out his name from the book of Life; but I will confess his name before My Father and before His angels. He who has an ear, let him hear what the Spirit says to the churches. He who overcomes, I will make him a pillar in the temple of My God, and he shall go out no more. I will write on him the name of My God and the name of the city of My God, the New Jerusalem, which comes down out of heaven from My God. And I will write on him My new name. He who has an ear, let him hear what the Spirit says to the churches.'" (Revelation 3:1–2, 5–6, 12–13)

Jesus uses the word "I," and He calls the Father "My Father" and "My God." We are told to hear what "the Spirit says."

Laodicea (The Lukewarm Church)

Although this church is not on fire for God, (Jesus said they were "lukewarm)," they will be given one of the most precious promises a believer can ever have. They will sit with Jesus on His throne in the same way He overcame and sat down with His Father in His throne.

John sat so close to Jesus that he could hear the heartbeat of the Son of God as he leaned on the chest (bosom) of Jesus. One day, you and I are going to get to sit that close to the Lord. Doesn't that make you long for the *harpazo*, the catching away of the saints, the Rapture of the church to be forever with the Lord? What a promise for the overcomer!

John reminds us to listen to the Spirit:

> To him who overcomes I will grant to sit with Me on My throne, as I also overcame and sat down with My Father on His throne. He who has an ear, let him hear what the Spirit says to the churches. (Revelation 3:21–22)

Revelation 4

We have covered the messages of Christ that speak of the Trinity to the churches of Asia Minor. We move from the earth (chapters 1, 2, and 3) to the throne room of God in heaven (chapters 4 and 5).

John sees God sitting on the throne:

> Immediately I was in the Spirit; and behold, a throne set in heaven, and One sat on the throne. And He who sat there was like a jasper and a sardius stone in appearance; and there was a rainbow around the throne, in appearance like an emerald. (Revelation 4:2–3)

This is important. After John sees God on His throne and describes Him in the above verses, he sees a book with seven seals in God's right hand. No one in heaven, on earth, or under the earth will be worthy to open the book—and John weeps.

One of the elders in heaven tells John not to weep for the "Lion of the tribe of Judah, the Root of David" has prevailed to open the book.

And don't miss this. John sees Jesus standing as a slain Lamb in the midst the throne of God with the seven Spirits of God. Jesus takes the book out of the hand of God on the throne.

John says the Lamb has redeemed the saints by His blood to God and makes them kings and priests to God.

We certainly can't miss verse 8 in chapter 4. Have you heard the term *thrice Holy God*? Have you ever wondered why there are three "holies" cried out in worship in heaven?

> The four living creatures, each having six wings, were full of eyes around and within. And they do not rest day or night, saying: "Holy, holy, holy, Lord God Almighty, Who was and is and is to come!" (Revelation 4:8)

Isaiah saw and heard the same thing:

> And one cried to another and said: "Holy, holy, holy is the Lord of hosts; The whole earth is full of His glory!" (Isaiah 6:3)

Why three Holies? God the Father is holy, God the Son is Holy (David said God would not let His "Holy One" see corruption), and the Holy Spirit has it in His name! John is referencing all three persons of the Godhead in chapter 4.

In chapter 5, John sees God the Father on His throne with a book in His hand that no one was worthy to open. That book contains the prophecies for future events, and John weeps because no one is worthy of opening the book.

John will be told not to weep because the Lion of the Tribe of Judah has prevailed to open the book. When John looks to see this Lion, he sees a Lamb that had been slain having the seven Spirits of God.

There, my friend, is the Trinity. God is on the throne, Jesus—as a Lamb—takes the book from the hand of God on the throne, and the seven Spirits of God are the Holy Spirit.

The scripture says that the redeemed in heaven were redeemed to God by the blood of the slain Lamb and that Jesus has made them kings and priests to God. There is no other way to be redeemed to God except by the blood of the Lamb. It is Jesus and what He did on Calvary's cross that brings lost mankind to God.

REVELATION 5

> And I saw in the right hand of Him who sat on the throne a scroll written inside and on the back, sealed with seven seals.
>
> Then I saw a strong angel proclaiming with a loud voice, "Who is worthy to open the scroll and to loose its seals?" And no one in heaven or on the earth

> or under the earth was able to open the scroll, or to look at it.
>
> So I wept much, because no one was found worthy to open and read the scroll, or to look at it. But one of the elders said to me, "Do not weep. Behold, the Lion of the tribe of Judah, the Root of David, has prevailed to open the scroll and to loose its seven seals."
>
> And I looked, and behold, in the midst of the throne and of the four living creatures, and in the midst of the elders, stood a Lamb as though it had been slain, having seven horns and seven eyes, which are the seven Spirits of God sent out into all the earth. Then He came and took the scroll out of the right hand of Him who sat on the throne.
>
> Now when He had taken the scroll, the four living creatures and the twenty-four elders fell down before the Lamb, each having a harp, and golden bowls full of incense, which are the prayers of the saints.
>
> And they sang a new song, saying: "You are worthy to take the scroll, And to open its seals; For You were slain, And have redeemed us to God by your blood out of every tribe and tongue and people and nation, and have made us kings and priests to our God and we shall reign on the earth." (Revelation 5:1–10)

We conclude from this that God the Father is on the throne with the scroll, Jesus is the Lamb standing before the throne of the Father, and Jesus takes the book from God's hand. Jesus has the Spirit of God, and Isaiah writes that the Spirit of the Lord would be upon Him (Isaiah 61).

In chapter 7, the redeemed have been moved from earth in chapters 2 and 3 to heaven in chapters 4 and 5. The rise of the Antichrist begins in chapter 6, and the tribulation is now underway on earth.

REVELATION 7

John sees a great multitude that no man can number. The Bible says they come from all nations, kindreds, people, and tongues. This is one of the many reasons why I believe the Rapture (harpazo) will occur before the tribulation. Those who have been redeemed by the blood are "people" in heaven before God's throne and in the presence of the Lamb while the tribulation is underway.

We also see the Trinity in these following verses. These people are before the throne of God "and" before the Lamb:

> After these things I looked, and behold, a great multitude which no one could number, of all nations, tribes, peoples, and tongues, standing before the throne and before the Lamb, clothed with white robes, with palm branches in their hands, and crying out with a loud voice, saying, "Salvation belongs to our God who sits on the throne, and to the Lamb!" (Revelation 7:9–10)

REVELATION 10

Jesus is seen (He's called a mighty angel). We can tell this by His description and the little book (scroll) in His hand. It is the scroll He took from the hand of God in chapter 5.

The book that was in God's hand is now in the hand of Christ. With the scroll in hand, He stands with one foot on the sea and another on the earth. He lifts His other hand to heaven and swears by Him the Creator. No one can deny that this angel is Christ Himself.

With His feet on the earth and sea, He lifts His hand and swears to God on the throne in heaven. This is one more clear difference between the two persons of our Holy God. Jesus is certainly not swearing to Himself. He is on earth and is swearing to God on the throne in heaven:

> I saw still another mighty angel coming down from heaven, clothed with a cloud. And a rainbow was on his head, his face was like the sun, and his feet like pillars of fire. He had a little book open in his hand. And he set his right foot on the sea and his left foot on the land, and cried with a loud voice, as when a lion roars. The angel whom I saw standing on the sea and on the land raised up his hand to heaven and swore by Him who lives forever and ever, who created heaven and the things that are in it. (Revelation 10:1–3, 5–6)

Revelation 12

We see our conjunction "and" again:

> Then I heard a loud voice saying in heaven, "Now salvation, and strength, and the kingdom of our God, and the power of His Christ have come, for the accuser of our brethren, who accused them before our God day and night, has been cast down. (Revelation 12:10)

Is it appropriate to use the term *power of his Christ*? We could spend much time on this question, but Jesus always freely submitted to the Father during His earthly ministry. In the Garden of Gethsemane, Jesus submits to the Father's will, and Paul wrote that the head of Christ is God (1 Corinthians 11:3). For now, that should suffice—although an entire book could be written on this topic alone. John uses the term "and the power of His Christ." "Christ" means "the anointed One, the Messiah." When it comes to God, Jesus is God's Messiah (His anointed one). This means this verse could read, "God and the power of His Anointed One" or "God and the power of His Messiah."

REVELATION 14

John next will speak of the Lamb (that's one), the 144,000 having "His" Father's name written on their foreheads (that's two), and ends with "saith the Spirit" (that's three). John also writes that the patience of the saints are they that keep the commandments of God "and" the faith of Jesus:

> Then I looked, and behold, a Lamb standing on Mount Zion, and with Him one hundred and forty-four thousand, having His Father's name written on their foreheads. Here is the patience of the saints; here are those who keep the commandments of God and the faith of Jesus. (Revelation 14:1, 12)

REVELATION 19

In this chapter, we come to the Second Coming of Christ to the earth. In theological terms this event is called the "Second Coming of Christ" or "the Second Advent." This is not to be confused with the Rapture where Jesus does not return to the earth. Instead, at the rapture He stops in the air, and those who are "in Christ" will rise to meet Him (I Thessalonians 4:13-18).

There are eleven verses here, which I'll summarize, but it would be good to read all the verses yourself. It's a great chapter with a lot of action. John first hears the voice of many "people" in heaven. Isn't it wonderful that the Bible tells us that "people" are in heaven. Some people don't believe people go to heaven, but John saw them there.

Revelation 5 says there are "people" in heaven who were there because they were redeemed by His blood. Where do redeemed people go when they die?

> And they sang a new song, saying: "You are worthy to take the scroll, And to open its seals; For You were

> slain, And have redeemed us to God by Your blood
> Out of every tribe and tongue and people and nation."
> (Revelation 5:9)

Yes, there are people in heaven; the Word of God says so!

To whom does the blood of Jesus redeem these people? The answer is right there before our eyes; the blood of Jesus redeems us to God! That's to whom we are redeemed; our faith in the blood of Jesus reconciles us back to God. John hears many people in heaven saying, "Glory, honor, and power unto the Lord our God."

Then he sees the twenty-four elders worshipping God on the throne. The twenty-four elders represent the Old Testament saints who died since Abel and the New Testament saints who died since the cross. There were twelve tribes in the children of Israel (Old Testament saints) and twelve apostles chosen by Christ (New Testament saints). Twelve plus twelve is twenty-four.

Still not convinced? How does the Bible describe the twenty-four elders? They are redeemed from every tribe, nation, tongue (language), and people!

The church was on earth in Revelation 2–3, and then these twenty-four elders are in heaven in chapters 4 and 5—but the tribulation doesn't begin until chapter 6! There is only one event that could move these "people" from earth to heaven before the tribulation gets started: the Rapture of the church. (For much more information, see my book *Will the Church Go through the Tribulation?*).

In Revelation 19, a voice from the throne says, "The marriage of the Lamb is come." He then goes on to use the term "marriage supper of the Lamb."

All of the above are the true sayings of God.

Verse 15 says that Jesus Himself treads the winepress of the fierceness and wrath of Almighty God.

In verse 10, the man speaking to John says, "I am your fellow servant, and of your brethren who have the testimony of Jesus. Worship God! For the testimony of Jesus is the spirit of prophecy."

The Trinity winds its way through these verses:

After these things I heard a loud voice of a great multitude in heaven, saying, "Alleluia! Salvation and glory and honor and power belong to the Lord our God!

For true and righteous are His judgments, because He has judged the great harlot who corrupted the earth with her fornication; and He has avenged on her the blood of His servants shed by her." Again they said, "Alleluia! Her smoke rises up forever and ever!"

And the twenty-four elders and the four living creatures fell down and worshipped God who sat on the throne, saying, "Amen! Alleluia!"

Then a voice came from the throne, saying, "Praise our God, all you His servants and those who fear Him, both small and great!" And I heard, as it were, the voice of a great multitude, as the sound of many waters and as the sound of mighty thunderings, saying, "Alleluia! For the Lord God Omnipotent reigns! Let us be glad and rejoice and give Him glory, for the marriage of the Lamb has come, and His wife has made herself ready." And to her it was granted to be arrayed in fine linen, clean and bright, for the fine linen is the righteous acts of the saints. Then he said to me, "Write: 'Blessed are those who are called to the marriage supper of the Lamb!'" And he said to me, "These are the true sayings of God."

And I fell at his feet to worship him. But he said to me, "See that you do not do that! I am your fellow servant, and of your brethren who have the testimony of Jesus. Worship God! For the testimony of Jesus is the spirit of prophecy." Now out of His mouth goes a sharp sword, that with it He should strike the nations. And He Himself will rule them with a rod of iron. He Himself treads the winepress of the fierceness and wrath of Almighty God. (Revelation 19:1–10, 15)

For whom does Jesus tread the winepress of fierceness and wrath? It is the fierceness and wrath of Almighty God that He will bring to the earth at His Second Coming.

Revelation 20

We are nearing the finish line with our conversation on the Trinity. We only have three more passages, and they are some wonderful scriptures in the Word of God. In chapter 20, we find ourselves at the end of the thousand-year millennial reign of Christ on earth.

Many think that the Battle of Armageddon will be the last battle, but there's still one more left. Armageddon happens at the end of the Great Tribulation and ushers in the thousand-year millennial reign. There's one more battle left; the Battle of Gog and Magog happens at the end of the millennium. Gog is a person, and Magog is a territory.

In these verses, we see the Trinity. Those included in the first resurrection will be made priests of God and of Christ. When the thousand years are complete, Christ's feet will have returned to touch the Mount of Olives. He is reigning from Jerusalem "on earth," which is important.

The revolt of Gog and Magog will occur at the end of the thousand years. Gog will gather an army to battle against Christ as He is reigning on earth in Jerusalem. At the Battle of Armageddon, which occurred a thousand years earlier, Jesus had to return from heaven to the earth to fight. At the Battle of Gog and Magog, Jesus is already on earth reigning, he's been back for a thousand years.

In the Battle of Gog and Magog, "fire came down from God out of heaven" and devoured them. Now don't miss this! The fire does not come down from Jesus who is ruling on earth. It comes from God who is still in heaven:

> Blessed and holy is he who has part in the first resurrection. Over such the second death has no

> power, but they shall be priests of God and of Christ, and shall reign with Him a thousand years. Now when the thousand years have expired, Satan will be released from his prison and will go out to deceive the nations which are in the four corners of the earth, Gog and Magog, to gather them together to battle, whose number is as the sand of the sea. They went up on the breadth of the earth and surrounded the camp of the saints and the beloved city. And *fire came down from God out of heaven* and devoured them. (Revelation 20:6–9)

The revolt of Gog and Magog happens at the end of the millennium. Jesus is on earth, ruling from His throne in Jerusalem, and the fire comes down from God out of heaven. People will receive the Holy Spirit (the third person in the Godhead) during the millennium.

Concerning of the restoration of Israel back to its own land and the millennium, let's read the following:

> For I will take you from among the nations, gather you out of all countries, and bring you into your own land. Then I will sprinkle clean water on you, and you shall be clean; I will cleanse you from all your filthiness and from all your idols. I will give you a new heart and put a new spirit within you; I will take the heart of stone out of your flesh and give you a heart of flesh. *I will put My Spirit within you* and cause you to walk in My statutes, and you will keep My judgments and do them. Then you shall dwell in the land that I gave to your fathers; you shall be My people, and I will be your God. (Ezekiel 36:24–28)

Notice the capital "S" and "I with put My Spirit within you." The Holy Spirit will be indwelling believers during the millennium, Christ will be ruling on earth from Jerusalem, God will put His Spirit within the hearts of Israel on earth and God will send fire down from heaven at the conclusion of the thousand years:

The Trinity is seen in the millennium.

- Jesus is reigning on earth.
- God is in heaven and sends down the fire.
- The Holy Spirit indwells believers during the millennium on earth.

Revelation 21

Ending on such a wonderful note feels so good. We only have two passages left. In chapter 21, our eternal home, the New Jerusalem, descends from God out of heaven. Could there be any mention of the Trinity here?

> But I saw no temple in it, for the Lord God Almighty and the Lamb are its temple. The city had no need of the sun or of the moon to shine in it, for the glory of God illuminated it. The Lamb is its light. (Revelation 21:22–23)

There it is! The Lord God and the Lamb are the temple and the glory of God, and the Lamb gives the New Jerusalem its light. But what about the Holy Spirit? Do we really think God—who began with the Trinity in Genesis 1—will end in any other way? We are about to see who gives the last invitation for salvation in the Bible.

Revelation 22

> "I, Jesus, have sent My angel to testify to you these things in the churches. I am the Root and the Offspring of David, the Bright and Morning Star." And the Spirit and the bride say, "Come!" And let him who

> hears say, "Come!" And let him who thirsts come. Whoever desires, let him take the water of life freely. He who testifies to these things says, "Surely I am coming quickly." Amen. Even so, come, Lord Jesus! The grace of our Lord Jesus Christ be with you all. Amen. (Revelation 22:16–21)

The Holy Spirit is here with us presently, and Jesus—in His body that He ascended with—is sitting at the right hand of God in heaven. Jesus said, "I am coming back." In Acts 1, Jesus ascended—and the disciples saw Him bodily go back to the Father. Angels stood by as He ascended, and they said, "This same Jesus who was taken up from you into heaven, will so come in like manner as you saw Him go into heaven" (Acts 1:11).

Jesus is not with us today in His body. He sent us the Holy Spirit—who is with us now—but the scripture says that the same Jesus who ascended is coming back just as He went away. He ascended from the Mount of Olives, and He's coming back to the Mount of Olives. He went away in a body, and He's coming back in a body (Zechariah 14:4). When Jesus told John that He would return, John cries out, "Even so, come, Lord Jesus!"

Before the Bible closes, the Holy Spirit gives one last invitation to be saved. Today, the Holy Spirit is saying, "Come." It's like the Holy Spirit was saying to John: "Before we close down the canon of scriptures, and before we say the last 'Grace of the Lord be with you all,' before we say that last "amen," John, I want to give one more invitation to "come."

My friend, if you don't know this wonderful Savior, let me say He is calling for you to "come." Will you hear what the Spirit says? You can know the One who left heaven's glory and came down to earth. He was born of a virgin, grew up and lived a sinless life, and then went to Calvary's cross and gave His blood and died so that we could be saved and have everlasting life. He arose again on the third day and lives today to bring us life more abundantly. If you don't know Him, all you have to do is believe and trust in Him, which means we place your faith in what He did on the cross for us for the forgiveness of our sins.

You may think that sounds pretty easy, but Jesus took care of the hard part when He went to the cross. Jesus said, "My yoke is easy." Jesus made it so easy that even a child can be saved. He made it so easy a person can be saved in a moments time. He did the hard part, and all we must do is believe in His giving of Himself on the cross for the forgiveness of our sins and receive Him as our Lord and Savior. I'm so glad I did, and I invite you to know Him too.

The canon of scripture concludes with the truth of the Trinity. We have seen the Trinity from Genesis to Revelation.

As we cross the finish line here in Revelation 22, what a journey it has been. From the opening verses in Genesis to the ending verses of Revelation, the Trinity, the Triune God, the Thrice Holy God has been with us the entire trip.

I leave you with the words of the great apostle Paul:

> Now may the God of hope fill you with all joy and peace in believing, that you may abound in hope by the power of the Holy Spirit … Now I beg you, brethren, through the Lord Jesus Christ, and through the love of the Spirit, that you strive together with me in prayers to God … Now the God of peace be with you all. Amen. (Romans 15:13, 30, 33)

CHAPTER 33

LAW VERSUS GRACE

Why is a chapter on law versus grace included in a book dedicated to the Trinity? This is an important chapter, especially if the reader is coming from a non-Trinitarian background. For those who have acquired this book to learn more concerning the Trinity or teach a series in their churches, this is something with which they will have to deal.

This is something I've had to confront when dealing with those who do not accept the Trinity. Almost everyone I know from a non-Trinitarian point of view struggles with law versus grace. In other words, they are in churches and synagogues where it is taught that one must keep the law or do good works to be saved.

We will first give the setting of how and why Galatians was written, which will lead us to the main topic concerning the law.

The Setting of the Book of Galatians

The churches in the region of Galatia were very special to Paul, and he actually visited these churches on each of his three missionary journeys, showing that the churches in this region were dear to the heart of Paul.

This book is actually not addressed to one single church but rather to "to the churches of Galatia" (Galatians 1:1). That means what Paul would write was something he wanted all the churches to know.

Why, this time, unlike his other books, did Paul address this letter to all of the churches in Galatia? There had to be a reason. Apparently, what Paul would write in Galatians was so critical that all the churches needed to be aware of it. Paul had founded these churches on the doctrine of "justification by faith." That seemed to be a scripture from Habakkuk that Paul was fond of. He had been a Pharisee and adhered to the works of the law.

Once Paul was arrested in Jerusalem, he said that "being zealous for God," he lived "strictly" according to the law (Acts 22:3). To the Galatians, he said he advanced in Judaism and was "extremely zealous" for his ancestral traditions (Galatians 1:14). Paul once was submerged in Mosaic works, and in three of his epistles, he repeats the following:

> But the just shall live by his faith. (Habakkuk 2:4)

Paul refers back to this verse in his epistles to Rome, Hebrews, and this great book of Galatians (Romans 1:17, Hebrews 10:38, and Galatians 3:11). Along with Habakkuk, this verse is found in scripture four times; apparently, the Holy Spirit wanted us to know this truth.

As we can see, this was the theme of Paul's message. Justification by faith really began with Abraham. Abraham believed God, and it was counted unto him for righteousness. That statement about Abraham is in the Bible three times: twice by Paul and once by James (Romans 4:3; Galatians 3:6; James 2:23).

THE JUDAIZERS

During Paul's day, he was continually facing Judaizers. This group of Jews believed in Christ, but they had a major flaw in their belief. They believed that Gentile Christians had to obey the Mosaic law and be circumcised to be saved.

These Judaizers would follow Paul around, and once he would leave, they would enter with their false teaching. Some of them attacked the apostleship of Paul and said he was not an apostle.

This is why the Pauline epistles began with "Paul, an apostle" (Romans 1:1; 1 Corinthians 1:1; 2 Corinthians 1:1; Galatians 1:1; Colossians 1:1; 1 Timothy 1:1; 2 Timothy 1:1; Titus 1:1). Paul was always having to defend his apostleship because of these Judaizers.

Paul was the hardest-working of all of the apostles (1 Corinthians 15:10). The New Covenant was revealed to him, and he was even more knowledgeable than the other apostles. After finally meeting the other apostles, Paul said they added nothing to him (Galatians 2:6).

If these Judaizers succeeded, then everything Paul taught on "justification by faith" would be completely void. Paul had to take a very hard stand, and the Gospel of justification by faith and the New Covenant depended on it.

In Galatians, he held back no punches. He came out swinging. Galatians doesn't even begin with compliments to the church like his other epistles. Paul is writing out of frustration and godly anger, and he reminds us of the anger of Jesus turning over the tables of the money changers in the temple. He uses some very strong words and repeats them more than once. He begins chapter 3 by calling them "foolish Galatians" and tells them they have been bewitched by the Judaizers (Galatians 3:1).

A preacher sometimes has to repeat himself. Jesus would often say, "Again I say unto you." Jude said, "I remind you, though you once knew this." Peter wrote that he wanted to stir up our pure minds by way of remembrance.

Someone once asked me if a preacher should ever repeat the same sermon. I said, "Yes, if they didn't get the message the first time." Jesus did this, Jude did this, Peter did this, and now we see Paul repeating himself in his holy anger. Any parent who has ever had to say something more than one time to their children can relate to Paul here.

When I read Galatians, I get a little angry, especially with James, Peter, and Barnabas. These foolish Galatians were listening to the Judaizers. Everyone should study Galatians.

GALATIANS 1

> But even if we, or an angel from heaven, should preach to you a Gospel contrary to what we have preached to you, he is to be accursed! As we have said before, even now I say again: if anyone is preaching to you a Gospel contrary to what you received, he is to be accursed! (Galatians 1:8–9)

To make sure they heard this, Paul said it more than once. He is coming down hard against the Judaizers. They would destroy the Gospel of grace by having people place their faith in their works rather than in the sacrifice of Jesus on Calvary's cross. What a man Paul was; he went from being a persecutor to a preacher!

> The man who once persecuted us is now preaching the faith which he once tried to destroy. (Galatians 1:23)

The bulk of Paul's opposition and sufferings did not come from outsiders. Most of his sufferings were caused by the religious crowd of his day. He even had problems with James, the senior pastor of the mother church in Jerusalem.

I sometimes am a little frustrated with James. Please don't take me wrong. James is definitely to be honored and respected. He was the half brother of Jesus, he was an apostle (Galatians 1:19), and he was a martyr who was killed in Jerusalem under Herod Agrippa. Some have said that the mother church in Jerusalem could have had as many as fifty thousand believers. James wrote inspired scripture, and the book of James bears his name. However, as a man, he could make mistakes. James dropped the ball at the Jerusalem council and created two Gospels—one for the Jews and another for the Gentiles.

In Acts 15:19–20, he placed no heavy yoke of circumcision on the Gentiles. However, he did not make it clear to the Jerusalem Jews that circumcision was no longer required, which left them zealous for the Mosaic law. James told Paul (just six chapters later) that the Jerusalem Christians were *all* zealous for the law (Acts 21:18–22).

As the senior pastor, it was his responsibility to teach the believers in Jerusalem that the Mosaic law had been nailed to the cross (Colossians 2:14). If creating two standards wasn't bad enough—a Jewish standard and a Gentile standard—James sent men from Jerusalem to Antioch to teach that circumcision was still required for salvation. This persuaded Peter and Barnabas to sway from justification by faith. This gives us three apostles in error (James, Peter, and Barnabas). Paul had to withstand Peter publicly. Paul held back no punches and told them what they were doing was hypocrisy (Galatians 2:11–14).

Paul was going to speak with "holy anger," and he was as tough on Barnabas and Peter as he was with the fickle Galatians. The Holy Spirit inspired Paul to put the name of James in writing and pen into scripture forever that he had sent the Judaizers to Antioch. Had Paul not taken such a stand, the doctrine of justification by faith would have been lost. Paul would not have it—even if he had to stand alone and confront other apostles.

Paul and Barnabas had "sharp disagreements." They went their separate ways over a disagreement about taking John Mark to journey with them (Acts 15:39). The scripture says their disagreement was "sharp." Paul later saw he was the one in the wrong and told Timothy to bring John Mark with him when they came to him (2 Timothy 4:11).

Paul was wrong concerning John Mark, and Barnabas was right. In Galatians 2 Paul was right—and James, Peter, and Barnabas were wrong. Even the apostles were not 100 percent right all the time. Folks, preachers don't have to be right all the time; they can make mistakes!

Jesus often became weary with His own disciples. There were times He was quite hard on them, and He called His own disciples "unbelieving and perverse" (Matthew 17:17). Jesus rebuked the disciples and corrected them many times. Jesus once looked at Peter and called him "Satan" (Matthew 16:23). Jesus was tough on the

Pharisees, Sadducees, scribes, money changers, and His followers. In Antioch, Paul was right in his righteous anger.

I repeat, James should be honored. Yet this teaches us that it can be dangerous to place our faith in a man—even if he's of high reputation, an apostle, a writer of scripture, a martyr, a pastor in a large church, or the chairman of a religious council. James was all of this, yet he could make big mistakes.

Many today make the mistake of placing all their trust in a minister of high reputation. We are to remember that we are to test all things and prove all things. Regardless of how popular the preacher is, we are to test what we are taught by the scriptures. We are to know when a minister is in error. Many are led to error far too often because of that which comes from a man.

May we all be like the Berean believers. "They received the word with all readiness of mind, and searched the scriptures daily, whether those things were so" (Acts 17:11).

Some denominations actually tell their lay members that they are not qualified to read the scriptures on their own and discourage them from reading the scriptures all together. This was certainly not the position of the Bereans. They tested everything Paul taught them, and they did so by searching the scriptures themselves. Every Christian should be doctrinally sound and be familiar with the Word of God by reading the Bible themselves.

We are spending so much time on law versus grace because those who struggle with the Trinity usually struggle with works too. Many of these precious people are held in bondage. They attend churches where the Trinity is not accepted, and they are taught that they won't get to heaven without honoring the law.

To be fair, many Trinitarians struggle with this too. We must say that. Many Trinitarian ministers and church denominations place a yoke of bondage on their hearers by requiring them to keep the law. Some of them have built some of the largest churches in the country, incorporating "man-made laws," and demand the membership keep them.

This problem of law versus grace occurs among some Trinitarians.

We must be fair in this discussion. I know some churches that practically believe everything is a sin; they preach against everything from drinking coffee to smoking to hair lengths and dress codes. Someone asked me, "Can a person smoke and go to heaven?" I said, "Yes, and they'll get there a lot quicker if they keep it up."

These people are some of the most judgmental people on earth. Folks, smoking is not mentioned in the Bible, but gossiping, stirring of discord, fault-finding attitudes, and plucking specks out of a brother's eye while they have a log in their own certainly are. I'm a nonsmoker in case you are wondering. Someone once said, "Smoking was wrong unless you smoke Camels." I asked, "Where'd you get that?" He said, "Rebekah lighted off her camel and ran to Isaac."

When we speak about law, we are speaking about the law of Moses and the laws we ourselves, our churches, our denominations, and our ministers make up on our own. It's legalism, but it's law! In the defense of non-Trinitarians, many Trinitarians have a big issue with this too.

I include this chapter because non-Trinitarians and salvation by law accompany each other. Anyone who deals with non-Trinitarians is going to come up against the issue of law versus grace.

I have had to deal with this issue quite a few times. Five families visited the church I pastored and wanted to join as members, but all five families were non-Trinitarians. In some churches, five families would be enough to change the church's "statement of faith" and turn the church non-Trinitarian. The five families also wanted to bring in salvation by works. They believed you had to be baptized to be saved—and only in the name of Jesus—speak with tongues, and abide by their dress code. This was the doctrine of the Pharisees! The Pharisees were non-Trinitarian and believed they had to keep the law. They implemented all types of works, including washing their hands before meals, keeping the Sabbath, paying tithes, fasting, wearing their phylacteries, and stoning their children if they were unruly.

When the Pharisees brought the woman caught in adultery to Christ, they said, "Moses said stone her—what do you say?" There have been many ideas about what Jesus wrote in the sand with His finger. I've heard everything from writing the personal sins of the crowd to "Where is the man?" The Pharisees were breaking the law by not bringing the man; they only brought the woman. According to Moses, they "both" were to be brought and stoned (Leviticus 20:10–12).

Although no one can say for sure what He wrote, I have an idea. The accusers were using the law for their grounds to kill the person. Every last one of them were lawbreakers. No one could ever—and no one has ever—kept the whole law except Jesus. The Bible says the law was written by the "finger of God" (Exodus 31:18; Deuteronomy 9:10). Jesus stooped down and wrote with His finger. What He wrote was enough to convict their own hearts and cause them to drop their stones and walk away. I can't prove it, but I think He wrote the Ten Commandments in the sand and then looked at them and said, "He that is without sin cast the first stone." The point for us to get out of this is that no one can keep the law!

If the reader does research, they will find that those who do not accept the Trinity also believe one has to be baptized under a certain formula, follow dress code restrictions, and speak with tongues. Some even believe a person has to join their church to be saved. Every bit of that is salvation by works (the works are made by man, but they are still works). Some sects in Judaism do the same thing and say, "No Trinity and righteousness by adhering to the law of Moses." They have added more than six hundred laws (rules and regulations) that are not found in the original Mosaic law. One can read a list of these 613 laws in the Mitzvot.

Many people are confused about the law of Moses. It was given at Mount Sinai to Israel only. Israel actually entered into a "covenant" with God to keep the law, but they broke the covenant. Nowhere in scripture have Gentiles ever been seen entering into a covenant with God to keep the Mosaic law.

The purpose of the law was not to bring salvation; it was to reveal that we have sinned. If they think the law was given to produce salvation, they are under the wrong impression. The law is good; it came from God, and everything that comes from God is good. It's good in that it reveals our need for a Savior. Without the law, we would never know that we are sinners:

> What shall we say then? Is the law sin? Certainly not! On the contrary, I would not have known sin except through the law. For I would not have known covetousness unless the law had said, "You shall not covet." (Romans 7:7)

The law was never meant to be permanent. When God gave it, He never planned to keep it in effect forever. Jeremiah, Ezekiel, and Moses all prophesied this:

> "Behold, days are coming," declares the Lord, "when I will make a new covenant with the house of Israel and the house of Judah, not like the covenant which I made with their fathers on the day I took them by the hand to bring them out of the land of Egypt, My covenant which they broke, although I was a husband to them," declares the Lord. "For this is the covenant which I will make with the house of Israel after those days," declares the Lord: "I will put My law within them and write it on their heart; and I will be their God, and they shall be My people." (Jeremiah 31:31–33)

> I will give you a new heart and put a new spirit within you; I will take the heart of stone out of your flesh and give you a heart of flesh. I will put My Spirit within you and cause you to walk in My statutes, and you will keep My judgments and do them. (Ezekiel 26:25–27)

In the Old Testament, the Holy Spirit sometimes would come "upon" some, but He did not dwell "within" them. The Holy Spirit was not yet given; that would happen in Acts 2 on the Day of Pentecost.

Today, the Holy Spirit dwells within the believer! This is a blessing the believer has today that the Old Testament saints did not have. This is huge (see also Ezekiel 11:19 and Deuteronomy 30:6).

As we can see, the Old Testament prophets said the covenant the Israelites made when they "came out of Egypt" would end someday. They said God would make a "new covenant" with them. Israel made this covenant with God concerning the law on Mount Sinai (Exodus 19:1–8, 24:1–3). I encourage you to read it. The law was given only to Israel, and it was only Israel that entered into covenant with God concerning the law. Gentiles have never been under a covenant with God concerning the law of Moses.

If a person who is living under condemnation of failure can grasp this, they will be able to find liberty in the new covenant. A load can be lifted, and the yoke of bondage can be broken. Paul called the law a "yoke of bondage" (Galatians 5:1). No one would know this better than Paul. He was a converted Pharisee who had the zeal for the law. Paul had lived under that bondage, and once he was saved on the road to Damascus, the bondage was broken—and he found himself living in liberty.

My friend, some of the most miserable people in the world are those who are trying to get to heaven by their own works and keeping of the law. In Galatians 5, Paul told them to stand fast in the liberty. He told them Christ had "made them free" and told them not be entangled again in the bondage of keeping the law. Jesus is a chain breaker! When Jesus sets someone free, they are free indeed (John 8:36).

Jesus quoted Isaiah and said He was sent to proclaim liberty to the captives. There is nothing that will bring one into captivity as much as the law. I know people who are not captive to outside influences—alcohol, drugs, immorality, and so on—but they are held captive as they sit under the teachings of the law and indoctrinated with keeping the law. The law brings one into captivity and bondage.

CHRIST IS THE END OF THE LAW

Let's take a look at some good news. What we are about to read cannot be said any better than the way the Holy Spirit wrote it:

> For Christ is the end of the law for righteousness to everyone who believes. (Romans 10:4)

I hope that sinks into our hearts deeply. Jesus is the "end of the law" for righteousness. I've met a lot of people who feel they are righteous because of all their good deeds. Doing good works for righteousness has ended. Paying tithes for righteousness has ended. Church membership for righteousness has ended. Fasting and praying for righteousness has ended. We could keep going here, but Christ is the "end of the law for righteousness."

This is how Paul addressed the Colossians about the law:

> Having wiped out the handwriting of requirements that was against us, which was contrary to us. And He has taken it out of the way, having nailed it to the cross. (Colossians 2:14)

The rules, regulations, requirements, keeping the law, and good deeds have been wiped out by the blood of Jesus. They were taken out! Paul said Jesus being nailed to the cross took the law out of the way. My parents used to ask me, "Have you taken out the trash?" In the eyes of God, all our good works "for righteousness" are trash. If one thinks I'm using a word that is too harsh, God said that our self-righteousness was "filthy rags (Isaiah 64:6). The Greek word for *filthy* is *idda*, which means *menstruation*. The Greek word for *rags* is *begged*, which means *fabric or cloth*. I trust by now we see how God sees our good works "for righteousness."

Paul told the church at Colossae that Jesus had picked up the law of Moses and "taken it out of the way." He did it by nailing it to the cross. When Jesus died on the cross, the law of Moses came to an end "for righteousness."

Jesus told us in His Sermon on the Mount that those who hungered and thirsted after "righteousness" shall be filled (Matthew 5:6). At the Last Supper, Jesus took bread (which remedies hunger) and the cup (which remedies thirst). They were the symbols of His body and blood and what He would do on the cross. When we go to the cross for righteousness, we shall be filled.

The Law Brings a Curse

I am fascinated with people who claim they are keeping the law. That's a very dangerous way to live because they are living under a curse. The Holy Spirit is the one who tells us that. Let's all chew on this for a moment.

According to Paul and James, if one desires to live under the law, they must keep every last bit of it. Law keepers are not allowed to break even one law—not even the smallest of laws—and remain righteous. Those who live under law need to be aware of this. It's important if they believe that are going to go to heaven by works:

> For as many as are of the works of the law are under the curse; for it is written, "Cursed is everyone who does not continue in all things which are written in the book of the law, to do them. But that no one is justified by the law in the sight of God is evident, for the just shall live by faith. Yet the law is not of faith, but "the man who does them shall live by them." (Galatians 3:10–12)

> For whoever shall keep the whole law, and yet stumble in one point, he is guilty of all. (James 2:10)

If a person was hanging from a tree by holding a chain with ten links, and all ten links broke, they would be "fallen" and land in the dirt. If they were holding the chain and only one link broke, they would be just as fallen as the one with ten broken links.

If a person tries to live by the law and breaks all the Ten Commandments, they are fallen. If they keep nine out of the ten and only break one, they are as fallen as the one who has broken the whole law. They are going to hit the ground just as hard as the other one. Paul and James tell us that if one lives under the law, they have to keep them all. There is not a person on the planet who can do that. If we have to keep all of the laws to go to heaven, we better start looking for fireproof suits quickly.

When Jesus came, He gave us the Sermon on the Mount. If we think that the law of Moses was hard—or impossible—to keep, try to keep the law of Christ from the Sermon on the Mount.

Moses said, "You shall not commit adultery," but Jesus said that if a man just "looks upon a woman" with lust in his heart, he has already committed adultery. Moses said, "You shall not kill," but Jesus said, "If we are angry with our brother with a cause," we have already committed murder. The law Christ gave is far more extreme than the law of Moses ever was.

I'm fascinated with today's law keepers. Mosaic law was easier than the law of Christ. No one could keep the law of Moses—much less the law of Christ. Someone can give it their best shot, but they'll see it's impossible. The law was not given to produce salvation; it was given to reveal our need for a Savior. Every last one of us sins continually. We sin by sins of omission as much as the sins of commission.

If a man knows to do good and doesn't do it, James says it is sin (James 4:17). Would it be good if you prayed more than you prayed today? Would it be good if you read your Bible more than you did today? Would it be good if you had witnessed for Christ better today? We didn't do it as we could have. If we knew how to do good, but we didn't do it, James said that's sin.

Paul taught us that anything we do that is not of faith is sin (Romans 14:23). Have you ever worried about something? Worry is not of faith; that means worry is a sin. Have you ever been discouraged? Since discouragement is not of faith, it is sin.

There is only one who ever lived sinless, and that was Jesus Christ, the Son of the living God. No one has ever even come close to that.

Jesus kept the whole law, and He never sinned—not even one time. When He died on Calvary, He died as a sinless and spotless Lamb of God. When we place our faith in His sacrifice on the cross, Jesus places His righteousness on our imperfect lives. God looks at us through the blood that has been applied to our hearts and says, "That person is righteous" because the righteousness of Jesus has been imputed on those of us who have believed on Him. Righteousness in the sight of God is something that is imputed to us:

> It shall be imputed to us who believe in Him who raised up Jesus our Lord from the dead. (Romans 4:24)

> Sin is not imputed when there is no law. (Romans 5:13)

If we read that in reverse, it says, "Where there is law, sin *is* imputed." My friends, if we do not want sin imputed to us, we cannot place our faith in the law. If we want the righteousness of Jesus imputed to us, we must place our faith in the sacrifice of Christ on the cross with nothing else added.

This is not giving a license to sin. The true believer, in their heart, hates sin. They know what it cost God to bring a remedy for sin: the death of His own Son. We will desire to live a life that is pleasing to Christ. We live our lives bearing the fruit of the Spirit because we love Him (Galatians 5:6), but that does not produce salvation.

Any person who feels they can be saved and continue to live in sin has some real self-examination to do. We are told to examine whether we are living in the faith. There is no such thing as a true Christian living in sin and not feeling conviction. If the Holy Spirit is in our hearts, He will convict the world of sin, righteousness, and judgment (John 16:8).

When a true Christian sins, they will desire to run to God as fast as they can and get that sin forgiven.

For those who say they never sin, John has a few words for them. When John is speaking to believers, he uses the word "we." He is speaking to the church. By using the word "we," John is including himself. John gives us three "if" statements and uses the word "we" five times.

> If we say that we have no sin, we deceive ourselves, and the truth is not in us. If we confess our sins, He is faithful and just to forgive us our sins and to cleanse us from all unrighteousness. If we say that we have not sinned, we make Him a liar, and His word is not in us. (1 John 1:8)

I was praying while writing this book, and I felt the need to add this chapter because it is something that many people struggle with. This struggle is familiar for Trinitarians and non-Trinitarians alike.

Although this chapter was not on the topic of the Trinity, I wanted to include it as a bonus chapter. I trust and hope this book has been a blessing in some way.

ABOUT GARY L. COX

Dr. Gary L. Cox, author and an ordained minister, has served as an evangelist, pastor, and conference speaker in many city and state meetings. He began his ministry in his early years and spoke his first sermon at the age of sixteen. He has delivered thousands of messages across the United States in Bible conferences, conventions, youth meetings, churches, and radio broadcasts. In seminary, he graduated highest in his class and was the recipient of the scholastic award. He has founded three churches during the past thirty years.

Printed in the United States
by Baker & Taylor Publisher Services